Increasing Multicultural Understanding

Second Edition

MULTICULTURAL ASPECTS OF COUNSELING SERIES

SERIES EDITOR

Paul Pedersen, Ph.D., *University of Alabama at Birmingham*

EDITORIAL BOARD

VOLUMES IN THIS SERIES

1. **Increasing Multicultural Understanding (2nd edition): A Comprehensive Model**
   by Don C. Locke

2. **Preventing Prejudice: A Guide for Counselors and Educators**
   by Joseph G. Ponterotto and Paul B. Pedersen

3. **Improving Intercultural Interactions: Modules for Cross-Cultural Training Programs**
   edited by Richard W. Brislin and Tomoko Yoshida

4. **Assessing and Treating Culturally Diverse Clients (2nd edition): A Practical Guide**
   by Freddy A. Paniagua

5. **Overcoming Unintentional Racism in Counseling and Therapy:
   A Practitioner's Guide to Intentional Intervention** by Charles R. Ridley

6. **Multicultural Counseling With Teenage Fathers: A Practical Guide** by Mark S. Kiselica

7. **Multicultural Counseling Competencies: Assessment, Education and
   Training, and Supervision** edited by Donald B. Pope-Davis and Hardin L. K. Coleman

8. **Improving Intercultural Interactions: Modules for Cross-Cultural
   Training Programs, Volume 2** edited by Kenneth Cushner and Richard W. Brislin

9. **Understanding Cultural Identity in Intervention and Assessment** by Richard H. Dana

10. **Psychological Testing of American Minorities (2nd edition)** by Ronald J. Samuda

11. **Multicultural Counseling Competencies: Individual and Organizational Development**
    by Derald Wing Sue et al.

12. **Counseling Multiracial Families** by Bea Wehrly, Kelley R. Kenney, and Mark E. Kenney

13. **Integrating Spirituality Into Multicultural Counseling**
    by Mary A. Fukuyama and Todd D. Sevig

14. **Counseling With Native American Indians and Alaska Natives: Strategies for
    Helping Professionals** by Roger D. Herring

15. **Diagnosis in a Multicultural Context: A Casebook for Mental Health Professionals**
    by Freddy A. Paniagua

16. **Psychotherapy and Counseling With Asian American Clients: A Practical Guide**
    by George K. Hong and MaryAnna Domokos-Cheng Ham

Increasing Multicultural Understanding

A Comprehensive Model
Second Edition

Don C. Locke

Multicultural Aspects of Counseling Series 1

SAGE Publications
International Educational and Professional Publisher
Thousand Oaks   London   New Delhi

For information:

SAGE Publications, Inc.
2455 Teller Road
Thousand Oaks, California 91320
E-mail: order@sagepub.com

SAGE Publications Ltd.
6 Bonhill Street
London EC2A 4PU
United Kingdom

SAGE Publications India Pvt. Ltd.
M-32 Market
Greater Kailash I
New Delhi 110 048 India

Printed in the United States of America

Library of Congress Cataloging-in-Publication Data

Locke, Don C.
    Increasing multicultural understanding : a comprehensive model /
by Don C. Locke.—2nd ed.
        p. cm.—(Multicultural aspects of counseling ; v. 1)
    Includes bibliographical references (p.) and index.
    ISBN: 978-0-7619-1119-7
      1. Pluralism (Social sciences)—United States. 2. Minorities—United States.
3. United States—Ethnic relations. 4. United States—Race relations. I. Title.
II. Series: Multicultural aspects of counseling series ; v. 1.
E184.A1L63 1998
305.8'00973—dc21   97-33920

05 06 07 08 09 11 10 9 8 7

Acquiring Editor:	Jim Nageotte
Editorial Assistant:	Fiona Lyon
Production Editor:	Astrid Virding
Production Assistant:	Lynn Miyata
Typesetter:	Marion Warren
Indexer:	Don C. Locke
Cover Designer:	Ravi Balasuriya
Print Buyer:	Anna Chin

Contents

Series Editor's Introduction

It is in everyone's best interest that we increase our comprehensive understanding of multicultural populations from the viewpoint of those populations themselves. Only after we have understood these multicultural viewpoints can we go on to assess the behavior of these populations accurately and to advocate changes appropriately. Don Locke's second edition provides a practical and popular approach to accomplish a comprehensive understanding. Locke's book has become the flagship of the **Multicultural Aspects of Counseling** series—both as the most popular book in the series and as the first book published in it, reflecting accurately the many goals and dreams we had when the series was conceptualized.

In this second edition, Locke has added chapters on the Jewish and the Muslim cultural contexts, with guidelines for counselors working with clients in those cultures. The other 10 chapters have been significantly updated since the 1992 first edition to include some of the extensive publications that have been written since that time.

Although thousands of publications have advocated increased understanding of multiculturalism, few step-by-step guidelines have been provided to suggest how that understanding can be accomplished. Locke provides a "blueprint" that approaches understanding in a systematic way and that balances the needs of the individual and the needs of the group to which the individual belongs. Readers can expect to develop increased understanding in several specific ways:

First, readers will increase their breadth of counseling-relevant information about 12 specific ethnocultural groups.

Second, readers will increase their comprehension of how these groups are both similar to and different from one another.

Third, readers will become more accurate in distinguishing each group from the dominant culture.

Fourth, readers will become more aware of their own culturally learned assumptions in contrast with these 12 groups.

A constant theme in Locke's book is the importance of diversity both between groups and within each group, and the dangers of a monocultural perspective both for counselors and for their clients. Locke writes in a conversational style that leads the reader toward both a better understanding of Locke and a better self-understanding without threat or verbal attacks. Although Locke does not avoid the obvious controversy of the multicultural topic, he respects the right of readers to disagree. Locke's book provides a safe and secure context for readers to grow in their better understanding of why multiculturalism has been so universally recognized as important.

Paul Pedersen
University of Alabama at Birmingham

Acknowledgments

I am indebted to many people whose help, support, and advice have been invaluable in writing this book. First, I thank the Counselor Education and the Adult and Community College Education faculties at North Carolina State University for their encouragement of this project. Dean Joan J. Michael of North Carolina State University has been a consistent and loyal supporter of my efforts, and I am grateful. The director of the Asheville Graduate Center, Gene McDowell, has been a great source of support and a valued colleague during the writing of this book. The staffs at the D. H. Hill Library at North Carolina State University and the D. Hiden Ramsey Library at the University of North Carolina at Asheville have been helpful in so many ways with the research necessary for the accuracy of this effort. Jim Nageotte and the Sage Publications staff made the effort an easy one as they directed the process from conception to completion.

Students in my classes—especially Marie Faubert, currently at the University of St. Thomas (Texas), and Sandy Peace, currently at North Carolina Central University—and members of the ACCE cohort at the Asheville Graduate Center have contributed directly or indirectly to the fine-tuning of my ideas and thoughts. I am deeply appreciative of their support throughout the process of trying to do justice to the cultural groups included in this book.

I express my appreciation to Allen Ivey, who read an early draft of the manuscript and made helpful suggestions. Paul Pedersen, Series Editor, took this project under his supervision and directed it to conclusion. For their helpful suggestions, I am particularly indebted to the reviewers: Augustine Baron, University of Texas, Austin; Rita Chi-Ying Chung, University of California, Los Angeles; Mary Fukuyama, University of Florida; Roger Herring, University of Arkansas at Little Rock; Morris L. Jackson, Ed.D., American University, Washington, D.C.; Evelyn Kalibala, New York Board of Education; Johnnie McFadden, University of South Carolina, Columbia; Jeff Mio, Washington State University, Pullman; Michelle Schwam, State University of New York at Albany; Satsuki Tomine, California State University; and Joe Wittmer, University of Florida, Gainesville.

Special thanks goes to my spouse, Marjorie, for being there in every way.

Introduction

A BLUEPRINT FOR
MULTICULTURAL UNDERSTANDING

We are living in an age of diversity. The roles of teachers and counselors have been expanded to include the consideration of the cultural identities of students and clients. Teachers and counselors have a responsibility to increase their awareness, knowledge, and skills so that all students and clients are taught and counseled with approaches that recognize the influences of cultural group membership. If teachers and counselors do not recognize the influence of cultural group membership, students and clients can be expected to profit only minimally from our interactions with them. Therefore, this book has an agenda and a point of view: to encourage interested readers to explore their own cultural backgrounds and identities and, in the process, come to better understand others.

Some readers will recall that Arthur M. Schlesinger, Jr. (1991) warned that competing ethnic groups, determined to tell the American story from their own vantage points, will cause the United States to lose its sense of uniqueness. He went on to predict that ethnic and racial conflict would remain an explosive issue. Schlesinger's proclamation was opposed by some people, including Takaki (1993), who concluded that United States Americans "have nothing to fear but our fear of our own diversity" (p. 427).

This book sets forth, one brick at a time, the process necessary to implement effective education and counseling strategies for culturally diverse populations. The practical suggestions offered are not presented as ends in themselves. Helping culturally diverse students and clients requires a focus of effort for each student or client that is based on both individual needs and cultural group membership needs.

This book is designed to provide one necessary step in gaining an overview of cultural groups. It will help readers identify characteristics of cultures, make comparisons between the dominant culture and the culturally different groups, make comparisons between culturally different groups, and use that information to develop strategies or interventions for students or clients. The book is designed to help make readers aware of their own ethnocentrism and to increase their awareness of the role that culture plays in determining the way people think, feel, and act.

In 1671, Governor William Berkeley of Virginia insisted, "I thank God that there are no free schools nor printing and I hope we shall not have these for a hundred years; for learning has brought disobedience, and heresy, and sects into the world and printing has divulged them, and libels against the best government. God keep us from both" (Stilgoe, 1982, p. 242). I hope that one result of this work will be obedience to a new set of principles, a belief system opposed to the status quo, and a meaningful recognition of the opinions, values, beliefs, and attitudes of diverse peoples.

Multiculturalism has been described as a fourth force in psychology (Pedersen, 1991). Although definitions of multiculturalism differ, the general premise underscores the rights of individuals to be respected for their differences. Multiculturalism rests upon the belief that all cultures have values, beliefs, customs, language, knowledge, and worldviews that are valid and viable and that these traits reflect the experiences of a particular group (Nieto, 1992). As we prepare to enter the 21st century, we are confronted with the demand for attention to diverse populations in education and counseling. The crisis in the United States today results from the alienation experienced by culturally different individuals and groups. The United States does not have one language, one set of values, one set of beliefs, or one set of customs. The "melting pot" theory of assimilation appears to have been rejected both by members of the dominant culture as well as by members of culturally different populations. More and more people are accepting the pluralistic nature of the culture of the United States. The methods of dealing with people who are different must be amended to provide for unique needs based on unique cultural group characteristics. We can no longer accept a singular method of teaching or counseling as useful for all our students or clients. We can no longer accept theories of teaching or counseling that do not include a focus broad enough to be applicable to students and clients who are different from the dominant viewpoint in education and counseling. The fourth force requires that we attend to student and client needs that may not be consistent with the predominant viewpoint of our professional training.

We must revise our educational practices and counseling strategies in a broad way. How and why have the experiences of culturally different groups been similar to and different from one another? How and why have the experiences of culturally different groups been similar to and different from the dominant culture? To answer these questions, we must not study statistics about groups only; we must ask the groups to write their own histories. We need to know what is on the minds of individuals from culturally different populations. Although we know that culturally different individuals and groups all face similar obstacles and issues related to acculturation in the United States, the key to understanding a particular cultural group lies in an appreciation of the wide diversity of their experiences.

Teachers and counselors may use the following questions to gain information on how cultural bias may be influencing their responses to students or clients:

- Does something about this person's appearance or behavior make me think that the behavior is abnormal?
- What is the basis for making these assumptions?
- What label(s) am I consciously or subconsciously applying to this person, and where did the label(s) come from?
- What other label(s) might be used to describe this behavior?
- To what cultural group am I assuming this person belongs, and what do I know about that group and that group's within-group differences?
- What is the source of my knowledge about the group?
- If the person was a referral, what is the cultural credibility of the person making the referral?

The model of multicultural understanding presented in this book has been designed to provide teachers and counselors with information that, when combined with their self-knowledge gained from answering the questions above and the pedagogy of the profession, will better enable the users to provide for the needs of all students or clients. The model is designed to provide no more than a basic foundation for teaching or counseling. The model does not attempt to answer all questions that might emerge about a particular cultural group. The model should serve as a beginning for more in-depth study of a particular cultural group. It serves as a springboard for understanding the cultures included and should be used with caution. Those who believe that the model is all-inclusive will soon discover it is virtually impossible for any model or scheme to be so comprehensive that no additional information will be needed.

The elements selected for inclusion in the model are those that appeared to be most relevant for use across cultures. Some elements are more useful and important in one culture than in another. For some elements, it was difficult to force the cultural group information to fit the model. For others, the information on the cultural group appeared to fit naturally with the model. In all cases, the model was used as the basis for providing information on the particular cultural group.

Weaver (1977) used the phrase "communities of interest" to describe the groups that are the subject of this book. I do not use the term *minority* to identify culturally diverse peoples because minority standing refers to power or the degree to which individuals identified with a specific group are denied access to privileges and opportunities available to others.

Each chapter was written with a clear understanding that cultures are heterogeneous and that any attempt at generalizations about a particular cultural group is dangerous. Readers are reminded to treat the information with caution. Students in a multicultural counseling course have used the material and provided their critiques. Faculty and students who used the 1992 edition have provided suggestions for improvement. Each chapter was submitted to a member of the cultural group discussed in that chapter for a blind review. Revisions were based on the recommendations of these reviewers.

Ethnic identity is a relational phenomenon having to do with cultural, historical, and social differences in relation to other groups in the same society. Ethnic identity includes, among other things, race, language, religion, cultural practices, socioeconomic status, political power, and country of origin. For many groups in the United States, ethnicity is less a question of essence than it is of position in the political and social structures of the society. Embedded within the concept of ethnic identity is the concept of "difference" or "diversity," which means that how a group is defined or how it defines itself includes how it is not like another group. Thus, many ethnic groups in the United States define themselves as how they are different from the dominant cultural group. Finally, ethnicity suggests membership in a group that (a) is different and less powerful than the dominant group, (b) is recognized as different by the dominant group, and (c) has a cultural heritage.

Teachers and counselors must acknowledge the following three identities:

1. All individuals are, in some respects, like all other individuals. All individuals are members of the human race and, as such, share many characteristics. All individuals share membership in our own species, *Homo sapiens.*
2. All individuals are, in some respects, like some other individuals as a result of cultural group membership. The cultural group serves as the basis for in-

dividuals to become humanized. Each individual becomes fully human through the process of participating in a cultural group or groups.

3. All individuals are, in some respects, like no other individuals in that each has some uniqueness. Individuals differ from one another both biologically and socially. No two individuals share the same experiences in their society.

For teachers and counselors, these three identities mean an awareness that individuals are seeking a personal identity, to a greater or lesser degree, by acknowledging an identity with a cultural group while living in a world community. By acknowledging the influences of cultural group membership on personal identity, teachers and counselors increasingly heighten their sensitivity to, and awareness of, issues related to the success of each student or client.

Just as there are three identities, there are three themes of the multiculturalism debate. The three major themes relevant to this book are

1. Competing visions of community
2. Educational quality
3. Social change

Advocates of multiculturalism see one nation in which differences and unique qualities are sources of strength, rather than of division. Advocates of multiculturalism call for equal attention to European influences and those of culturally diverse peoples. They believe that education will be enriched by the inclusion of multiple perspectives. Evident in multiculturalism is a social justice attitude that helps students understand the nature of difference and dominance and the effects of power and privilege.

Each chapter is divided into an introduction, a discussion of the 10 elements from the model, implications for education or counseling or both, questions for reflection, and references. Taken as a whole, each chapter presents my interpretation of what I consider the most important and useful information on the cultural group discussed. In no way is the material presented to be considered exhaustive of information about any particular cultural group. Readers who wish more detailed knowledge about a particular cultural group are encouraged to begin with the references at the end of the appropriate chapter and then to seek additional information from other sources.

The book is intended for undergraduate or graduate courses in multicultural education or counseling. It may be used as a supplement to a text for a course in which the instructor wants students to have specific information on different cultural groups.

Controversy is likely to be one product of this book. Because there is no consensus about what constitutes relevant cultural group information, whether certain facts are historically or currently relevant, the degree of homogeneity among cultural group members, and what methods are best for interventions with culturally different populations, readers may disagree with what I have written about some cultural groups. The controversy will be useful if it leads to a clearer understanding of cultural groups and how best to provide for their educational and counseling needs.

References

Nieto, S. (1992). *Affirming diversity: The sociopolitical context of multicultural education.* White Plains, NY: Longman.

Pedersen, P. B. (1991). Multiculturalism as a fourth force in counseling [Special issue]. *Journal of Counseling and Development, 70*(1).

Schlesinger, A. M., Jr. (1991). *The disuniting of America: Reflections on a multicultural society.* New York: Norton.

Stilgoe, J. R. (1982). *Common landscape of America.* New Haven, CT: Yale University Press.

Takaki, R. (1993). *A different mirror.* Boston: Little, Brown.

Weaver, J. L. (1977). *National health policy and the underserved.* St. Louis, MO: C. V. Mosby.

To Tonya Elizabeth and Regina Camille

1

A Model of Multicultural Understanding

The model of multicultural understanding presented in this volume is a comprehensive model that can be used as a guide to gain knowledge and understanding of culturally diverse individuals and groups. This knowledge and understanding can then be reflected appropriately in educational and counseling situations. The model was designed to include all the elements of personal awareness and information necessary for a person to engage in positive and productive relationships with culturally diverse individuals or groups. It is useful for teachers, individual counselors, family counselors, and those involved in any intervention within culturally diverse communities.

The model (Figure 1.1) provides a solid foundation for exploring ethnic differences. Although thorough and comprehensive, it is succinct enough to be useful in examining the cultural patterns, social relationships, and experiences of culturally diverse individuals and groups.

Awareness of Self

One uses the model by beginning with *awareness of self*. This component refers to the traditional "know thyself" element of Greek philosophy. In helping relationships with the culturally diverse, it might be necessary and

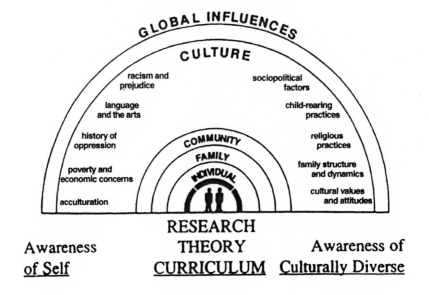

Figure 1.1. Multicultural Understanding

useful for those involved to share their personal experiences as well as their worldviews. *Worldview* means contemplation of the world or a view of life. It connotes a personal theory composed of knowledge and beliefs about the meaning of the world. Knowing one's own personal biases, values, interests, and worldview—which stem from culture—as well as knowing one's own culture will greatly enhance one's sensitivity toward other cultures. Awareness of self is the first step to understanding others (Locke, 1996); in seeking that awareness, one might attempt to answer the following questions:

- What is my worldview?
- What is my cultural heritage? What was the culture of my parents and my grandparents? With what cultural group(s) do I identify?
- What is the cultural relevance of my name?
- Which values, beliefs, opinions, and attitudes do I hold that are consistent with the dominant culture? Which are inconsistent? How did I learn these?
- How did I decide to become a teacher or counselor? What cultural standards were involved in the process? What do I understand to be the relationship between culture and education or counseling or both?
- What unique abilities, aspirations, expectations, and limitations do I have that might influence my relations with culturally diverse individuals?

Global Influences

What happens in our world often becomes more meaningful if where it happens has some relevance at a personal level. The culturally sensitive individual must be cognizant of world events and how members of various cultures translate those events into personal meaning. The world is becoming smaller and smaller, and events in a cultural group's country of origin may produce significant emotional reactions in group members. Some culturally diverse individuals may have relatives who still live in their countries of origin and may be quite sensitive to events in those countries, the policies of the U.S. government toward those events, and the attitudes of helpers toward the events. Such interest on the part of culturally diverse individuals necessitates some knowledge of world affairs. Shifts in the economic and political scenes in the United States greatly influence the state of affairs in South America, Africa, and Asia. Knowledge of the culture in a client's country of origin provides the helper with a more complete picture of that client's worldview.

Dominant Culture

This model uses the general culture of the United States as the backdrop for understanding culturally diverse individuals and groups. The model is useful in any setting with two reasonably different cultural groups. It seems appropriate for teachers and counselors to have a clear knowledge of the values of the dominant culture.

Culture is a construct that captures a socially transmitted system of ideas—ideas that shape behavior, categorize perceptions, and give names to selected aspects of experience. The primary mode of transmission of culture is language, which enables people to learn, experience, and share their traditions and customs. Hughes (1976) formulated a definition of culture that presents it as "a learned configuration of images and other symbolic elements widely shared among members of a given society or social group which, for individuals, functions as an orientation framework for behavior, and, for the group, serves as the communicational matrix which tends to coordinate and sanction behavior" (p. 13). Thus, the cultural process is a means for conveying values across generations. Cassirer (1944) described the symbolic system as unique to humans when he pointed out that humans "live not merely in a broader reality . . . but live, so to speak in a new dimension of reality . . . [humans] cannot escape their own achievement. [Humans] cannot but adapt the conditions of life. [Humans] live in a symbolic universe" (pp. 42-43).

The root concept for the term *ethnicity* is culture. Ethnicity is a derivative concept that recognizes the in-group values conceptualized by a particular cultural group, such as African Americans, Jewish Americans, or Vietnamese in the United States. Ethnic identity is measured by self-perception, identification, and participation in ethnic activities. Thus, *culture* and *ethnicity* refer to the same generic processes.

Nash (1989) reduced the core elements of ethnicity to three:

1. Kinship
2. Commensality (e.g., food preferences, lifestyle)
3. The shared ideology he calls a *common cult* (body of beliefs and ritual activities that celebrate the community's historical experience)

The essence of ethnicity is contrast, the recognition of difference.

Alba (1990) categorized theories of ethnic identity into four types:

1. Ethnicity as class (e.g., working class)
2. Ethnicity as a political movement (e.g., "power" movements of the 1960s)
3. Ethnicity as revival (e.g., ethnic foods, clothing, festivals)
4. Ethnicity as a token identity (e.g., passing down a Swedish cookie recipe)

Steward (1972) identified five components of culture in his summary of cultural assumptions and values:

1. *Activity:* How do people approach activity? How important are goals in life? Who makes decisions? What is the nature of problem solving?
2. *Definition of social relations:* How are roles defined? How do people relate to those whose status is different? How are sex roles defined? What is the meaning of friendship?
3. *Motivation:* What is the achievement orientation of the culture? Is cooperation or competition emphasized?
4. *Perception of the world:* What is the predominant worldview? What is the predominant view on human nature? What is the predominant view on the nature of truth? How is time defined? What is the nature of property?
5. *Perception of self and the individual:* How is self defined? Where is a person's identity determined? What is the nature of the individual? What kinds of persons are valued and respected?

Robin M. Williams, Jr. (1970), a noted sociologist, identified 15 cultural themes and orientations that generally reflect the Anglo-Saxon influence on the culture of the United States. Although not all Anglo-Saxons value these themes and orientations, these nevertheless reflect what many determine to be predominant in the culture of the United States. Noted historian John Hope Franklin (as cited in Fersh, 1978) concluded that, by the end of the 19th century, United States American standards of ethnicity accepted Anglo-Saxons as the norm, placed other White people on what might be called "ethnic probation," and excluded all others from serious consideration. Thus, it seems logical to describe Anglo-Saxon values as representative of the culture of the United States. The themes and orientations identified by Williams are as follows:

1. *Achievement and success:* The emphasis is on rags-to-riches success stories.
2. *Activity and work:* This is a land of busy people who stress disciplined, productive activity as a worthy end in itself.
3. *Humanitarian mores:* People spontaneously come to the aid of others and hold traditional sympathy for the underdog.
4. *Moral orientation:* Life events and situations are judged in terms of right and wrong.
5. *Efficiency and practicality:* The emphasis is on the practical value of getting things done.
6. *Progress:* An optimistic view is held that things will get better.
7. *Material comfort:* Emphasis is placed on the good life. Many are conspicuous consumers.
8. *Equality:* The avowal of the commitment to equality is constant.
9. *Freedom:* The belief in individual freedom takes on almost a religious connotation.
10. *External conformity:* Uniformity in matters of dress, housing, recreation, manners, and even expression of political ideas is great.
11. *Science and secular rationality:* The sciences are esteemed as a means of asserting mastery over the environment.
12. *Nationalism-patriotism:* The sense of loyalty to what is called "American" is strong.
13. *Democracy:* The people believe that every person should have a voice in the political destiny of the country.
14. *Individual personality:* Every individual should be independent, responsible, and self-respecting. The group should not take precedence over the individual.
15. *Racism and related group superiority:* This theme represents the chief value conflict in the culture of the United States because it emphasizes differential evaluation of racial, religious, and ethnic groups.

We must understand the dominant culture from the perspectives of the individual, the family, and the community. We need to know how that culture defines a psychologically healthy individual, defines and reinforces the family for its acculturation function, and defines the concept of community in terms of size and who is included in it.

Cultural Differences

The model has many elements of the culture to examine: sociopolitical factors, the culture's history of oppression, the experience of prejudice and racism, poverty within the culture, the influence of language and the arts, the influence of religious practices, child-rearing practices, family role and structure, values and attitudes, and degree of opposition to acculturation. This model is similar to Sue and Sue's (1990) model in that they stress the impact of sociocultural forces as well as the psychological and developmental influences on the behavioral expressions of different racial and ethnic groups.

Thus, as immigrants come to the United States, they are influenced by one set of factors: the existing environmental conditions. They bring with them a second set of factors: their own psychological and behavioral qualities, including language and the arts, child-rearing practices, religious practices, family structure, and values and attitudes. These two sets of factors work either against each other or together to form and shape the new immigrant into a participant in the culture of the United States. The "Americanization" process is designed to blend the many ethnic ingredients so that one nationality is produced. The degree to which an immigrant group is assimilated into the culture of the United States occurs by mutual consent. For some, the dominant culture resists assimilation. For others, the immigrant group itself elects to remain outside the main cultural group. Under either circumstance, the gap between the dominant culture and the immigrants' culture-of-origin is likely to present major problems for helping professionals from the dominant culture who do not have knowledge about, and sensitivity to, culturally diverse individuals or groups.

The model employs a circumstantialist view of culture and ethnicity (Glazer & Moynihan, 1975) wherein cultural identity is seen as primarily socially constructed and reactive. This view explains why some cultural groups define themselves along lines of ethnicity (e.g., common history, kinship, language, religion), whereas other groups define themselves along factors of class. This view also brings issues of power and position into focus and helps explain why, at certain points in history, different ethnic groups are more or less aware of their ethnicity.

It is important to see cultural differences as contrasts, and not just as differences. By looking at contrasts, both the helper and the helpee are required to evaluate their cultural practices and to determine how these practices affect their relationship. Statements of cultural contrast are only starting points because the objective truth of cultural differences may be less important than beliefs about what the truth may be. In terms of how people differ along psychological dimensions, McGoldrick and Giordano (1996) reported that people differ according to the following six characteristics:

1. Their experience of psychological distress
2. How they describe symptoms of the distress
3. How they communicate about their distress and its symptoms
4. Their attribution of cause(s)
5. Their attitudes toward helpers
6. Their expectations for treatment

The model allows for scrutiny of the following cultural elements: acculturation, poverty and economic concerns, history of oppression, language and the arts, racism and prejudice, sociopolitical factors, child-rearing practices, religious practices, family structure and dynamics, and cultural values and attitudes. When investigating these cultural elements to find out about a particular cultural group, one must remember that the differences *within* a cultural group may be greater than the differences between the dominant culture and other cultures. Helping professionals should bear in mind that the uniqueness of the individual must be respected at all times, along with the uniqueness of the cultural group. Giving too much attention to the individual encourages neglect of the impact of the cultural group on the individual. Giving too much attention to the cultural group runs the risk of stereotyping the individual as a member of that cultural group and forgetting individual uniqueness. The helper must keep both the individual's uniqueness and the cultural group membership foremost in mind as he or she works with the culturally diverse.

Following are brief discussions of the 10 elements of the model. I believe that these represent the most important elements in terms of knowledge about, and sensitivity toward, other cultures for counselors and other helping professionals to understand.

Acculturation

Members of any given cultural group are not all alike. One major difference among members of the various cultural groups is the degree to which they have immersed themselves into the culture of the United States. Members of culturally diverse groups might be classified as follows:

- *Bicultural:* Able to function as competently in the dominant culture as in their own while holding on to manifestations of their own culture
- *Traditional:* Holding on to a majority of cultural traits from the culture of origin while rejecting many traits of the dominant culture
- *Acculturated:* Having given up most cultural traits of the culture of origin and assumed traits of the dominant culture
- *Marginal:* Neither completely at ease in the culture of origin nor minimally a part of the dominant culture

Pinderhughes (1982) suggested that a "victim system" operates among marginal individuals. This system is a set of self-reinforcing beliefs and practices that contribute to the perpetuation of poverty and helplessness.

Royce (1982) used the term *cultural brokers* to characterize biculturalism. She defined cultural brokers as "individuals who span both the world of the immigrants and the home they have chosen. . . . They take a personal interest in the individual who is trying to make the connections and tailor their strategies to his particular needs" (p. 135). Rouse (1992) used the term *cultural bifocality* to describe the capacity to see the world through two different value lenses.

Redfield, Linton, and Herskovits (1936) described acculturation as the phenomena that result when individuals from different cultures come into continuous firsthand contact, resulting in changes in the original pattern for either or both groups. When looking at the degree of acculturation, one might also seek to determine at what level(s) individuals belonging to culturally diverse groups have acculturated in terms of marital, attitudinal, behavioral, civic, structural, and identification factors. An early study by Ellman (1977) found that the more American an ethnic individual feels, the less fearful he or she is of exhibiting his or her ethnic background. This finding supports the notion that bicultural persons are likely to be more patriotic and to exhibit more ethnic identification.

Hansen (1952) hypothesized that children of first-generation immigrants were likely to focus primarily on acculturating, whereas third-generation offspring tended to reassert their ethnicity. Although his theory has stimulated much interest, it fails to fully explain why and how members of certain cultural groups are more bicultural, acculturated, traditional, or marginal than others.

Bogardus (1949) identified three types of overlapping acculturation:

1. *Accidental acculturation* occurs when individuals of various cultures in close proximity to each other exchange goods and services and incidentally adopt cultural patterns from each other in a hit-or-miss fashion.
2. *Forced acculturation* imposes cultural patterns, behavior, or beliefs on ethnic populations and immigrants.

3. *Democratic acculturation* respects the history and strengths of different cultures and demonstrates the equivalency of social and psychological patterns of all cultures. Individuals may choose either to adopt cultural patterns of other groups over time or to retain the patterns of their culture of origin.

Bicultural conflict occurs when the values and behaviors of the culture of origin are different from those of the dominant culture. It can lead to bicultural tension, which occurs when an individual's coping skills are based on only one value system—either that of the culture of origin or of the dominant culture. The rejection and abandonment of the culture of origin is called *overacculturation* (Galan, 1992).

Pinderhughes (1989) asserted that culture defines the problem perspective, the expression of the problem, the treatment provider, and the treatment options. Fabrega (1969) hypothesized that less acculturated individuals tend to experience greater psychological distress than more acculturated people. Graves (1967), in contrast, hypothesized that more acculturated individuals tend to be alienated from their own ethnic support systems and are more likely to suffer psychological disorders. The bicultural hypothesis (Ramirez, 1984) suggests that the relationship between mental health and acculturation is a curvilinear one; people who can maintain the balance between two cultures have fewer psychological disorders than the more extreme groups, the less acculturated, or the more acculturated. Less acculturated individuals have been reported by Vega, Warheit, and Meinhardt (1984) to experience greater psychological distress, whereas Krause, Bennett, and Tran (1989) hypothesized that the more acculturated individuals would experience greater psychological distress.

Poverty and Economic Concerns

Some 39 million United States Americans live in poverty. Persons living below the poverty level in the United States include inordinate numbers of ethnic/racial culture group members. The effective helper of culturally diverse individuals or groups has a clear view why poverty exists within a society. Knowledge of the historic causes of poverty, the political and economic factors that perpetuate poverty, and the networking being carried out in the client's local community to eradicate poverty enhance the ability of the culturally sensitive helper to work with culturally diverse individuals. Factors such as housing, employment, educational opportunity, and life expectancy are often clearly associated with poverty among members of culturally diverse populations.

Some might even argue that discrimination, prejudice, and racism, which express themselves differently in different countries, are more a reflection of economic status than of racial or ethnic group membership. Helpers need to have empathy for poor people. Good helpers have a repertoire of strategies to recommend that include alternatives to the traditional dominant culture's view of poverty and how to overcome it.

History of Oppression

Educators and counselors cannot explore only those factors relating to individuals' experiences in the present. They must understand and have empathy for those events from the past or future that have an impact on the present. Likewise, although much evidence confirms that the history of culturally diverse groups in the United States often is unpleasant, helpers must be willing to explore this unpleasant material so that culturally diverse individuals can better deal with events in the present. For some culturally diverse persons, a recollection of the past or even the reading of history contributes to their willingness or unwillingness to interact with the dominant culture. Teachers and counselors must explore what this actual or vicarious oppression has done to the psychological adjustment of culturally diverse students or clients.

Language and the Arts

A major question within the dominant culture is how much the culture should tolerate those who do not speak Standard English. Hurtado and Rodriguez (1989) stated that language is perceived by some White Americans as the one mutable feature of culturally diverse groups and therefore the place to demand assimilation. Because it appears that the dominant culture wishes the culturally diverse to acculturate, and because language is the means by which culture is transmitted, it seems logical that the dominant culture would desire that all persons learn the dominant language as soon as possible. The ability to speak Standard English thus becomes a symbolic measure by which members of culturally diverse groups are often judged. Scant attention is given to fostering bilingualism, and many people hold contempt for individuals whose spoken language or dialect is noticeably different from Standard English.

Likewise, similar emotions are generated regarding art or art forms. For example, the standard artistic form of the dominant culture in the United States is linear, with a progressive organization that drives toward climax, catharsis, and closure. The artistic forms prevalent in many culturally diverse groups place heavy emphasis on circular organization, involvement through repetition of sound and movement, and short units leading to a succession of mini-climaxes. For example, African American audiences interact with a performer through a great deal of "call and response"; the better known and respected the performer, the greater and more enthusiastic the response. Dominant culture audiences in the United States, in contrast, indicate their approval of an artistic expression through silence, quiet attention, and mild response to the performer; the greatest sign of approval is given at the conclusion of the performance.

Significant attention should be given to nonverbal communication as well. Helping professionals need to know that culture determines such elements of communication as tone of voice, rate of speech, pitch, volume, proxemics, haptics, kinesics, smiling, occulism, and greetings and farewells. Albert Mehrabian (1981) concluded that, in any given total message, 7% of communication is verbal, 38% is vocal, and 55% is facial. His findings clearly demonstrate the need for understanding and appreciation of nonverbal communication within the cultural context.

Racism and Prejudice

Prejudice is defined as judgment formed before fully examining the object of evaluation. *Racial prejudice* refers to judgment based on racial/ethnic/cultural group membership before getting to know the person. *Racism* combines prejudice with power—power to do something based on prejudiced beliefs.

In our urgency to categorize people, we all use some prior knowledge in the process. Thus, all people are prejudiced. Prejudice may be personal, institutional, or cultural. *Personal prejudice* includes beliefs about individuals as members of a particular group. *Institutional prejudice* is prejudice that has been incorporated into the structure of an institution and is based on the beliefs of the people who have influenced the institution. *Cultural prejudice,* or *ethnocentrism,* is demonstrated in an assertion of a cultural group's superiority in accomplishments, creativity, or achievements.

One way to understand prejudice and racism is through the use of a matrix that views the expression of prejudice/racism along two dimensions: overt versus covert, and intentional versus unintentional (Locke & Hardaway, 1980). The matrix yields four types of prejudice/racism:

1. *Overt intentional:* Openly espousing a doctrine of inferiority of culturally diverse groups
2. *Overt unintentional:* Counseling culturally diverse clients toward lower socioeconomic status jobs/careers; cultural blindness that equates underuse of mental health services with mental health status
3. *Covert intentional:* Expecting culturally diverse individuals to communicate nonverbally exactly as members of the dominant culture do
4. *Covert unintentional:* Explicitly identifying the races of members of particular cultures when certain behaviors are described

Racism and prejudice are inextricably entwined in the oppression of culturally diverse groups in the United States. From the moment White European settlers first stepped onto the soil of the Atlantic coast, attitudes of superiority and lack of understanding of other cultural group members have been predominant. Many of those attitudes persist today, and many have been absorbed into the training and education of counselors and other helping professionals. Helping professionals have an opportunity and a responsibility to communicate honestly and directly regarding the views they hold about culturally diverse groups. Wellman (1993) identified two perspectives that are often used *unsuccessfully* to confront racism:

1. Racism continues because of our failure to communicate.
2. Racial misunderstanding comes from our ignorance about each other.

The truth is that racism persists even when we communicate well across cultural lines and even after we have learned quite much about each other.

Terry (1970) described six attitudes/beliefs/behaviors of dominant group members who wish to be positive influences with culturally diverse populations: Dominant group members must

1. Move beyond guilt
2. Value the self-worth of persons
3. Understand power
4. Take risks
5. Be proactive
6. Value pluralism

Adherence to these attitudes should enhance the attractiveness of dominant-culture members who work with persons culturally different from themselves.

Sociopolitical Factors

Helping professionals need to understand the culturally unique social factors that affect a culture. Many items in this category overlap other areas (e.g., family structure, child-rearing practices), but others are quite different. The celebration of holidays, the roles of social organizations, and how friendship is determined are examples of social factors unique within cultural groups.

Political factors include the area of self-determination within the cultural group. The level of involvement in the political process at local, state, and national levels may be a function of the dominant culture's imposing restrictions, as well as the degree of interest and belief in the political system as an avenue for group advancement. Singer (1994) pointed out that many young people are silenced in school because they are stereotyped in the media and in textbooks. He posited that the debate over multiculturalism has little to do with academic scholarship, but is rather a political battle over who will hold power and shape policy in United States American society.

Child-Rearing Practices

The family is the primary socialization agent of a culture, and thus the process of child rearing itself can be very revealing of a culture's structure and values. By examining specific child-rearing practices in a culture, one can learn much about kinship networks, how sex roles are socialized, how respect is taught, who is respected, when children are taught to be assertive, the obligations of children to parents and of parents to children, and the place of competition in the culture.

Religious Practices

Religion is an organized system of the belief in a god, gods, or other supernatural beings. Religion helps a cultural group determine relationships with other peoples and with the universe. Canda (1989) posited that religion is an aspect of human culture and experience that significantly affects both individual and collective behavior. All human beings possess spiritual needs for a sense of meaning and purpose in life, including expressions both within and without formal religious institutions. Religious beliefs and practices often play a crucial role in the understanding of self and world, especially regarding the way they establish meaning and purpose in relationships among self, others, the environment, and the ultimate reality. In some cultural groups, religion and local politics are closely tied. Some cultural protest organizations had their beginnings in religious organizations. For some cultural groups, religion has been a primary source of strength for coping with the demands of the dominant culture. For others, religion has been the primary determinant of a sense of community, providing a basis for cohesion and moral strength within the cultural group.

Family Structure and Dynamics

The family, the oldest human institution, is the basic unit of a culture. The family is responsible for the production of children who will continue the culture, as well as for the socialization of those children. The way the culture organizes itself in kinship patterns provides useful information on its structure. Individuals who are biologically unrelated but who are treated as "family" are called *fictive kin*. Factors such as who has authority in families and in what areas, the impact of marriage outside the cultural group, the nature of relationships among members of the family, and how lineage is determined are useful in understanding the impact of family structure on the culture.

McGill (1992) recommended the use of the cultural story as a nonthreatening way to access relevant background information. He stated,

> The cultural story refers to an ethnic or cultural group's origin, migration, and identity. Within the family, it is used to tell where one's ancestors came from, what kind of people they were and current members are, what issues are important to the family, what good and bad things have happened over time, and what lessons have been learned from their experiences. At the ethnic level, a cultural story tells the group's collective story of how to cope with life and how to respond to pain and trouble. It teaches people how to thrive in a multicultural society and what children should be taught so that they can sustain their ethnic and cultural story. (p. 340)

Congress's (1994) culturegram comprises 10 categories of cultural information for a specific family:

1. Reasons for immigration
2. Length of time in the community
3. Legal or undocumented status (student or work permit; remaining in the country after expiration of visa)
4. Age of family members at time of immigration
5. Spoken language
6. Contact with cultural institutions (churches, social clubs)
7. Health beliefs (native attitudes on health, illness, and treatment)
8. Holidays and special events
9. Crisis events or stressors (losing a job, death of a family member, relocation)
10. Family, education, and work values

The culturegram is especially useful for counselors. Use of the culturegram helps us understand the complexities of family culture, individualize treatment plans specific to the target family, and discover specific areas for intervention.

Cultural Values and Attitudes

Kluckhorn and Strodtbeck (1961) provided five categories of questions that are useful in examining cultural values and attitudes:

1. *Time:* Is the orientation based on the past, the present, or the future?
2. *Human relations:* Are individuals, collateral relationships, or lineal relationships valued most?
3. *Human activity:* Is the focus on doing, being, or becoming?
4. *Human nature:* At birth, are people considered basically good, bad, neutral, or mixed?
5. *Supernatural:* Is the relationship with the supernatural one of control, subordination, or harmony?

Some of these concepts are cognitive in that they stress what people know and how they interpret their world. Others emphasize behavior and customs and how they are transmitted from generation to generation. Counselors and educators need to realize that culture inevitably influences personality orientation, acculturation, manifestations of behavior, effectiveness of procedures, and the language used.

Research, Theory, and Curriculum

The 10 elements in the model, when related to culturally diverse groups, provide insight into specific research questions that may be investigated. Various assumptions of traditional educational and counseling theories may also be challenged and even altered to fit the specifics of members of culturally diverse populations. Curriculum modifications may be implemented, from elementary schools to graduate-level training, that reflect sensitivity to members of culturally diverse populations. In communities, services must first be available to members of culturally diverse groups. Once services are available, they must be culturally sensitive. Marin (1993) argued that culturally appropriate interventions must be based on the cultural values of the group of interest, must adopt strategies that "reflect the subjective cultural characteristics" of the group, and must take into account their behavioral preferences (p. 155).

The nature of many culturally diverse groups limits their accessibility as communities, and therefore it is difficult to conduct direct research without being intrusive. Important questions may be answered, however, through observations, discussions, and participation of the researcher in the culture of the group under study. The current need is for research perspectives that place culturally diverse peoples' interests, values, beliefs, and ideals at the center of any cultural analysis. Research questions might focus on examination of the conditions under which members of culturally diverse groups seek assistance from members of the dominant culture; the relationship between education/counseling and ethnically diverse people; the tendency to write about people of color as victims; the failure to distinguish between differing aspirations of ethnic communities and multicultural educators and counselors; and the need for theoretical frameworks that analyze the consequences of acculturation and the goals of ethnically diverse peoples in a neoconservative society. In the final analysis, however, this research is best conducted by professionals who are themselves members of the cultural groups under investigation.

From information obtained by examining the 10 elements in the model and derived from research, several considerations for educational and counseling theory emerge and require evaluation if useful and effective counseling strategies are to be developed for use with the culturally diverse. These areas are definitions of normality within the cultural group, the place of the individual within the system, how independence is treated within the culture, the place of support in the culture, and the meaning of personal change (Pedersen, 1987).

Giordano and Giordano (1995, pp. 23-24) suggested eight considerations useful in responding to cultural diversity:

1. Assess the importance of ethnicity to clients and families.
2. Validate and strengthen ethnic identity.
3. Become aware of clients' support systems.
4. Help clients identify and resolve value conflicts.
5. Become aware of "cultural camouflage" (use of ethnic, racial, or religious identity as a defense against change or pain).
6. Recognize the advantages or disadvantages of being of the same ethnic group as your clients.
7. Avoid the goal of having to know everything about other ethnic groups.
8. To avoid polarization, always try to think in categories that allow for at least three possibilities; for example, if you are exploring African American and White differences, consider how a Japanese American might view the same situation.

Often, "normality" is judged by how much a person or group of persons varies from the dominant culture in the larger society. Most educational and counseling theories are based on the assumption that a single standard is the norm by which all individuals should be judged. Given this rather narrowly focused assumption, culturally diverse individuals might be considered deviant with respect to socialization, religion, education, and other areas. All cultures have folk syndromes, locally defined conditions of distress, diagnostic categories, and appropriate intervention techniques. Normality in a culturally diverse population must be considered within the context of the individual's subgroup and its own esoteric rules.

Although most theories of development in the United States are based on the assumption that the *individual* is the basic building block of society, this notion does not hold for many other cultural groups. In many cultures, the family unit and, ultimately, the entire community operate as a strong bonding system that supports each individual. Considering the goals of an individual group member to be more important than group welfare might be offensive in a group-centered culture. In a similar vein, independence is viewed as "good" or "healthy" in the dominant culture of the United States, but among many other cultural populations, dependence on the family or the community or both is the accepted standard for survival.

Cazden (1986) warned helpers to distinguish between differential treatment that individualizes favorable and differential treatment based on bias. Students or clients who have specific needs deserve differential treatment. Those who do not have specific needs but who receive differential treatment nonetheless are probably the subjects of bias.

Shweder (1991) discussed five cultural modifiers that highlight the context of language in cross-cultural relationships:

1. Culturally sensitive counselors must know the types of emotional states commonly reported in a given population.
2. All emotional illnesses have a situational aspect.
3. Counselors need a sense of the culturally generated meanings attached to specific emotions.
4. Counselors need to understand the extent to which individuals from specific cultural groups are willing to talk openly about emotional functioning.
5. Counselors must understand that in all descriptions of emotional states are issues of power, its distribution, and its availability.

It is necessary that counseling be properly and sufficiently used with different ethnic groups by well-trained ethnic- and language-matched helpers so that a claim can be made for its acceptance and effectiveness. Atkinson, Thompson, and Grant (1993) proposed a three-dimensional model for use in selecting roles and strategies when working with culturally diverse clients: (a) client level of acculturation, (b) internal or external problem etiology, and (c) whether goals of helping are prevention or remediation.

After considering the 10 elements of culturally diverse populations addressed in the model and exploring specific research questions and implications for theory, it is possible to propose strategies for curriculum modification and change. Curriculum alterations are needed from the elementary level through the graduate level. Elementary school students can study various perspectives derived from many cultures. In schools with large concentrations of students from culturally diverse groups or in communities where they live, specific attention needs to be directed to the study of these groups. Such programs should stress the positive aspects of these cultures, along with the principle of mutual respect for one another's cultural differences.

Curricula for college and graduate students, especially in teacher education and counselor education programs, should include the study of many cultures, with emphasis on appreciation of contributions of all groups to the society. Courses in areas such as multicultural education, multicultural counseling, and cross-cultural communication can help students become aware of perspectives other than their own.

The need for research perspectives that place the interests of culturally diverse groups in proper focus is clear. Specific needs for specific groups must be at the center of any analysis. Cultural traditions and multiple ways of knowing must be a part of any research that claims to be culturally relevant.

Summary

To meet the needs of culturally diverse populations, helping professionals who work with them must have an understanding of culturally consistent assessment, evaluation, and treatment skills, as well as theoretical content. To ensure that methods are ethnically sensitive, one must design programs or organizations that are responsive to the culture of the target group. The model of cross-cultural understanding presented above offers a framework for such action. This model does not specifically address skills; rather, it is meant to provide a foundation upon which counselors and educators can build relationships with students and clients from culturally diverse populations through the knowledge they gain from the study of culturally diverse groups. Effective education and counseling of the culturally diverse can occur only when teachers and counselors have knowledge of both education/counseling theory and the particulars relevant to the individuals and groups they are trying to help.

Questions for Review and Reflection

1. Define the following terms:

   culture

   bicultural

   marginal

   culturally diverse

     proxemics

     kinesics

     melting pot

     prejudice

     racism

     acculturated

2. Using the questions in the section on awareness of self, identify how you have been influenced by your cultural background. What specific benefits have you enjoyed as a consequence of your ethnicity?

3. What world events have had the greatest impact on your work as an educator or a counselor?

4. What is your metaphor for "America," and what are the advantages or disadvantages of each possibility?

5. Which of R. Williams's (1970) cultural themes appears most relevant to you personally? How has this cultural theme helped or hindered your development as an educator or a counselor?

6. Which of the 10 elements used to describe culturally diverse groups do you think is most important in your work? Why?

7. How does the model help you as an educator or a counselor understand the importance of using culture-specific strategies/techniques with culturally diverse populations?

8. Describe what might be called a "typical" person from the dominant culture of the United States. How do you differ from this typical person?

9. Identify and explain three major assumptions underlying the model presented in this chapter.

10. Explain some potential hazards inherent in sending inconsistent nonverbal messages.

11. How does an acculturation viewpoint differ from a culturally diverse (pluralist) viewpoint in terms of the qualities necessary for success in the United States?

12. Create a genogram for yourself, using as a reference Monica McGoldrick and Randy Gerson, 1985, *Genograms in Family Assessment,* New York, Norton.

References

Alba, R. D. (1990). *Ethnic identity: The transformation of White America.* New Haven, CT: Yale University Press.

Atkinson, D. R., Thompson, C. E., & Grant, S. K. (1993). A three-dimensional model for counseling racial/ethnic minorities. *Counseling Psychologist, 21,* 257-277.

Bogardus, E. S. (1949). Cultural pluralism and acculturation. *Sociology and Social Research, 34,* 125-129.

Canda, E. R. (1989). Religious content in social work education: A comparative approach. *Journal of Social Work Education, 25*(1), 36-45.

Cassirer, E. (1944). *An essay on man: An introduction to a philosophy of human culture.* New Haven, CT: Yale University Press.

Cazden, C. B. (1986). Classroom discourse. In M. C. Wittrock (Ed.), *Handbook of research on teaching* (pp. 432-463). New York: Macmillan.

Congress, E. P. (1994). The use of culturegrams to assess and empower culturally diverse families. *Families in Society, 75,* 531-540.

Ellman, Y. (1977). The ethnic awakening in the United States and its influence on Jews. *Ethnicity, 4,* 133-155.

Fabrega, H. (1969). Social psychiatric aspects of acculturation and migration: A general statement. *Comprehensive Psychiatry, 140,* 1103-1105.

Fersh, S. (1978). *Asia: Teaching about/learning from.* New York: Teachers College Press.

Galan, F. J. (1992). Experiential focusing with Mexican American males' bicultural identity problems. In K. Corcoran (Ed.), *Structuring change: Effective practice for common client problems* (pp. 236-238). Chicago: Lyceum.

Giordano, J., & Giordano, M. A. (1995). Ethnic dimensions in family treatment. In R. H. Mikesell, D. D. Lusterman, & S. H. McDaniel (Eds.), *Integrating family therapy* (pp. 5-30). Washington, DC: American Psychological Association.

Glazer, N., & Moynihan, D. P. (1975). *Ethnicity: Theory and experience.* Cambridge, MA: Harvard University.

Graves, T. D. (1967). Acculturation, access, and alcohol in a tri-ethnic community. *American Anthropologist, 69,* 306-321.

Hansen, M. L. (1952). The third generation in America. *Commentary, 14,* 492-500.

Hughes, C. C. (1976). *Custom made: Introductory readings in cultural anthropology.* Chicago: Rand-McNally.

Hurtado, A., & Rodriguez, R. (1989). Language as a social problem: The repression of Spanish in South Texas. *Journal of Multilingual and Multicultural Development, 10,* 401-419.

Kluckhorn, F., & Strodtbeck, F. (1961). *Variations in value orientations.* Evanston, IL: Row, Peterson.

Krause, N., Bennett, J., & Tran, T. V. (1989). Age differences in the acculturation process. *Psychology and Aging, 4,* 321-332.

Locke, D. C. (1996). Multicultural counseling issues. In A. J. Palmo & W. J. Weikel (Eds.), *Foundations of mental health counseling.* Springfield, IL: Charles C Thomas.

Locke, D. C., & Hardaway, Y. V. (1980). Moral perspectives in interracial settings. In D. Cochrane & M. Manley-Casimir (Eds.), *Moral education: Practical approaches* (pp. 269-285). New York: Praeger.

Marin, G. (1993). Defining culturally appropriate community interventions: Hispanics as a case study. *Journal of Community Psychology, 21,* 149-161.

McGill, D. W. (1992). The cultural story in multicultural family therapy. *Families in Society, 73,* 339-349.

McGoldrick, M., & Giordano, J. (1996). Overview. In M. McGoldrick & J. Giordano (Eds.), *Ethnicity and family therapy.* New York: Guilford.

Mehrabian, A. (1981). *Silent messages.* Belmont, CA: Wadsworth.

Nash, M. (1989). *The cauldron of ethnicity in the modern world.* Chicago: University of Chicago Press.

Pedersen, P. (1987). Ten frequent assumptions of cultural bias in counseling. *Journal of Multicultural Counseling and Development, 15,* 16-24.

Pinderhughes, E. (1982). Family functioning in Afro-America. *Social Work, 27,* 91-96.

Pinderhughes, E. (1989). *Understanding race, ethnicity, and power: The key to efficacy in clinical practice.* New York: Free Press.

Ramirez, M. (1984). Assessing and understanding biculturalism-multiculturalism in Mexican American adults. In J. L. Martinez & R. H. Mendoza (Eds.), *Chicano psychology* (pp. 77-94). San Diego: Academic Press.

Redfield, R., Linton, R., & Herskovits, M. J. (1936). Memorandum for the study of acculturation. *American Anthropologist, 38,* 149-152.

Rouse, R. (1992). *Power in popular culture.* Ann Arbor: University of Michigan Press.

Royce, A. P. (1982). *Ethnic identity: Strategies of diversity.* Bloomington: Indiana University Press.

Shweder, R. A. (1991). *Thinking through cultures: Expectations in cultural psychology.* Cambridge, MA: Harvard University Press.

Singer, A. (1994). Reflections on multiculturalism. *Phi Delta Kappan, 76,* 284-288.

Steward, E. C. (1972). *American cultural patterns.* La Grange Park, IL: Intercultural Network.

Sue, D. W., & Sue, D. (1990). *Counseling the culturally different: Theory and practice* (2nd ed.). New York: John Wiley.

Terry, R. W. (1970). *For Whites only.* Grand Rapids, MI: Eerdmans.

Vega, W., Warheit, M., & Meinhardt, K. (1984). Marital disruption and the prevalence of depressive symptomatology among Mexican American farm workers. *Social Science and Medicine, 20,* 39-45.

Wellman, D. T. (1993). *Portraits of White racism.* London: Cambridge University Press.

Williams, R. M., Jr. (1970). *American society: A sociological interpretation.* New York: Knopf.

2

African Americans

Since coming to the United States from Africa, Black Americans' experiences have been paradoxical: hardship and uncertainty on the one hand, and accomplishment and determination on the other. The institution of slavery, followed by emancipation, with its sanctioned institutional arrangements of political, social, and economic segregation and discrimination, produced a people who provide the greatest challenge to the democratic principles of the dominant culture's emphasis and focus on equality and egalitarianism.

The African American population has undergone significant changes during its history in the United States in terms of growth, distribution, and composition. At the time of the first U.S. census in 1790, about 757,000 African Americans lived in the United States. By 1990, 29.9 million African Americans lived in the United States (12.1% of the total population), projected to grow to 53.7 million by 2060. Winbush (1996) reported that African Americans constitute the largest culturally diverse group in the United States and have large numbers of the very old and very young. Prior to World War II, three out of every four African Americans lived in the South. By 1970, 81% of African Americans lived in urban areas and only 50% lived in the South.

Women outnumber men in the population as a result of the loss of African American boys and young men to homicide, suicide, and substance abuse. This gender difference is sustained throughout the life cycle, with accidents and medical problems contributing to the loss of African American men in later years (Task Force on Black and Minority Health, 1986).

Throughout this chapter, the term *African American* is used because it is consistent with terms used to describe other groups. It is also used because the term *Black* is inadequate to convey the rich history of descendants of the peoples who came to the United States from the continent of Africa. The term also includes recent immigrants from the West Indies, Brazil, and a host of other countries, including those from Africa. For most of the history of African Americans in the United States, the tendency has been to omit the history of this group in Africa and to begin the history as of the time the first Africans arrived in the "New World" in 1619. *African American* is used because the term *Black* has been associated with darkness, evil, and ignorance, whereas the term *White* has been associated with brightness, good, and intelligence.

Acculturation

Valentine (1971) believes that most of the African American community is bicultural. He concluded that the collective behavior and social life of the Black community is bicultural in the sense that each African American ethnic segment draws on both a distinctive repertoire of standardized African American behaviors and, simultaneously, patterns derived from the dominant culture. Socialization into both systems begins at an early age and continues throughout life, and both systems are generally of equal importance in individuals' lives. Root (1992) estimated that, in terms of family history and genealogical lines, one half or more of all African Americans are multiracial.

Pinderhughes (1989) described a meeting with a group of teachers in which one teacher had this to say about the bicultural condition:

> A mother explained when I was questioning her values about allowing him to fight, "I'll take care of his behavior; you take care of his education. Where we live he has to be tough and be able to fight. I'm not going to stop that. You set your standards here and see that he understands he has to abide by them."
> (p. 181)

Staples (1976) suggested that the bicultural nature of African Americans is forced on them and is often antithetical to their own values. He went on to say that the commitment to Eurocentric values is not necessarily positive and that although African Americans may engage in Euramerican cultural practices (e.g., individualism, materialism), this should not be taken as a strong commitment to those values.

Essien-Udoms's (1962) concept of the dilemma of duality suggests that African Americans must choose to act either "the Black way" or "the non-Black way." The dilemma is resolved when African Americans distinguish between themselves and their "role."

Myrdal (1944) concluded that "it is to the advantage of American Negroes as individuals and as a group to become assimilated into American culture, to acquire the traits held in esteem by the dominant White culture" (p. 929).

Poverty and Economic Concerns

Historically, African American unemployment rates have been at least twice those of members of the dominant culture (Dovidio & Gaertner, 1986). Dickson (1993) reported that African American males earn only 58% of the income of their White counterparts and that 35% of African American families report incomes below the poverty line. Sassen (1990) reported that, as a function of a combination of poverty, unemployment, and discrimination, African Americans are overreported among residents in poor, inner-city neighborhoods. Blake and Darling (1994) concluded that joblessness and substandard employment of African American males contribute to family instability, mental illness, somatic symptoms, and increased rates of crime.

Wilson (1987) called the truly disadvantaged African Americans an "underclass." These individuals are concentrated in inner cities where they are effectively isolated. This underclass emerged as a result of the growing joblessness during the 1970s and 1980s, and now these people lack the educational and technical skills to participate in the labor market. They are also isolated from other African Americans who have fled the inner cities for the suburbs. Malveaux (1988) reported that income distribution has changed for African Americans in three ways since 1970: (a) The proportion of African Americans in poverty has increased; (b) the proportion of African Americans with incomes between $15,000 and $34,999 has declined; and (c) the proportion of African Americans at the highest income levels (over $35,000) has risen by almost one third.

Swinton (1983) characterized the economic plight of African Americans thus:

Blacks have consistently experienced a relatively disadvantageous labor market position in good times and bad. Black workers typically have higher rates of unemployment, obtain fewer high paying jobs, more low paying jobs, and have lower wage rates than Whites. The combination of obtaining less work and lower paid work results, as we have seen, in Blacks obtaining significantly smaller amount of income from labor than Whites. (p. 62)

Between 1970 and 1980, the median income of African American families decreased from $13,325 to $12,674, whereas median income for Whites rose from $21,722 to $21,904 for the same time period (U.S. Bureau of the Census, 1980). In 1994, African American men working year round, full-time earned a median income of $25,350, 72% of the income of White men. In the same year, African American females earned $20,610, representing 85% of the income of White women (U.S. Bureau of the Census, 1995).

Cone (1994) concluded,

[D]espite the progress in middle-class Black America, the Black underclass are poorer today than they were in the 1960s. One half of Black babies are born in poverty, and nearly 25% of the Black men between the ages of 19 and 28 are in jails, prisons, or awaiting their day in court. (p. 28)

Sleeter and Grant (1993) reported that 43.5% of African American children are living in poverty.

Traditionally, African Americans experience higher rates of joblessness, underemployment, mortality, morbidity, family instability, poor housing, homicide, and institutionalization than their White counterparts. No greater issue faces African Americans than the economic one.

History of Oppression

African Americans were enslaved and subjected to a system of bondage with few parallels in human history. Formal slavery ended following the Civil War, and a social system developed that continued to relegate former slaves and their descendants to a position of inferiority. This oppressed status has been recognized as a major social problem with current ramifications in all categories of the lives of African Americans. Events such as the "Red Summer," so named because African American soldiers returning from World War I were assaulted and lynched by White mobs fearful of armed men who had been treated as equals abroad, serve to accentuate oppression.

Racism is still the dominant force in the United States insofar as attitudes and behavior toward African Americans are concerned. Changes in the status of African Americans have occurred, but the lack of significant change in the first 100 years after emancipation compounded the problems. Racism sustains and reinforces the privileges that members of the dominant culture enjoy, thereby maintaining the dominant culture and oppressing African Americans.

Hale-Benson (1986) found that even the literary treatment of slavery by the dominant culture has influenced the view that African Americans have of themselves. She recommends the following:

> We need an extensive investigation of the acculturative process and the reaction of Black people to enslavement and slave status. The traditional interpretation of Black history has emphasized the acquiescence of Blacks to slavery. Recognizing the resistance to slavery is important because slaves who acquiesced in their status would be more prone to accept the culture of their masters than those who rebelled. Similarly, if they were reluctant to accept slave status, they would have struggled harder to retain what they could of their African culture and heritage. (pp. 12-13)

Many differences between the primary social institutions in the African American community and in the dominant culture are a result of the long history of oppression. Although changes have occurred in the 20th century, the racism of the dominant culture and the African American consciousness will promote the distinctive aspects within the social institutions. President Bill Clinton appointed a national task force on race in the United States during the summer of 1997.

In a classic study, Myrdal (1944) developed the following rank order of types of segregation and discrimination against African Americans:

1. The bar against intermarriage and sexual intercourse involving White women
2. Several etiquettes and discriminations that specifically concern behavior in personal relations (barriers against dancing, bathing, eating, and drinking together, and social intermingling generally)
3. Segregations and discriminations in the use of public facilities, such as schools, churches, and means of conveyance
4. Political disenfranchisement
5. Discriminations in law courts, by the police, and by other public servants
6. Discriminations in securing land, credit, jobs, or other means of earning a living, and discriminations in public relief and other social welfare activities

It is important to note that African Americans in the Myrdal study ranked their concerns with the areas of segregation and discrimination in a parallel, but inverse, order. Likewise, it is interesting to note that the items in the discrimination rankings of more than 50 years ago remain as issues separating African Americans from the dominant culture. Such a pattern of relations results in isolation of African Americans and members of the dominant culture and vice versa, and this isolation provides the opportunity for stereotypes to persist as significant racial issues.

Language and the Arts

Two major positions relate to the spoken language of African Americans: The first, the language deficit position posited by Deutsch (1965), holds that the lack of appropriate early language stimulation in African American homes results in immature or deficient language development. Those who adhere to this position believe that the speech patterns of African American children are incorrect and must be corrected according to the linguistic rules of Standard English.

Linguists such as Baratz (1969) and Smitherman (1977) take the second position, that all human beings develop some form of language, and contend that African Americans employ a well-ordered, highly structured, highly developed language system that in many aspects is different from Standard English. Although Black English is similar to Standard English in many aspects, it is different in its phonological and grammatical structure. Smitherman (1977) concluded,

> African slaves in America initially developed a pidgin, a language of transaction, that was used in communication between themselves and Whites. Over the years, the pidgin gradually became widespread among slaves and evolved into a Creole. Developed without benefit of any formal instruction, this lingo involved the substitution of English for West African words, but within the same basic structure and idiom that characterized West African language patterns. (p. 5)

Smitherman (1977) identified some West African language rules that still operate in Black English today. Included among the rules are the repetition of the noun subject with the pronoun ("My father, he work there"), question patterns without *to do* ("What it come to?"), and an emphasis on the character of action without the tense indicated in the verb ("I know it good when he ask me"). West African sound rules that are found in Black English include no consonant pairs (*jus* for *just*), no /r/ sound (*mo* for *more*), and no /th/ sound (*souf* for *south*).

Black English appears to be maintained by social pressures within the African American community, although the speakers are often unaware that they are maintaining it. Group identity provides a strong subconscious pressure to maintain the dialect even while the speaker's conscious effort may be to speak Standard English. For some, especially among writers, speaking Black English has become a symbol of African American unity. Baugh (1994) concluded that the "lingering linguistic differences found in minority speech communities reflect that the United states still strives to attain the status of a color blind society it has yet to become" (p. 195).

Some researchers have identified a unique cultural form expressed in African American arts. Hale-Benson (1986) characterized the African American style as circular with a "heavy emphasis on involvement through repetition of sound and movement" and with an "episodic arrangement calling for small, short units leading to a succession of mini-climaxes." There is also a tendency to retreat from closure in favor of the ongoing and open-ended (p. 41). Black (1996) posited that it is quite clear the "rhythms of jazz and the blues, calypso and reggae, salsa and other Latin beats all trace their roots back to Africa" (p. 61). Black also found that the intensity of form and color in the paintings and sculpture of artists of African descent echoes the style of their mother continent.

Racism and Prejudice

The issue of race and racism has engaged much attention and preoccupied many as it relates to African Americans in the United States. W. E. B. DuBois noted in 1909, with particular reference to race relations between the dominant culture and African Americans, that "the problem of the Twentieth Century is the problem of the color line" (p. 41).

A persistent disparity and inequality exists in the economic conditions of African Americans and members of the dominant culture that are a result of the racism of the past. Numerous civil rights laws, affirmative action regulations, and other public policies have not been able to remove these unequal conditions; indeed, in some areas they are becoming worse. Ford (1994) reported,

> [T]hree of every five African Americans live in neighborhoods with hazardous waste sites. In Houston, Texas, with 25 percent population of African Americans, 100 percent of landfills and 75 percent of garbage incinerators are located in Black neighborhoods. One of the nations largest landfills housing waste from all of eastern United States, is located in Emelle, Alabama, with a population that is 79 percent African American. (p. 188)

Inequality in income, educational and occupational patterns, unemployment, and housing are influenced to a great extent by institutional racism and show minor changes, if any.

Inequality in educational opportunity, performance, achievement, and outcomes is one major area in which racial differences are apparent. School funding, quality, and completion rates at all levels are significant variables to note when studying racial differences. Of those African Americans 25 years old or older in 1996, 74% had graduated from high school, whereas

86% of Whites in the same age-group had graduated. A decline occurred in the annual high school dropout rate of African Americans in Grades 10 to 12 from 11.2% in 1970 to 5.3% in 1993 (U.S. Bureau of the Census, 1996). It is not surprising that Wilcox (1970) declared that "education must become a process that educates for liberation and survival—nothing less" (p. 11).

Despite these encouraging signs, some areas of concern still must be addressed. Although the dropout rate is decreasing, in 1980, 16% of African American 14- to 24-year-olds had dropped out of school (U.S. Bureau of the Census, 1981). Although it is important to keep students in school, it is even more important for them to graduate from school with skills or abilities to make them useful citizens. In 1990, 4.2% of African Americans 25 years old and over had graduated from college, whereas 9.2% of Whites in the same age-group had done so (U.S. Bureau of the Census, 1991). Far too many youngsters who are functionally illiterate, lacking the basic skills of reading, writing, and computation, leave school. As a result, they are relegated to the lower-paying and least-desirable jobs. Mullins (1995) reported that when education, performance rating, and other factors are held constant, African Americans are twice as likely as Whites to be dismissed from government jobs and that the reasons are not explained. African Americans are also turned down for loans at two-and-one-half times the rate of Whites. Although affirmative action, problematic as it is, speaks to the inequality structured into the social system, the attack on affirmative action presumes that systematic, institutional discrimination no longer exists. In any case, the ability of the dominant group to define the terms of the debate and thereby to control dissent is evident.

The outlook for major changes in these and other areas of importance to African Americans is grim. Perhaps the most important impediment to change is the extent to which racism has become institutionalized. Cose (1993) suggested that the foundation of a solution to problems of racism involves recognizing the sense of oppression, grievance, and rage that many African American men feel, including men of professional standing. African Americans have worked to achieve equality through legal means, and the dominant culture has refused to accept African Americans as equals. African Americans are more likely than members of the dominant culture to view the racial situation in the United States with greater urgency. The likelihood of major progress in eliminating racism is remote.

Sociopolitical Factors

With rare exceptions, African Americans have played a minor role in the formal political life of the United States (holding elected or appointed positions in government). Historically, African Americans have been heavily concentrated in the South, where various techniques have been used to keep them from participating in the electoral process. African American politics has reflected an extensive range of forms and strategies, such as electoral politics, civil rights organizations, civic organizations, and policy process (through the courts).

The Fifteenth Amendment to the U.S. Constitution, passed in 1870, was the first attempt at ensuring participation of African Americans in the electoral process. The Voting Rights Act of 1965 and its subsequent amendments have helped overcome the disenfranchisement of millions of potential African American voters. The Voting Rights Act was an attempt by Congress to enforce the Fifteenth Amendment. It mandated direct federal action, which allowed African Americans to register and vote without having to rely on litigation (U.S. Civil Rights Commission, 1968).

The success of the civil rights movement changed politics in the United States. In the first election of African American mayors in 1968, the African American candidates ran against the established political machine. C. Young (1986) summarized the mood and focus of the dominant culture:

> The general approach of the government to policy issues concerned with Afro-American affairs has been at best one of benign neglect. Disregard for the economic, social, political, and psychological well-being of Black citizens is apparent in the deterioration of services, resources, and quality of life available to inner city residents. (p. 71)

Child-Rearing Practices

The role of African American fathers has been explored within the context of the contemporary sociopolitical environment of all African Americans. In a study of child socialization patterns, Allen (1981) found that the child-rearing patterns of African American parents reflected the reality that their sons were being socialized to be confrontive. He concluded that African American parents recognize that future success for their sons hinges on an ability to be alternately and selectively assertive and acquiescent. According to Allen, the African American mother's central role in her sons' lives is concerned with their interpersonal relations and their social life, whereas the father serves as a supporter in these areas.

Willie (1976) described the environment of African American children not only as including the special stresses of poverty or discrimination but also as an ambiguous and marginal one in which they live simultaneously in two worlds—the African American world and the world of the dominant culture.

McGoldrick (1993) noted that the African American approach to discipline—in which children are expected to obey parental commands immediately and are not permitted to talk back, question parental authority, or have angry tantrums—is necessary to the survival of children who must learn to face the harsh realities of life. An inescapable aspect of the socialization of African American children is that it prepares them for survival in an environment that is covertly, if not overtly, hostile, racist, and discriminatory against them.

Religious Practices

Religion has traditionally played an important role in the lives of African Americans. The African American church has served as an important socializing institution for individuals and as a source of leadership for the community. Jemison (1982) described the African American church as "the first welfare organization on earth" (p. 9). The African American church has provided service functions such as senior citizen services, day care centers, credit unions, housing developments, and education in survival skills. Lefley (1986) noted that the role of the church in African American survival is well established:

> It has served both as a social and spiritual resource, providing collective human support and a reference point for meaningfulness in life. Therapeutic aspects of the religious experience are so profound that it has been suggested that the Black church service is a functional community mental resource for its participants. (p. 32)

African American religious practices are an outgrowth of a complex historical process. The cultural traditions of West Africa were preserved directly in the lives of the slave population in the United States. Jules-Rosette (1980, p. 275) identified six distinctive features of African spirituality that survived and became incorporated into the practices of African Americans:

1. The direct link between the natural and the supernatural
2. The importance of human intervention in the supernatural world through possession and spiritual control
3. The significance of music to invoke the supernatural
4. The strong tie between the world of the living and the world of the dead in defining the scope of community

5. The importance of participatory verbal performance, including the call-response pattern

6. The primacy of both sacred and secular verbal performance

The central focus of African American religion has been its ability to interpret the African American experience in a meaningful way. The chief function of the African American preacher has been and remains to make the Bible relevant to current events. As Henry (1990) stated: "Black preaching is based on the Bible but not tied to pat legalistic or literalistic answers. Black worshipers are seeking the strength and assurance to survive another day rather than solutions to abstract theological problems" (p. 65).

With the emphasis on civil rights in the 20th century, the African American church has taken on a major role in advocating social change. African American ministers have become leaders in the civil rights movement, and the movement has continued to have a religious base. Henry (1990) characterized the role of religion thus: "Black theology condemns capitalism, does not condemn violence, contends that God is actively working for Black liberation, and demands reparations for past injustices" (p. 66).

The African American church has always been more than a religious institution. Jones (1983) indicated that a strong religious orientation has always been an important sustaining element in the struggle to cope with racism. During slavery, the church was a center for the development of leadership, an educational institution, and an agent for the transmission of traditions and values of the African American community. After emancipation, the functions of the church increased as it became an agent for strengthened family ties, an employment agency providing assistance to newcomers in locating housing and jobs, and a cultural center providing opportunities for African Americans to learn about and appreciate their own heritage. The church served as a major promoter of several themes: belief in the unity of the race, belief in self-help as the primary means of addressing problems and social conditions, and a commitment to improving the race. According to DuBois (1909), it was natural that "charitable and rescue work among Negroes should first be found in the churches and reach there its greatest development" (p. 6).

The majority of African American Christians are affiliated with the Baptist and Methodist denominations. The largest segments of these denominations are as follows: the National Baptist Convention U.S.A., 6.8 million members; the National Baptist Convention of America, 3.5 million members; the Progressive National Baptist Convention, 1.1 million members; and the African Methodist Episcopal Church, the African Methodist Episcopal Zion Church, the Christian Methodist Episcopal Church, and the United Methodist Church, a combined membership of approximately 6 million (Blackwell, 1985).

Some African Americans have joined other religions and cults but in relatively small numbers. Readers will find a discussion of Black Jews and Black Muslims in Chapters 11 and 12, respectively.

Family Structure and Dynamics

Franklin (1988) posited that the family is one of the strongest and most important traditions in the African American community. Moynihan (1965) described the African American family as a "tangle of pathology . . . capable of perpetuating itself without assistance from the White world" (p. 47). Moynihan's "blame-the-victim" deficiency-oriented explanation ignored the strengths of these families. Bass, Acosta, and Evans (1982) identified five strengths of the African American family that lead toward survival, advancement, and stability:

1. Strong kinship bonds
2. Strong work orientation
3. Adaptability of family roles
4. Strong achievement orientation
5. Strong religious orientation

He argued that these factors, not unique to African American families, have been functional for the survival, advancement, and stability of African American families. These strengths have been found in African American communities in the form of informal day care services, informal foster care, services to unwed mothers, and services to the elderly. Hale-Benson (1986) suggested that the common use of words such as *brother, sister,* or *cousin* for those without actual kinships are instrumental in modeling this loyalty for the children of each generation.

Asante (1981) identified four aspects of Afrocentric male-female relationships that are based on teachings that man and woman are equally the source of strength and genius of African Americans:

1. Sacrifice
2. Inspiration
3. Vision
4. Victory

These elements provide the source and inspiration for all that men and women do together. Jones (1983) defined the African value system of "we-ness" as a focus on interdependence and cooperation in the face of racism and discrimination. Furthermore, the focus on we-ness is not only an adaptation to racism in the United States but also a tradition passed on in families through early training in self-transcendence that has been culturally inherited from the family's African tribal roots.

Staples (1981) provided insight on how external forces affect the internal stresses and strains that accompany the process of living in families. He challenged the myth of the African American matriarchy, a myth that still exists to a great extent despite numerous studies that have cast doubt on it. He concluded:

> It has been functional for the White ruling class, through its ideological apparatus, to create internal antagonisms in the Black community between Black men and Black women to divide them and to ward off attacks on the external system of White racism. It is a mere manifestation of the divide-and-conquer strategy, used by most ruling classes through the annals of man, to continue the exploitation of an oppressed group. (p. 33)

No discussion of African American family structure would be complete without some attention to the extended family. Martin and Martin (1978) defined the African American extended family as

> a multigenerational, independent kinship system which is welded together by a sense of obligation to relatives, is organized around a dominant figure; extends across geographic boundaries to connect family units to an extended family network; and has a built in mutual aid system for the welfare of its members and the maintenance of the family as a whole. (p. 1)

Edelman (1993) reported that the basic family unit among African Americans is the multigenerational informal extended family, wherein, in addition to one or both parents and their biological children, true kin, fictive kin (long-time friends or informal adoptions), and visiting relatives may be included. The extended family might simply be described as all those who see themselves as family.

Hatchett and Jackson (1993, p. 92) summarized the characteristics of the African American extended kin system as follows:

- High degree of geographic propinquity
- Strong sense of family and familial obligations

- Fluidity of household boundaries, with great willingness to absorb relatives as the need arises
- Frequent interactions with relatives
- Frequent get-togethers for holidays and special occasions
- System of mutual aid

In addition to the extended family, Pinderhughes (1982) pointed out, the struggle to create a family system that can withstand the stress of the victim system has spawned a variety of family forms other than the traditional nuclear family. It is evident that the meaning of the term *parents* includes natural parents and grandparents as well as others who, at different times, assume parental roles and responsibilities. Roles within the African American family must be viewed as having developed from an interplay of at least three factors:

1. African heritage
2. Interaction with the dominant culture in the United States
3. Method of coping with years of oppression

Cultural Values and Attitudes

Distinctive characteristics of African American cultural traits give strong credibility to the uniqueness of an African American culture. Many characteristics of African American culture are not found in the dominant culture. A connection exists between the cultural traits of African Americans and other Afrocentric communities, such as the Caribbean. Finally, many elements of African American culture are quite similar to the same elements found in West Africa, the location from which most slaves came.

Herskovits (1958) and Woodson (1968) identified cultural elements that have been carryovers from Africa and that have survived in the United States: dialect, folklore, adult-child relationships, family structure, music, generosity or hospitality, respect for the law, religion, a sense of justice, and the work ethic.

One specific cultural value of Africans that is different from that of the Western world is the concept of time. This difference exists because Africans have no way of expressing a distant future. Another difference is that, in traditional African societies, people emphasize whether something is done only at the current moment or habitually. The Western view of time is linear, with an emphasis on the point on the time line at which an event occurs—that is, whether it is past, present, or future.

In becoming African Americans, the Africans had to develop a new framework capable of holding their beliefs, values, and behaviors. What was useful from Africa was retained, what was useless was discarded, and new forms evolved on the old. This adaptive strategy allowed African Americans to carve out a world where they could get on with the business of living, building families and kinship groups, and a way of life capable of sustaining them under the conditions they found in the United States. African American culture is testimony to the process of adaptation and cultural exchange (Turner & Perkins, 1976). Although the cultures of West Africa differ in many ways, the traditional worldview of these cultures is that they are remarkably similar. Among other things, each culture places a great deal of importance on family and kinship relationships, religion, and the care of children.

Hilliard (1976, pp. 38-39) described the core cultural characteristics of African Americans as follows:

- They tend to respond to things in terms of the whole picture instead of its parts. The Euramerican tends to believe that anything can be divided and subdivided into pieces and that these pieces add up to a whole. Therefore, art is sometimes taught by numbers, as are dancing and music.
- They tend to prefer inferential reasoning to deductive or inductive reasoning.
- They tend to approximate space, numbers, and time, rather than stick to accuracy.
- They tend to focus on people and their activities, rather than on things. This tendency is shown by the fact that so many African American students choose careers in the helping professions, such as teaching, psychology, and social work.
- They tend to have a keen sense of justice and are quick to analyze and perceive injustice.
- They tend to lean toward altruism, a concern for one's fellow humans.
- They tend to prefer novelty, freedom, and personal distinctiveness. This is shown in the development of improvisations in music and styles of clothing.
- They tend not to be "word" dependent. They tend to be very proficient in nonverbal communications.

A cultural nation is formed by a people with a common past, a common present and, one would hope, a common future. The society may be that of the United States, but the values are African American. African American values come only through an African American culture. Culture is stressed because it gives identity, purpose, and direction. It tells you who you are, what you must do, and how you can do it. Without a culture, African American values are only a set of reactions to the dominant culture. African American culture is an expression of the desire of African Americans to decide their own destiny through control of their own political organizations and the formation and preservation of their cultural economic and social institutions.

Implications

African American children must be taught and believe that deviations from the normative patterns of the dominant culture are not indications that they are abnormal. They must be helped to understand that negative social and psychological views have resulted in images of low self-esteem, identity crisis, and self-hatred. An appreciation of African American cultural values is essential for African American children if they are to develop positive self-identities. Despite the dominant culture's representations of deficiency or abnormality, many strengths serve as the foundation of African American culture. Educators and counselors can work more effectively with African Americans if they begin from their students' or clients' points of strength.

Gibbs (1981) described a five-stage process through which African Americans interpret their meetings with White counselors. Stage 1 is the *appraisal stage,* wherein the client "sizes up" the counselor and minimizes the intensity of the interaction. Stage 2 involves the client's more assertive investigation of who and what the counselor is about. During this stage, the subject of race is likely to emerge. Stage 3 involves the exchange of information, personal favors, and mutual obligations. Stage 4 is the client's commitment to the relationship. Stage 5 involves actual work on the issue that brought the client to the counselor in the first place. Gibbs (1990) recommended short-term, ego-oriented treatment for African American youths experiencing nonpsychotic behavioral and emotional problems. Family therapy is appropriate where the adolescents' problems are symptomatic of a dysfunctional family system, a breakdown in family communication, or a family scapegoating process.

The strengths of the family (Bass et al., 1982) and the core African American cultural characteristics (Hilliard, 1976) should serve as background for any specific strategies developed for use with individuals or groups. Individuals from the dominant culture should not use themselves as sole reference points for how African American children should behave. An individual's family and community and how one measures up to his or her peers should provide additional reference points. In other words, the interactions of African American children with the dominant culture should be filtered through an African American frame of reference.

Questions for Review and Reflection

1. What event do you think has had the greatest influence on African Americans? Why?

2. What ethnic group labels have been associated with people of color whose roots are in Africa? What is the value associated with being called "African American"?

3. Most African Americans are descendants of individuals who came to the United States as slaves, whereas most other ethnic groups are descendants of individuals who came voluntarily to the United States. What influences did this difference create in terms of cultural identification? In terms of other factors?

4. Why has the African American church had so much influence on the African American culture?

5. How does Black English (Ebonics) influence the education of African Americans? Should African Americans be forced to abandon Black English? Why or why not?

6. Which African American cultural trait has influenced the education or counseling of African Americans the most? How?

7. Discuss E. U. Essien-Udoms's (1962) concept of "dilemma of duality."

8. How would you describe the rank order of discrimination now in comparison with the rank order found by G. Myrdal in 1944? How does the rank today influence educational or counseling practices?

9. W. R. Allen (1981) concluded that African American fathers socialize their sons to be confrontive. How can educators or counselors use this knowledge in working with African American males?

10. How can educators or counselors use the cultural values reported by A. Hilliard (1976) in devising strategies and techniques for their work with African Americans?

References

Allen, W. R. (1981). Moms, dads, and boys: Race and sex differences in the socialization of male children. In L. E. Gary (Ed.), *Black men* (pp. 99-114). Beverly Hills, CA: Sage.

Asante, M. (1981). Black male and female relationships: An Afrocentric context. In L. E. Gary (Ed.), *Black men* (pp. 75-82). Beverly Hills, CA: Sage.

Baratz, J. C. (1969). *Language and cognitive assessment of Negro children: Assumptions and research needs.* Washington, DC: Center for Applied Linguistics.

Bass, B. A., Acosta, F. X., & Evans, L. A. (1982). The Black American patient. In F. X. Acosta, J. Yamamota, & L. A. Evans (Eds.), *Effective psychotherapy for low-income and minority patients* (pp. 83-108). New York: Plenum.

Baugh, J. (1994). New and prevailing misconceptions of African American English for logic and mathematics. In E. R. Hollins, J. E. King, & W. C. Hayman (Eds.), *Teaching diverse populations* (pp. 191-206). Albany: State University of New York Press.

Black, L. (1996). Families of African origin: An overview. In M. McGoldrick, J. Giordano, & J. K. Pearce (Eds.), *Ethnicity and family therapy* (pp. 57-65). New York: Guilford.

Blackwell, J. E. (1985). *The Black community: Diversity and unity.* New York: Harper & Row.

Blake, W. M., & Darling, C. A. (1994). The dilemmas of the African American male. *Journal of Black Studies, 24,* 409-415.

Cone, J. H. (1994, April). Demystifying Martin and Malcolm. *Theology Today, 51*(1), 28.

Cose, E. (1993). *The rage of the privileged class.* New York: HarperCollins.

Deutsch, M. (1965). The role of social class in language development and cognition. *American Journal of Orthopsychiatry, 35,* 78-88.

Dickson, L. (1993). The future of marriage and family in Black America. *Journal of Black Studies, 23*(4), 472-491.

Dovidio, J. F., & Gaertner, S. L. (1986). *Prejudice, discrimination, and racism.* San Diego: Academic Press.

DuBois, W. E. B. (1909). *Efforts for social betterment among Negro Americans.* Atlanta: Atlanta University.

Edelman, M. W. (1993). The Black family in America. In L. Tepperman & S. J. Wilson (Eds.), *Next of kin* (pp. 241-245). Upper Saddle River, NJ: Prentice Hall.

Essien-Udoms, E. U. (1962). *Black nationalism: A search for an identity in America.* Chicago: University of Chicago Press.

Ford, C. (1994). *We can all get along: 50 steps you can take to end racism at home, at work, and in your community.* New York: Dell.

Franklin, J. H. (1988). A historical note on Black families. In H. P. McAdoo, *Black families* (pp. 23-26). Newbury Park, CA: Sage.

Gibbs, J. T. (1981). The interpersonal orientation in mental health consultation: Toward a model of ethnic variations in consultation. In R. H. Dana (Ed.), *Human services for cultural minorities* (pp. 163-184). Baltimore: University Park.

Gibbs, J. T. (1990). Mental health issues of Black adolescents: Implications for policy and practice. In A. R. Stiffman & L. E. Davis (Eds.), *Ethnic issues in adolescent mental health* (pp. 21-52). Newbury Park, CA: Sage.

Hale-Benson, J. E. (1986). *Black children: Their roots, culture, and learning styles.* Baltimore, MD: Johns Hopkins.

Hatchett, S. J., & Jackson, J. S. (1993). African American extended kin systems. In H. P. McAdoo (Ed.), *Family ethnicity* (pp. 90-108). Newbury Park, CA: Sage.

Henry, C. P. (1990). *Culture and African American politics.* Bloomington: Indiana University Press.

Herskovits, M. J. (1958). *The myth of the Negro past.* New York: Beacon Press.

Hilliard, A. (1976). *Alternatives to IQ testing: An approach to the identification of gifted minority children.* Final report to the California State Department of Education. Sacramento, CA: Department of Education.

Jemison, T. J. (1982). As Christians we must do more to help other people. *The Crisis, 89,* 9.

Jones, R. (1983). Increasing staff sensitivity to the Black client. *Social Casework, 29,* 419-425.

Jules-Rosette, B. (1980). Creative spirituality from Africa to America: Cross-cultural influences in contemporary religious forms. *Western Journal of Black Studies, 4,* 273-285.

Lefley, H. P. (1986). Why cross-cultural training? Applied issues in culture and mental health service delivery. In H. P. Lefley & P. B. Pedersen (Eds.), *Cross-cultural training for mental health professionals* (pp. 11-44). Springfield, IL: Charles C Thomas.

Malveaux, J. (1988). The economic statuses of Black families. In H. P. McAdoo, *Black families* (pp. 133-147). Newbury Park, CA: Sage.

Martin, E. P., & Martin, J. M. (1978). *The Black extended family.* Chicago: University of Chicago.

McGoldrick, M. (1993). Ethnicity, cultural diversity, and normality. In F. Walsh (Ed.), *Normal family processes* (pp. 331-360). New York: Guilford.

Moynihan, D. P. (1965). *The Negro family: The case for national action.* Washington, DC: U.S. Department of Labor.

Mullins, L. (1995). Racism remains pervasive. *New Politics, 5*(3), 31-34.

Myrdal, G. (1944). *An American dilemma.* New York: Harper & Row.

Pinderhughes, E. (1982). Family functioning of Afro-Americans. *Social Work, 27,* 91-96.

Pinderhughes, E. (1989). *Understanding race, ethnicity, and power.* New York: Free Press.

Root, M. P. P. (1992). *Racially mixed people in America.* Newbury Park, CA: Sage.

Sassen, S. (1990). Economic restructuring and the American city. *Annual Review of Sociology, 16,* 465-490.

Sleeter, C. E., & Grant, C. A. (1993). *Making choices for multicultural education: Five approaches to race, class, and gender.* New York: Macmillan.

Smitherman, G. (1977). *Talkin and testifyin: The language of Black America.* Boston: Houghton Mifflin.

Staples, R. (1976). *Introduction to Black sociology.* New York: McGraw-Hill.

Staples, R. (1981). The myth of the Black matriarchy. *Black Scholar, 12,* 26-34.

Swinton, D. H. (1983). The economic status of the Black population. In National Urban League, *The state of Black America* (pp. 45-114). New York: National Urban League.

Task Force on Black and Minority Health. (1986). *Homicide, suicide, and unintentional injuries.* Washington, DC: U.S. Department of Health and Human Services.

Turner, J., & Perkins, W. E. (1976). Slavery and Afro-American culture: Review essay. *Journal of Ethnic Studies, 3,* 80-87.

U.S. Bureau of the Census. (1980). *1980 census of the United States.* Washington, DC: Government Printing Office.

U.S. Bureau of the Census. (1981). *Statistical abstract of the United States.* Washington, DC: Government Printing Office.

U.S. Bureau of the Census. (1991). *Statistical abstract of the United States.* Washington, DC: Government Printing Office.

U.S. Bureau of the Census. (1995). *Current population survey.* Washington, DC: Government Printing Office.

U.S. Bureau of the Census. (1996). *The social and economic status of the Black population in the United States: A historical view, 1790-1971* (Current Population Reports, Special Studies, Series P-23, No. 80). Washington, DC: Government Printing Office.

U.S. Civil Rights Commission. (1968). *Political participation.* Washington, DC: Government Printing Office.

Valentine, C. (1971). Deficit, difference, and bicultural models of Afro-American behavior. *Harvard Educational Review, 41,* 137-157.

Wilcox, P. (1970). Educating for Black humanism. In N. Wright (Ed.), *What Black educators are saying* (pp. 3-17). San Francisco: Leswing.

Willie, C. V. (1976). *A new look at Black families.* New Bayside, NY: General Hall.

Wilson, W. J. (1987). *The truly disadvantaged: The inner city, the underclass, and public policy.* Chicago: University of Chicago.

Winbush, G. B. (1996). African-American health care: Beliefs, practices, and service issues. In M. Julia (Ed.), *Multicultural awareness in the health care professions.* Boston: Allyn & Bacon.

Woodson, C. G. (1968). *The African background outlined.* New York: Negro Universities Press.

Young, C. (1986). Afro-American family: Contemporary issues and implications for social policy. In D. Pilgrim (Ed.), *On being Black: An in-group analysis* (pp. 58-75). Bristol, IN: Wyndham Hall.

3

Old Order Amish

Old Order Amish culture has changed little in 300 years. It varies only in minor ways in districts across the United States despite the absence of telephones and the limits of horse-and-buggy travel. Their agrarian life-style is defined by simplicity, hard work, integrity, order, and community. Hostetler (1992) characterized the Amish as "a church, a community, a spiritual union, a conservative branch of Christianity, a religion, a community whose members practice simple and austere living, a familistic entrepreneuring system, and an adaptive human community" (p. 70). Amish life is distinctive in that religion and custom blend into a way of life.

Followers of Mennonite elder Jacob Amman broke from the Mennonite church in Germany in the late 1600s. The first Amish settled in the United States around 1737 (Wittmer, 1990). The Amish, the Mennonites, and the Moravians, collectively referred to as the "Pennsylvania Dutch," settled at William Penn's invitation in his colony. The European Amish gradually assimilated into other religions and no longer exist separately. Although the Amish have never been averse to relocating, the largest Amish settlements remain in Lancaster County, Pennsylvania. To the west, Holmes County, Ohio, and Buchanan County, Iowa, are also home to large Amish communities (Hudson, 1981).

The Old Order Amish, the most conservative and traditional, are known as the House Amish because they hold services in private homes. They are distinguished from the New, Church, or Beachy Amish, who do not thoroughly accept modern American culture but have fewer qualms about using labor-saving technology and associating with "the English," their term for the non-Amish (Hostetler, 1980). They are also distinguished from the Mennonites, Moravians, and Black Car Amish. The census of 1990 used the category "Pennsylvania German" to code the 246,461 persons called Amish in this chapter (U.S. Bureau of the Census, 1991). Krabill (1993) reported the existence of some 900 congregations in the United States and Canada. Wittmer (1996) predicted that the Amish population will double in 15 to 20 years.

Acculturation

Old Order Amish culture is based on two verses of Scripture: "Be not conformed to this world: but be ye transformed by the renewing of your mind, that ye may prove what is that good, and acceptable, and perfect, will of God" (Romans 12:2) and "Be ye not unequally yoked together with unbelievers; for what fellowship hath righteousness with unrighteousness? And what communion hath light with darkness?" (II Corinthians 6:14). Accordingly, the Amish seek as complete a separation from the world as possible.

The Amish do many things to maintain their culture and identity. These practices, values, and beliefs include the exclusion of the outside world for all things except the purchase of essential necessities; the observance of strict rules for behavior, dress, language usage, education, and religion; the sequential socialization process; the strong involvement of the extended family; and the rich sense of community and mutual aid that is woven through the Amish way of life (Good, 1985). Their way of life in refusing to be acculturated has resulted in "hostility and harassment and it is becoming increasingly more difficult for the Amish to preserve their peace-loving values in America" (Wittmer, 1990, p. 6). Emery (1996) reported that it is becoming increasingly difficult for those who leave the Amish faith and community to make a successful transition into the dominant culture.

Poverty and Economic Concerns

Unlike most oppressed groups in the United States today, the Amish are not deprived of the ability to secure enough to eat and living in suitable quarters. To some outsiders, however, the Amish choice of a way of life may seem much like poverty. The Amish can live very inexpensively by dressing plainly; by building or making most of their clothes, houses, and barns; by not using electricity; and by not owning any modern conveniences or machines. If anyone in the community is in need, all come to that person's assistance. Their simple way of life, coupled with a tradition of community aid, has enabled the Amish to be both healthy and prosperous.

History of Oppression

Oppression of the Amish has its origins in the social, economic, and religious upheavals experienced in Europe as far back as the 16th century. The Amish are direct descendants of the Anabaptist movement in Switzerland. The Anabaptists, which literally means "rebaptizer," were severely persecuted by the Roman Church and the Reformers, such as the Lutherans, because they represented a "third" option: a belief that Christians are a group of adults who voluntarily confess their faith and subsequently are baptized, as in the early Christian Church.

The torment faced by the Anabaptists in Europe was implemented by secret police called "Anabaptist hunters," who were trained to spy on the Anabaptists and finally arrest them. Their fate was then imprisonment or banishment, coupled with confiscation of property (which was ultimately sold to defray the costs of the spies). Special rewards were given to any hunter who captured an Anabaptist leader.

Children of Anabaptists were deemed "illegitimate" because their parents had not been married by reformed ministers and, therefore, could not inherit their parents' estates. Because of the Anabaptists' refusal to baptize infants, serve in the military, or take oaths, even in the face of imprisonment, they were often sold as galley slaves. Often, Anabaptist men were taken to the border, branded with hot irons, and then forced into exile.

The Amish history of persecution forced them to develop dependence on the mutual assistance of their own, gave them a reluctance to change, and created a distrust of those outside their group. In part because of their reluctance to change, the Amish, led by Jacob Amman, split from the Mennonites in the late 17th century over the use of Meidung (shunning of the excommunicated). The Amish believed in this practice; the Mennonites did not. The Amish have suffered many other divisions since their beginnings.

Ironically, the Amish migrated to the New World to escape religious persecution, both during the first half of the 1700s and between 1815 and 1860. Once in the United States, however, they encountered problems because they would not take an oath of allegiance or join the military. During the Revolutionary War, the Amish were viewed as patriots aligned with the British. They were not allowed to serve on juries, sue within the law, hold public office, or buy or sell land. Some Amish were charged with treason and were held in jail.

In later wars, the Amish were initially granted agricultural releases. According to Nolt (1992), some Amish were given exemptions under the provision for religious conscientious objectors. They often had to report to an army camp anyway, however, where they received verbal abuse, beatings, and wirebrush treatments, and many were made to stand for long periods of time without anything to drink.

The oppression served to galvanize the Amish, who stressed "man's duty to glorify God by full and unyielding obedience." They risked coming to the New World to "make a beginning free from the restraints to which they were subjected back home" (Hudson, 1981, p. 21). The Amish struggle for freedom to exercise their beliefs continues to be challenged in the 20th century as the Old Order Amish are pitted against the U.S. government in matters concerning educational freedom and the freedom to live apart from society and apart from the advances of technology.

Language and the Arts

The Amish create scant art for art's sake. Their art is manifest in the simplicity and symmetry of their gardens, solid furnishings, and hand-fashioned household items. They do not create art by writing poetry or novels or by painting or drawing. Although *art* is probably not a term the Amish would use to describe their work skills, Amish art is found in the crafts and vocational skills that the Amish possess and use.

Most Amish are farmers by trade, but all participate in the 1-day craft of barn raising. By bringing an entire community together in 1 day for the sole purpose of building a barn, the task is completed with incredible artful skill. This form of mutual aid also extends into other Amish "art forms," such as the beautiful quilts made by the women. In general, the arts of the Amish are utilitarian products that are always completed by a group of people and not by individuals.

An Amish home may be decorated with a calendar or a photograph of the farm, but no pictures of people are used. The Amish do not allow themselves to be photographed. Colorful braided rugs may cover the floors, especially in winter, for insulation. Quilts, many completed in the same dark colors as Amish clothing with the addition of white backgrounds, are made for use, not display. Friendship quilts are popular. Each woman in a group creates an original square, often sewing in the names of family members. The group meets to assemble the quilt and presents it as a gift. The same process is used to produce quilts for sale (Hostetler & Huntington, 1971).

Just as Amish art is utilitarian in nature, the languages spoken by the Amish have specific uses and purposes. The Amish speak three distinct tongues:

Pennsylvania German, High German, and English. Their native Pennsylvania German is primarily an oral language; they have a passing command of High German for reading the Bible or for quoting it aloud with their own distinctive pronunciation; and they can read, write, and speak English without interference of their other languages.

Pennsylvania German, or "Pennsylvania Dutch" as it is sometimes called, is the preferred spoken language and is used exclusively in the home and the community. It is the mother tongue of children born to Amish parents. Amish High German, or "the language of the Bible," is used exclusively for the preaching service and on formal ceremonial occasions. The Amish do not converse in High German. The children are taught how to read High German in school, but many do not fully understand its meaning.

English is learned out of necessity. It is the responsibility of the school teacher to teach English. English is spoken all the time at school except for designated High German classes or perhaps on the playground when the children might speak Pennsylvania Dutch. English is considered the language of the world. The fear in the Amish community is that English is being preferred by the children over the traditional Pennsylvania Dutch.

Four current Amish publications, which support Amish values and teachings through stories, poems, and editorials, can provide additional information for those interested in the most contemporary information about the Amish. *The Budget* is a weekly newspaper published in Sugarcreek, Ohio, by non-Amish for the Amish. This newspaper uses a reporter from each Amish community who writes a weekly column with information on births, illnesses, deaths, and the like. It contains no comics or editorials. The other three publications, *Young Companion, Family Life,* and *Blackboard Bulletin,* are published by Pathway Publishers, whose writers and publishers are Old Order Amish. They use innovative, nonmodern methods for these publications (Wittmer, 1990).

Racism and Prejudice

Since the founding of the Amish way of life, religious, social, and legal persecution has limited the group's freedom. During the 17th century, the Amish were hunted, sold as slaves, and stripped of their dignity as a result of differences in their religious beliefs compared with those of the dominant churches.

After migrating to the United States in hopes of living in a freer environment, the Amish were met with skepticism when they refused to fight for "their country." They were treated as traitors by people who could not understand their pacifist position.

As a result of their distinctive customs, many people deride them for being different. They are often referred to as "backward" or "ignorant." The movie *Witness* included a scene, based on reality, in which a group of outsiders began to hit and spit on a group of Amishmen, taking advantage of their nonviolent stance. Some of these negative attitudes have translated into tragedy. In one case, an Amish baby in Indiana was killed by an object thrown into a buggy by scornful neighborhood youths passing by in a speeding truck (Hostetler & Huntington, 1971).

Like other ethnic minorities, the Amish endure verbal affronts as well. In Buchanan County, Iowa, they are often pejoratively called "hookies," a term that refers to the Amish use of hooks and eyes instead of buttons.

More recently, the Amish have been victims of crimes against their property and their people. One incident in March 1992, in an Amish settlement in the Big Valley of Pennsylvania, involved fires that torched seven barns, six of which burned to the ground. The fires destroyed Amish farm equipment, buggies, and animals. Because violence is unknown among the Amish, the police assumed it was the work of urban or suburban vandals out on a spree. The FBI suspected the arson as a possible hate crime ("Barn Raising in Los Angeles," 1992).

Laws have also made it difficult for the Amish to practice their religious beliefs fully. For many years, one major issue that threatened the Amish culture was compulsory school attendance. Following a long struggle and a Supreme Court decision, however, an exemption clause was written for the Amish, exempting them from compulsory high school attendance. Another legal issue that created a problem for the Amish was compulsory social security payments. The Amish believe in taking no aid from the government; thus, the law that forced them to pay social security taxes violated their beliefs. The Amish were eventually excluded from mandatory payments.

Sociopolitical Factors

Despite their separatist tendencies, the Amish interact with the outside world in a continuum spanning from global generosity to governmental confrontation via passive resistance. On the one side of the issue, the Amish strongly support local charities and specific worldwide relief organizations. On the opposite side, the Amish have been forced into numerous legal battles that have threatened open practice of their religious beliefs and ideals. Because the Amish are "defenseless Christians," they will not defend themselves in court. Their cases are usually argued by the National Committee for Amish Religious Freedom, a non-Amish group. The Amish people's resistance to change, or rather their steadfastness in their beliefs, has compelled the courts to consider landmark decisions supporting freedom for the Amish to practice their beliefs.

The Amish are active in supporting local charities that aid the general welfare of the community, such as fire and emergency services. Benefit auctions for specific needs, such as a new ambulance, are attended and heavily supported by the Amish. Many Amish support their Mennonite cousins in two worldwide relief organizations. They participate in global assistance through the Mennonite Central Committee (MCC), which distributes millions of dollars of aid and service to many countries in the name of Christ. Quilts, crafts, and food are sold at public relief sales to benefit the MCC and a second relief organization called the Mennonite Disaster Service. When major disasters strike, groups of Amish volunteer their time to work in the ruined areas throughout North America (Good, 1985).

Although generous in supporting the general welfare of all people throughout the world, the Amish hold a less open position toward the U.S. government, perhaps, in part, because of their ancestral persecution by governments in Europe and by the U.S. government as well. The Amish are respectful of local, state, and federal governments, but they are also wary. Like their ancestors, the Amish acknowledge the need for government to maintain order in the "carnal" world; however, the authority of the state is not applicable to the spiritual realm.

Given the latter statement, the Amish do not run for public office and do not resort to courts of law to settle disputes among themselves or with outsiders. They cannot take oaths, serve on juries, or collect debts by using the courts. The Amish do pay their taxes, except for the social security tax, which was exempted under the Johnson administration in 1965. Crime rates in general tend to be low in Amish communities (Warner & Denlinger, 1969).

Nonetheless, many beliefs of the Amish have been analyzed and questioned by the courts. Nearly 300 years after the first Amish settlers came to the New World to escape religious persecution, the Amish still are threatened by the dominant culture in exercising their constitutional freedom. Examples of the governmental analysis of their rights are the Iowa school incident, the compulsory education issue, and the compulsory welfare problem, described below.

The Iowa school incident during the mid-1960s involved conflict between Buchanan County officials and the Amish community. In short, the community was forced to send their children to nearby "adequate" schools because the two Amish schools did not have "appropriately certified teachers," did not teach "adequate curriculum," and did not provide "proper facilities." After many conflicts, the Amish were allowed to keep their schools intact through a special grant from a private foundation that paid for the certified staff. Some saw this as an overwhelming victory for the Amish (Keim, 1975).

The compulsory education issue involves the fact that many in the Amish community perceive compulsory education as a threat and obstacle to the Amish way of life. In the past, some states required school attendance for all children until they were 16 years old. After imprisonment of Amish fathers unwilling to pay fines or to comply with the compulsory education law, believing that it violated their religious beliefs, the landmark case *Wisconsin v. Yoder* was heard by the U.S. Supreme Court. The court ruled that "enforcement of the State's requirement of compulsory formal education after the eighth grade would gravely endanger if not destroy the free exercise of . . . (Amish) religious beliefs" (Keim, 1975).

The compulsory welfare problem involved another law that compelled the Amish to violate their beliefs. The Amish are opposed to any dependency on government; rather, they support the principle of self-sufficiency in caring for the elderly, widows, and orphans. They refuse any type of governmental assistance. In 1955, when social security benefits were extended to cover self-employed persons, including farmers, the Amish were required to make payments in the form of social security taxes. After much resistance, however, an exemption was granted to the Amish that excludes them from compulsory welfare payments.

In summary, the relationship between the Amish community and the outside world has been one of mixed exchanges. Although generous in giving to those in need, whatever their political identifications, the Amish continue to resist any changes created by technology and the so-called upgrading of U.S. society. They remain passive but determined and firm in their convictions.

Child-Rearing Practices

Unlike most of mainstream America, the Amish are child centered in their structuring of everyday life. Some would argue that Amish children are forced to lead restricted lives that stifle their individualism; however, Amish child-rearing practices have many positive aspects. Amish children are content and surrounded by security, have clear expectations and structures set for them, and have numerous role models both inside and outside their extended families, as well as a sense of community belonging. Both parents are intimately involved in the socialization of the children as teachers, role models, and consistent disciplinarians.

Parents are an integral part of their children's development at each of the recognized stages: infancy, preschool, scholars, and young people. Each stage corresponds with specific responsibilities to accept and use and specific tasks to learn. The first stage, *infancy,* covers the period of time from birth until the child walks; children in this stage are called "babies." The second stage, *preschool,* spans the period between walking and entrance to school, which is usually age 6 or 7; preschool children are sometimes called "little children." In the third stage, children attending school are called *scholars,* and they fulfill the eighth-grade minimum requirement for school attendance. After schooling is complete, the children, now called "youth" or *young people,* are in the fourth stage and are required to complete a regular adult day's work. Baptism signifies religious adulthood and marriage, and the birth of the first child signifies social adulthood (Hostetler, 1989; Hostetler & Huntington, 1971).

Babies are considered special gifts from God and not primarily extensions of the parents. A baby is considered blameless and can do no wrong. There is no such thing as a bad baby, although there may be a difficult one. If a baby cries, he or she is comforted, not disciplined. Within the security of the home, babies are lovingly handled by persons of all ages and are rarely alone. They are rarely fed on a strict schedule; rather, they are fed when they are hungry. The openness and affection displayed toward babies within the community contrasts with the way babies are exposed to the outside world. When a mother goes outside the community, she wraps her baby up tightly and carries him or her under her shawl.

During the preschool years, the children learn to respect and obey those in authority, to care for those younger and less able, to share with others and help others, to do that which is right and avoid that which is wrong, and to complete work responsibilities pleasantly. Obedience is based on love and respect; the child learns that the adult authority has her or his best interest always in mind. Blind obedience is not encouraged. There are consistent consequences for disobedience, defiance, or stubbornness, however. A switch may be used (Hostetler, 1989; Hostetler & Huntington, 1971).

Work is viewed as a collective helping of others, and independence is discouraged. Little children are expected to complete certain tasks, such as running errands around the farm, and are never thanked for carrying out these responsibilities. Boys and girls at this age do similar tasks. Finally at this stage, the asking of "why" questions is stifled; children are encouraged to observe and imitate behavior, not to ask intellectual questions.

At the scholars stage, children between the ages of 6 and 15 continue to be reinforced with the cultural values of the Amish community by their parents. Scholars are motivated, not by fear of punishment, but by concern for other people. Although scholars attend Amish schools or public schools, the primary responsibility for religious and social training lies with the parents. Parents fear that their children will become indoctrinated by outside ideas and that, thus, the unity of faith, family, and community would be broken.

Despite parental fears, laws require Amish children to attend school at least up until the eighth grade. Before the 1930s, all Amish children attended public schools, but in recent decades, Amish communities have maintained their own schools. Most Amish schools have one room and one teacher for all eight grades. Younger children learn by listening to older children recite their lessons. The schools teach the three R's—reading, 'riting, and 'rithmetic—and do meet state standards concerning the number of school days and the length of school days.

After the completion of the eighth grade, the young people are discouraged from going on to high school because this is considered unnecessary and worldly. Instead, the boys are taught the essentials of farming, and the girls are taught the basics of homemaking. Often, the young people will test the limits of their community by engaging in "non-Amish" activities, such as owning a radio or wearing non-Amish clothing. The young people are not forced to join the Amish religion; a child may decide to be baptized and thus enter religious adulthood. Marriage usually does not occur until they are in their 20s.

During all their stages of development—as babies, little children, scholars, and young people—Amish children are influenced by the consistent but compassionate care of their parents. Although seemingly rigid in methods, Amish parents do allow their children to make the major decision of religious and social inclusion; of course, the consequence of not choosing the Amish way is lifelong shunning from the community.

Religious Practices

Religious considerations determine all aspects of Amish life: hours of work; daily, weekly, seasonal, and yearly rituals; occupation; means and destinations of travel; choice of friends; and marriage partners (Hostetler, 1992).

The Amish are primarily users of the New Testament. The *Dortrecht Confession of Faith,* written in Holland in 1632, is the basis of the *Ordnung,* district rules and standards. The sense of community and togetherness permeates the religious practices of the Amish. For them, the sacred power is found within the community, and not outside it. The Amish have no religious scholars who interpret the Bible; rather, each person models the teachings of the sacred book without debating its content. The Bible is to be used ritualistically, never didactically or intellectually. Amish rituals include the preaching service, communion, foot washing, and baptism (Schwieder & Schwieder, 1975).

An all-day preaching service is held every other week at the home of various members of the church on a rotating basis. Much preparation is required in the hosting of the service, including preparing the house and the stables and cooking the common meal that is shared. Everyone attends the services, even infants. The formal part of the service may last up to 3 hours, including the singing of hymns a cappella (one hymn may take 20 to 30 minutes to sing), prayers, Bible readings, several sermons, testimonials, and community announcements. People must enter and exit from the room in a set order, and special seating assignments are also used.

Communion, a ritual practiced twice a year, binds the Amish members together in mutual dependency. It also requires the Amish person to experience a personal examination 2 weeks prior to the communion service to prepare for the taking of communion. During the day-long communion service, children are kept in a separate place while the adults participate in the ritual. Communion includes the humble practice of washing one another's feet as Jesus did at the Last Supper.

Finally, baptism is offered once a year to young people who have decided to join the Amish faith as spiritual adults. The Amish do not believe in infant baptism: this is one focal issue that separates the Amish from other religious groups.

Although the rituals of the Amish Christian faith are practiced with other community members, only the parents teach their children about the Bible; adults never teach children other than their own about the Bible. Religion is not taught specifically at school. It is thought that because Christianity pervades all life, it will naturally emerge in all subjects at school. It is believed that the Bible is taught by example, not by lecture. For example, the parents dress, behave, and make decisions according to the proper Christian way to set an example for their children. The Amish do not proselytize. Their aim is to preserve, rather than promote, their way of life (Hostetler, 1989; Hostetler & Huntington, 1971). The church has no hierarchy beyond the bishop, no conferences, archbishop, or further organization. Each Amish community is made up of several families who comprise their district. A bishop is named by the church community of families and is the leader inside the community and in all official interactions with the outside world.

Overt appearance and behavioral practices that the adults model include taking a passivist stand on violence or the bearing of arms; refraining from pleasurable activities such as dancing or attending card parties, theaters, or amusement parks; abstaining from drinking liquor or smoking cigarettes; and refusing to own radios, jewelry, telephones, or other modern technological advances. Through parental example, children are to learn the appropriate morals of the Amish culture.

Louden (1991) reported that, despite separation from the world, many Amish settlements have "phone shanties" that house public telephones for community use, or telephones may be located in barns or businesses. Louden concluded that "the Amish do not strive for total independence from the rest of American society, but realize that in fact their very existence depends on a healthy relationship with the world that surrounds them" (p. 120).

Like all other aspects of Amish life, religious practices are structured, consistent, simple, and unchanging. The Amish favor close ties with the soil. The two most important lessons learned from nature and the soil are the main focus of the Amish religion. First, a seed, placed in the earth, must die before it can give birth. The images of death and resurrection surround the farmer. Second, one reaps what one sows, either in this life or the next. Thus, two Biblical parables connect the people with nature and the land.

Family Structure and Dynamics

The family is the basic unit of Amish culture; it provides nurturing, stability, and socialization. One illustration of this is that the size of a church district is measured, not by the number of baptized persons, but by the number of families or households in the district. An Amish schoolteacher will tell you how many families attend the school, and when she introduces the children, she will often introduce them by family, rather than by grade. The Amish emphasize the group over the individual. The family has authority over the individual in childhood, adolescence, and beyond.

The main functions of the Amish family are procreation, nurture, and socialization of the children. Families are monogamous in formation and patriarchal in authority. The family comes first. A job is of no intrinsic importance; it is only necessary to provide economic support for one's family. Activities of the community, such as church services, are centered around family units joining together.

The average Amish household has 7 children, but some have as many as 14. Married couples are expected to take on the responsibility of having and rearing children. Parents spend much of their time teaching their children appropriate behaviors and useful skills in maintaining the Christian life.

In marriage, husband and wife become "one flesh," a union that can be terminated only in death. Divorce is not an option in the Amish community. In keeping with biblical law, the man is the head of the woman and the household, although the wife does have some voice. For example, in the church, although the woman must be silent for the most part, she does have an equal vote. A woman is also allowed to decide individually whether she is ready to take communion. She does follow her husband's decisions for the family, but often some mutual discussion takes place before he makes the final decision. Should her husband sin to the extent that he is placed under the ban, however, she, like all other members of the community, will shun him. The husband would do the same if his wife were under the ban.

In practice, the farm is the Amish man's kingdom, and his wife is his general manager of household affairs. The man helps only nominally in household tasks. The wife's duties include caring for the children, cooking and cleaning, preparing food for market, making clothes for the family, preserving food, and gardening. Children assist with these tasks as they are able.

Marriage partners are to be considerate of each other and never disagree in public. Similarly, their personal relationship is quiet and reserved, and affection is never openly displayed. The expectation of the romance popular in the mainstream U.S. culture is not part of Amish culture; no terms of endearment or physical gestures are used. The marriage norm is not love, but respect.

As with all community activities, the extended family is involved in the socialization and modeling for the children. Often, grandparents, who may retire as early as age 50, will assist in the care of young children. The older people of the community are respected and often consulted about questions regarding farming, cooking, building, and so on.

Retirement is gradual unless children need farms. Older people are revered as keepers of knowledge and tradition and may work or rest as they like, gradually taking more time for visiting and for avocations like needlework, toy making, or raising flowers. As a son and his family take over the running of the farm, they also take over the house. The older couple may move to the "Grossdawdy's (grandfather's) house," a smaller house to the side of the main house (Wittmer, 1990). Older people remain active and useful. When the end comes, they are cared for and die at home (Hostetler, 1989; Hostetler & Huntington, 1971).

The family is the stabilizing structure in the Amish community. It is central to the activities of all community members' daily lives. Only God comes before the family. The family bond spreads out to the community to form a unified, mutually nurturing group of people.

Cultural Values and Attitudes

The Amish people hold a unique set of cultural values and attitudes. According to Good (1993), the Amish culture is "not a static culture or a dying curiosity, as some would suggest" (p. 42). Although living solely in the here and now, they are working toward the ultimate everlasting life in Heaven with God. Children are born into the world without sin or evil; this is illustrated in the practice of adult baptism rather than infant baptism. They live in subjugation to God, following God's will as revealed in the Bible. An Amish person interacts with others in the community in a collateral way; everyone is part of the "family." This method of communication is not extended to the "outside" world.

Hostetler and Huntington (1971) identified five main values of the Old Order Amish. The first is separation from the world. The Amish view the world as containing opposites, such as good and evil, light and darkness. It is the duty of each person to keep him- or herself "unspotted from the world." This is accomplished, in part, by minimizing contact with the outside world, sanctioned only to secure essential necessities with which to live.

The Amish also set themselves apart from the world by not participating in any form of violence or war. They do not use any type of self-defense and will more readily move from an area than try to defend their rights. Their refusal to serve in the military has caused considerable difficulty with the U.S. government, dating to the Revolutionary War. Zook (1989) concluded that the doctrine of separation is a major religious tenet. Separation from the world is based on scripture, articles of confession, and church tradition.

Second, voluntary acceptance of high social obligations is symbolized by adult baptism. This is a serious commitment, from which there is no turning back. Men vow at baptism to accept the call to minister if they are chosen. Through voluntary adult baptism, the Amish person becomes a member of the Amish Christian faith, which has many social and moral obligations. These include the responsibilities of raising children under the proper rules, contributing to the continuance of the society, and being a part of community activities, such as barn raisings.

Third, a disciplined church community is maintained. Few rules are in writing, and the *Ordnung* may vary with the district. Questionable issues must be resolved "with unanimous expression of peace and good will" (Hostetler & Huntington, 1971, p. 6) twice a year before communion is offered. The religious symbolism of the Amish is conveyed in dress and physical appearance. The style of dress is a protest against the proud and disobedient world. An Amish man wears a full beard, simple black clothing with no outside or hip pockets or suspenders, and a black hat with a 3-inch brim. Women may not wear silk or showy garments; they must wear plain dresses cut within 8 inches from the floor; and the hair must remain uncut, with no styling or curling. Women must also wear aprons, shawls, and bonnets of proper size and color at appropriate times.

Fourth, the practices of excommunication and shunning are strictly enforced. In an effort to keep the church pure, the Amish use excommunication (*Bann*) and shunning (*Meidung*) with members who break the rules of the faith. Members not "in fellowship" with the group, meaning not living according to the *Ordnung,* must be "expelled from the fellowship just as the human body casts off an infectious growth" (Hostetler & Huntington, 1971, p. 7). Excommunication bans the person from sharing communion. Shunning involves the total avoidance of a person in social, economic, and religious realms. No member can eat at the same table with an excommunicated/ shunned person. If the person under the ban is a husband or wife, the couple must suspend marital relations. Members may not exchange favors or services nor have social or sexual interaction with shunned members until they publicly repent.

Fifth, life must be in harmony with soil and nature. Humanity is viewed as caretaker, not conqueror or exploiter, of nature. The Amish austere lifestyle ensures few expenses and few repairs. Each farm can be self-sufficient, raising vegetables, pigs, and dairy cows and selling eggs, extra horses, honey, maple syrup, lumber, and handmade quilts. The Amish use steel wheels on their vehicles, which reduces possible farm size because steel wheels cannot be run on public roads between fields (many Amish communities now permit a small strip of rubber on each vehicle wheel). Small farms mean enough farms for all, which prevents affluence and a tenant class, especially important because affluent young work less, have more time to explore worldly ways, and are more likely to leave the church.

Like their pacifist, Anabaptist ancestors, the Amish will move rather than fight to protect their way of life. Mobility is a respected safety valve in the preservation of culture. When a district grows too large, when land prices increase beyond the means of young marrieds, and when disagreement cannot be mediated, Amish communities separate and move in friendship. When the differences are not too great, the groups maintain "kinship ties and visiting patterns."

Implications

Emery (1996) offered professional guidelines for those who provide services to Amish who either remain in their communities or have left their culture:

- Avoid helping an individual evolve a sense of self and personal pride that will place the individual in conflict with his or her culture.
- Use care in exploring subjects concerning family or community problems.
- Be sensitive to issues of gender roles.
- Be cautious of counseling instincts that lead you to encourage someone to leave the community.
- Be open to learning about their world.

Wittmer (1996) made points that may be added to the above guidelines:

- Recognize the limitations of tests, especially those that might use items unfamiliar to individuals in the Amish culture.
- Be cautious in activities that involve speed. Amish children are taught to work steadily and to do well what one does, rather than do a great deal and make careless mistakes.

- Recognize that Amish children and parents are not interested in career exploration.
- Respect the need for social distance that Amish children have with non-Amish children.
- Accept the fact that parents of an Amish child may have asked him or her to avoid counselors.

When the Amish came to the United States, their ways and outward appearance differed little from those of their neighbors. As the world grew increasingly complex, the Amish maintained their simple, self-sufficient ways, bringing differences into sharper focus. Despite the lure of the world, the Amish continue to hold on to a large majority of their youths. Schwieder and Schwieder (1975) estimated an Amish defection rate—that is, young people refusing to join the church—of 10% to 15%. Of that group, 95% stay "close to home," joining either Beachy Amish or Mennonite groups.

Old Order districts are found in more than 20 states, with the largest concentrations in Illinois, Iowa, Kansas, Minnesota, Mississippi, Oklahoma, and Wisconsin, in addition to the extensive communities in Pennsylvania and Ohio. They have also migrated into Central and South America and Canada. As the dominant culture encroaches on and restricts their way of life, the Amish will no doubt continue to move as long as affordable farmland is available. Perhaps they will concentrate in Arkansas, where one Beachy Amish community and one Amish Mennonite community are already established. Because of the modern irrigation and farm practices required on the Great Plains, they will not likely go farther west (Schwieder & Schwieder, 1975).

Zook (1989) concluded it is reasonable to assume that the traditional ways and strong religious beliefs of the Amish will continue to come into conflict with legal and economic structures and perceptions of the modern American society. The Amish are resilient, compromising only when absolutely necessary to maintain their families and communities and moving on when compromise is too threatening. As long as there is affordable land to farm, the Amish will compromise, relocate, and survive.

Questions for Review and Reflection

1. What influence does the practice of limiting education to the eighth grade have on the Amish culture?
2. What is shunning? How does this practice affect the psychological health of the shunned person?

3. Which Amish cultural practice do you find most desirable for you as a member of your cultural group? Why?

4. What Amish cultural traits appeal to you as desirable and potentially useful to the dominant culture? Why?

5. What stereotypes do you hold, relative to the Amish people? How might the stereotypes facilitate or hinder your work with Amish students or clients?

6. What is the basis of Amish separation from the world?

7. How do Amish art and language differ from those of the dominant culture?

8. How does the stereotype of "ignorant" and "backward" influence your view of Amish culture?

9. What steps would you take to resolve a conflict between the Amish culture and laws in the dominant culture?

10. What principles would guide your interactions with an Amish youth who desires to leave the Amish community?

References

Barn raising in Los Angeles. (1992, June 27). *Economist, 323*(7765), 29-33.

Emery, E. (1996). Amish families. In M. McGoldrick, J. Giordano, & J. K. Pearce (Eds.), *Ethnicity and family therapy* (pp. 442-450). New York: Guilford.

Good, M. (1985). *Who are the Amish?* Intercourse, PA: Good Books.

Good, M. (1993). *An Amish portrait: Song of a people.* Intercourse, PA: Good Books.

Hostetler, J. A. (1980). *Amish society.* Baltimore: Johns Hopkins University Press.

Hostetler, J. A. (1989). *Amish roots: A treasury of history, wisdom, and lore.* Baltimore: Johns Hopkins University Press.

Hostetler, J. A. (1992). The Amish: A small society. In J. J. Macionis & N. V. Benokraitis (Eds.), *Seeing ourselves: Classic, contemporary, and cross-cultural readings in sociology* (pp. 69-72). Upper Saddle River, NJ: Prentice Hall.

Hostetler, J. A., & Huntington, G. E. (1971). *Children in Amish society: Socialization and community education.* New York: Holt.

Hudson, W. S. (1981). *Religion in America.* New York: Scribner.

Keim, A. (1975). *Compulsory education and the Amish: The right not to be modern.* Boston: Beacon.

Krabill, D. B. (1993). *The Amish and the state.* Baltimore: Johns Hopkins.

Louden, M. L. (1991). The image of the Old Order Amish: General and sociolinguistic stereotypes. *National Journal of Sociology, 5*(2), 111-142.

Nolt, S. M. (1992). *The history of the Amish.* Intercourse, PA: Good Books.

Schwieder, E., & Schwieder, D. (1975). *A peculiar people: Iowa's Old Order Amish.* Ames: Iowa University Press.

U.S. Bureau of the Census. (1991). *Statistical abstract of the United States.* Washington, DC: Government Printing Office.

Warner, J., & Denlinger, D. (1969). *A portrait of the Amish.* New York: Grossman.

Wittmer, J. (1990). *The gentle people: Personal reflections of Amish life.* Minneapolis: Educational Media Corporation.

Wittmer, J. (1996). Old Order Amish. In P. B. Pedersen & D. C. Locke (Eds.), *Cultural and diversity issues in counseling* (pp. 13-15). Greensboro, NC: ERIC/CASS.

Zook, L. (1989). The Amish in America: Conflicts between cultures. *Journal of American Culture, 12*(4), 29-33.

4

Native American Indians

One of the great tragedies of the exploitation of culturally different groups in the United States has been the consistent and long-standing maltreatment of Native American Indians. Native American Indians throughout the Americas found themselves virtually stripped of their cultural identities and relegated to land unwanted by Whites.

It is believed that Native American Indians migrated from Asia over a land bridge at the Bering Strait during a recent ice age, sometime about 20,000 to 27,000 years ago (Snow, 1979). Before the coming of the Europeans, two large geographic areas were largely occupied by Native American Indians who practiced farming (Dobyns, 1983). One area followed the Rocky Mountains; the other area occupied the eastern half of the United States from Canada to the Gulf of Mexico.

Motivated by self-interest and a quest for power over people and natural resources, White Europeans and their descendants invaded the territorial homelands of this country's aboriginal inhabitants well into the 20th century. Berkhofer (1978) stated that "White hopes for the exploration of Indians and their lands certainly shaped their perceptions of Native American Indians from the very beginning of contact. . . . Images of the good Indian suggested the ease of exploration" (p. 118). In many respects, Native American Indian culture has been approached superficially by historians and other researchers, whose writings have traditionally concentrated on the development and expansion of Anglocentric culture in the United States. The popular entertainment media have almost invariably distorted accurate views of Native American Indian culture. The results of these biases often have been misunderstanding by the general populace and a broad stereotyping of richly complex peoples.

Some ambiguity exists about the name that should be used for the population discussed in this chapter. The name *Amerind* or *Amerindian* has been used to designate the 2.5 million nomadic people who lived in the Americas before the arrival of the Europeans. Historically, the name *Indian* was used, followed by *American Indian,* and more recently, *Native American* and *Native American Indian.* The Bureau of Indian Affairs (BIA) (1988) defines a Native American Indian as a person who is a registered or enrolled member of a federally recognized tribe or whose blood quantum is one fourth or more Indian, genealogically derived, and who can legally demonstrate that fact to the BIA. This fact makes Native American Indians the only *legally* defined ethnic group living in the United States. The Lumbee Regional Development Association in Pembroke, North Carolina, issues American Indian Tribal Membership cards that state, "[T]he bearer of this card is a duly enrolled member of the Lumbee Tribe and is entitled to all privileges as a member" (Alfred Bryant, Jr., personal communication, April 1997).

Hirschfelder (1982) reported that one Native American Indian law center has assembled 52 legal definitions of Native American Indians. The U.S. Bureau of the Census, in contrast, records anyone who claims native identity as Native American Indian. Although there appears to be no consensus on the most appropriate term, *Native American Indian* is used here because it connotes both their original inhabitation of this country and their current U.S. citizenship. The term includes people who are descendants of pre-Columbian inhabitants of North America. Native Hawaiians are not included although they are also deserving of the title "Native American."

Many tribal groups of Native American Indians live throughout the United States, and it is impossible to say that any one culture is associated with all Native American Indians per se. The modern notion of a "tribe" as a centralized political system, with firm geographic boundaries and a common culture and language, is a European conception (Berkhofer, 1978). Native American Indians constitute less than 1% of the U.S. population, numbering 1.9 million in 1990 (U.S. Bureau of the Census, 1991). The Native American Indian population increased nearly 65% from 1980 to 1990. The rate of growth is one of the fastest in the country. This heterogeneous, geographically dispersed group speaks some 150 tribal languages in 505 federally recognized and 365 state recognized tribal groups (BIA, 1988). The largest are the Navajos of Arizona and New Mexico (approximately 160,000); the smallest are the Chumash of California and the Modocs of Oklahoma, each numbering fewer than 100. The majority of Native American Indians live west of the

Mississippi River, with 40% of the total population living in Arizona, California, New Mexico, Oklahoma, and Washington. More than one half of the total population reside in urban areas, and about 637,000 live on the 52 million acres of land identified as reservations (Hodgkinson, 1990; Stock, 1987). It is important to distinguish population distribution from tribal distribution. In some states, a tribe or group of unrelated tribes, such as the Navajo, Hopi, and Pueblo peoples, may live in the same geographic area because of the presence of reservations; other states may have rural Native American Indian communities but no reservations.

In the face of this vast diversity, "it can be said that it is possible to isolate unifying and consistent patterns of behavior among Indian individuals as well as among Indian tribes" (Washburn, 1975, p. xvi). And Thomason (1991) concluded that "there are some similarities in the basic values and beliefs of many Native Americans" (p. 326). On the premise that similarities exist among Native American Indians, a composite view of Native American Indian culture may be drawn. The existence of these similarities, however, should not result in a conclusion that Native American Indians are one group with one need. In fact, the material in this chapter emphasizes qualities/characteristics of reservation Native American Indians, individuals quite different from nonreservation Native American Indians.

Acculturation

Despite the assault by the overarching dominant U.S. culture on Native American Indian life, many Native American Indians have not become acculturated. Neumann, Mason, Chase, and Albaugh (1991) reported that many Native American Indians, especially those on reservations and in rural areas, think of themselves as Indians, rather than as members of a minority group. This opposition to being defined by the dominant culture shows dramatically how very different their perspectives on, and assumptions about, the world are from Eurocentric values and traditions. As Yates (1987) stated:

> On the whole, American Indian tribes are remarkable in that they have withstood attempts at extermination, removal from their traditional lands, extreme poverty, deployment of their youth to boarding schools, relocation policies, and last but not least, the White man's poison—alcohol. (p. 1135)

Ethnic reorganization accounts for changes in Native American Indian culture but simultaneously provides for ethnic distinctiveness. This occurs when a group "undergoes a reorganization of its social structure, redefinition of ethnic group boundaries, or some other change in response to pressures or demands imposed by the dominant culture" (Nagel & Snipp, 1993, p. 204).

Despite the willingness of some Native American Indians to become bicultural, the newcomers to their world were intent on acculturating or terminating Native American Indians almost from the beginning. This policy was and still is most easily seen in the U.S. educational system. Thomas Jefferson espoused an educational system that would "educate men to manners, morals, and habits perfectly homogeneous with those of the country" (Foreman, 1987, p. 2). The "manners, morals, and habits" of which Jefferson spoke were those of his native Englishmen, not those of Native American Indians. This attempt to force the acculturation of Native American Indians is still prevalent in our educational system today (Pertusati, 1988). The clash of cultures has caused many Native American Indians to experience a general lack of self-confidence and a sense of helplessness.

Poverty and Economic Concerns

The dominant culture has forced Native American Indians to become intimate with the concept of poverty. According to O'Connell (1985), "Native Americans represent the most economically disadvantaged and underserved group in America. They have the lowest average income, lowest educational level and lowest standard of living" (p. 5). Although one would think that Native American Indians could continue to live their cultural lifestyle on the reservations, this possibility has been virtually eliminated by the federal government's establishment of reservations on useless land, which forced Native American Indians to live a difficult and impoverished existence. Educational and employment opportunities on the reservations are often poor, at best, creating a cycle of poverty (Beuf, 1977). John (1985) noted that the "deprivation experienced by reservation Indians is substantially greater than urban Indians. In general, the reservation group is poorer, supports more people on its income, has fewer social contacts, lower life satisfaction, and poorer health" (p. 237).

Unemployment in both rural and urban areas remains high, although the number of Native American Indian businesses increased by 64% between 1982 and 1987. Poverty also continues to plague Native American Indian families. In the 10 states with the largest Native American Indian populations, between 17% and 47% live in poverty (Hodgkinson, 1990).

Despite John Colliers's "Indian New Deal" in the 1930s, Glenn Emmons's economic development program in the 1950s, and President Lyndon Johnson's Great Society of the 1960s, Native American Indians still suffer severe problems in the areas of employment, education, income, and health.

Unemployment is a result of the geographic isolation of the reservations, the lack of transportation, the lack of skilled labor, and the absence of capital. Unemployment on reservations ranged from 20% to over 70% in 1985 (Senate Select Committee on Indian Affairs, 1985). Few industrial jobs appear on the reservations, and those that do become available pay very low wages. In 1983, only 25% of reservation workers earned more than $1,000 a year. In fact, average yearly income for the Native American Indian family was $1,500 in 1983. More than 40% reside in households that earn less than $15,000 annually. Off the reservation, racism and the lack of education cause high unemployment rates among urban Native American Indians (Harrington, 1984; Hodgkinson, 1990).

Unemployment and low income lead to poor housing, malnutrition, and poor community sanitation, which in turn cause health problems. In 1980, the rate of tuberculosis among Native American Indians was 6 times the national average. Native American Indians are 70 times more likely than Euramericans to suffer dysentery. Their suicide rate is 6 times that of any other ethnic group, and their alcoholism rate is the highest in the nation. Arrest and incarceration rates are 30 times higher for Native American Indians in towns near reservations than for non-Native American Indians (Olson & Wilson, 1984). Blum, Harmon, Harris, Bergeisen, and Resnick (1992) reported that inadequate health care and poor nutrition continue to be major sources of stress for Native American Indians.

Unemployment, poverty, and lack of education are all symptoms of the cultural alienation that Native American Indians experience when trying to live in the dominant culture of the United States. Many of these problems were brought to this continent by the Europeans and are the direct result of oppression of Native American Indians.

The land, to Native American Indians, could no more be owned or divided than could the air. In traditional culture, the individual worked toward the improvement of the tribe, and the accumulation of material goods for personal use was an offense. Time was seen as a constant. Living in the present was seen as important. Planning for the future or dwelling on the past was futile. These basic cultural views led to economic "failure" of Native American Indians when judged by Anglocentric standards, which value material possession and accumulation, planning for the future, and individual achievement.

History of Oppression

Native American Indians have a long history of oppression at the hands of European settlers. As early as 1524, Native American Indians were seized by European settlers and sold as slaves in the West Indies. Native American

Indians were also oppressed by settlers who expected them to adhere to European standards of conduct, cultural values the Europeans spent little or no time teaching to Native American Indians. Disease, slavery, and warfare often contributed to the early extinction of Native American Indian tribes. As the tribes weakened, the Europeans were able to encroach further on Native American Indian land (Wetmore, 1975). Although the policies and actions of the Whites toward Native American Indians in the 19th century appeared to be aimed at termination, it is interesting to note that when a tribe of Native American Indians attempted to move into Canada, they were pursued by the cavalry and forced back into the United States. Fueled by the doctrine of Manifest Destiny, Whites believed in their divine right to the land and their supremacy over Native American Indians (Beuf, 1977; Wetmore, 1975).

By the end of the 18th century, the 2.5 million people who lived in the Americas before the arrival of the Europeans had been reduced through annihilation to fewer than 250,000. Native American Indians were described as vanishing, but they did not vanish. In 1980, approximately 1.5 million Native American Indians lived in the United States, and they are considered one of the fastest growing ethnic groups in this country. More than 500 tribes are federally recognized, and some 365 tribes are state recognized (Olson & Wilson, 1984).

The oppression of Native American Indians has continued on the reservations. Native American Indians were given land that was believed to be useless. When it was found that some reservation land contained gold or other valuable resources, the land was taken away. In his autobiography, Chief Clinton Rickard (1973) of the Tuscaroras noted that it had become a 200-year-old custom among his people that when gold is discovered on the reservation, it is covered up and never spoken of again. Treaties between Native American Indians and the federal government were broken by Whites more often than they were kept. Disputes over reservation land and boundaries, which are usually settled to the disadvantage of Native American Indians, have continued to the present. It has even been proposed that reservation land be broken up and sold to the public at large. Native American Indian tribes seeking official recognition by the federal government often find it a difficult process; usually, the result is that they do not receive official recognition (South, 1980; Wetmore, 1975).

Language and the Arts

Language is often thought of as merely a set of words, spoken or written, that communicates thoughts. Many cultures, however, including the Native

American Indian, also have a rich heritage in nonverbal language. One may learn much by "listening" to what Native American Indians are expressing through body language, eye movements, silence, and tone of voice (Sue & Sue, 1990). Many speak softly and at a slow rate, often avoiding direct eye contact with the speaker or listener. Spoken language varies quite a bit among tribes, with some 300 tribal languages and dialects in use in contemporary Native American Indian communities. Most Native American Indians know and use English, but many do not, and many do not use it comfortably.

One method used by European settlers to refer to groups of Native American Indians, along with a tribal name, village name, and European geographic name, was by linguistic families (Wetmore, 1975). The Cherokee were the only Native American Indian tribe to develop a written language (South, 1980). Although the absence of a written language is often viewed as evidence of the primitive nature of Native American Indians and the supremacy of the European settlers, this is a viewpoint taken out of cultural context. Native American Indians live and learn holistically. They learn through listening, by watching others, and through experience. They pass on traditions and customs through oral myths and legends. They live in the present, rather than in the past or future. When the entire culture is taken into account, it is easy to see that a written language was not necessary for Native American Indians until they were forced to interact with the dominant American culture.

The holistic lifestyle of Native American Indians is also reflected in their arts, in their traditions of music, dance, and crafts. Their art is woven throughout the fabric of everyday Native American Indian life and is insepa- rable from nature, religion, and the universe. The holistic approach of Native American Indian artists can be seen in their methods: In creating a mural, an artist, not using any sketch or outline, paints in all the blue parts first, then all the red, and so forth. It is difficult for linear-thinking individuals to envision being able to approach painting in this manner (South, 1980). Today, the ancient traditions of most tribes are transmitted only through occasional ceremonies and existing legends, art, and folklore.

Native American Indian art is best understood from the viewpoint of Native American Indian religious values. The importance that Native Ameri- can Indians place on mystical experiences is also central in their art. When these values are kept in mind, one can more easily begin to understand and appreciate Native American Indian art forms. Pottery, masks, basketry, jewelry, weaving, and sculpture are all subject to the regional styles and designs of the hundreds of tribes that engage in creative artistry.

For the Native American Indian, a "work of art" is functional first and foremost, regardless of whether it is aesthetically pleasing to the viewer. Native American Indian painting is seen as an evolutionary process that runs the gamut from "primitive" to modern, from traditional to abstract (Wade & Strickland, 1981). Most experts agree on its remarkable continuity in themes and styles, while at the same time it returns to many of the ancient forms and ideas. This dichotomy may reflect one basic element of the Native American Indian value system: The old ways are best and change only results in problems for the culture.

Racism and Prejudice

Even some early European settlers recognized the prejudices of Whites toward Native American Indians, as evidenced by the following comments of John Lawson, who traveled among, and wrote about, North Carolina Native American Indians:

> They were really better to us than we have been to them, as they always freely give us of their victuals at their quarters, while we let them walk by our doors hungry, and do not often relieve them. We look upon them with disdain and scorn, and think them little better than beasts in human form; while with all our religion and education, we possess more moral deformities and vices than these people do. (Rights, 1947, p. 44)

Some hidden or covert prejudice that may be intentional or unintentional, depending on the source, is seen in the constant message that if Native American Indians are to succeed, they need to become like Whites. The covert message is that Native American Indians and their culture are inferior.

Institutional racism by the federal and state governments has been readily apparent over the years through such policies as Manifest Destiny, the loss of Native American Indians' citizenship rights of voting and bearing arms under the 1835 North Carolina state constitution, and the relocation of Native American Indians under the Indian Removal Act of 1830 (Beuf, 1977; Rickard, 1973).

Native American Indians have met continual opposition to their attempts to benefit from life in the United States. One example points to this continuous discrimination against them: In 1910, the Lumbee were formally recognized by the state of North Carolina. A bill passed by the U.S. Congress in 1956 recognized the Lumbee as an Indian tribe but denied them access to services from the Bureau of Indian Affairs (Alfred Bryant, Jr., personal communication, April 1997).

In a discussion of how children learn about each other, Pang (1991) identified examples of stereotypes about Native American Indians. She cited the use of Native American Indians as objects to be counted ("Ten Little

Indians"), a practice that usually includes showing identical pictures of Native American Indians, from which students concluded that they were a homogeneous population; depicting Native American Indians as objects from the past; and the use of Native American Indians as mascots for athletic teams. She concluded that these examples "make it seem natural that Whites would enjoy some aspects of Indian culture as historic relics, but continue to abrogate treaties with Indians when they 'stand in the way of progress' " (p. 183).

Language is another area in which prejudice can be found. For example, the expressions "Indian giver" and "give it back to the Indians" are used pejoratively. Prejudice is also frequently encountered in the educational system, where school counselors tend to direct Native American Indian students into technical areas and away from college. Studies have shown the discouraging trend that prejudice toward Native American Indians is staying the same or even increasing (Beuf, 1977). Lomawaima (1993) suggested that this trend continues to plague contemporary life on reservations.

Sociopolitical Factors

Tribal government varies among the tribes. Historically, most tribes were ruled by chiefs with matriarchal lines of succession. A war chief and council members were usually chosen from among the elders in a tribe (Rights, 1947). Currently, most tribes use a tribal council type of government, with variations on whether members are appointed or elected. Some tribes still have chiefs; some are elected, and some are hereditary successors. Decisions are usually made either through council consensus or through the spiritual leader.

Native American Indians are represented in city, state, and federal governments, but at a lower rate than proportional to the U.S. population (Rickard, 1973). Native American Indians seemed to have relatively little power over their own lives in the United States until the 1960s. The Red Power movement brought about positive change and put more power into the hands of Native American Indians, primarily through three Native American Indian organizations: the National Indian Youth Council, the National Congress of American Indians, and the American Indian Movement. These changes in social and political power are reflected in the following quote by Chief Clinton Rickard (1973):

> We tried to live in peace, but the government would give us no peace. In the old days the Indian was always going on the warpath to protect his rights. Now in our own day, we still have to go on the warpath. The only thing that has

changed is that today we Indians use peaceful weapons. We organize, we write letters, we make speeches, we go to court, we have demonstrations, and we rouse up friendly White people to support us. We are determined to fight to the end for those things that are most precious to us. (p. 137)

The BIA (1988), an agency in the Department of the Interior, provides services to approximately 650,000 Native American Indians via 123 offices in 12 geographic areas. The BIA provides child welfare services, family services, consultant services, and advisory services to Native American Indian youths and adults. Native American Indian leadership in emerging social and political action movements offers promise for improving social conditions through political activity.

Child-Rearing Practices

Native American Indian children are reared by the extended family, clan, or tribe, with grandparents and other elders usually responsible for teaching the children. Children are given a great deal of freedom and are allowed to explore and be independent quite early in their lives. Disliking a show of temper, Native American Indians rarely discipline their children unless real danger exists. They believe that a child should be allowed to make mistakes and to learn the natural consequences of misbehavior. The elders also do not want ill feelings to arise because this might prove harmful to the elders in their old age or may offend an ancestral spirit dwelling in the child (Johnson, 1967).

Many Native American Indians use noncoercive parenting styles that encourage the child's self-determination and that are not encumbered by expectations about developmental timing (Everett, Proctor, & Cartnell, 1983). Child-rearing practices are characterized by early training in self-sufficiency, and psychological development is in harmony with knowledge gained from the natural world. Shomaker (1989) reported that childhood naming ceremonies often establish lifelong linkages between infants and adults who will share in responsibilities of child rearing along with biological parents.

Children develop an inner motivation to learn by "seeking out knowledge of human experience and skills by being present in practice or their telling" (More, 1987, p. 23). The Native American Indian style of child rearing is, therefore, a holistic one that fits in with the rest of the Native American Indian lifestyle.

Indian parents are generally quite permissive in their training, and children have no fixed schedules for eating or sleeping. Interestingly, among Native

American Indian mothers who had attended secondary schools outside their childhood community, changes in this practice have been found that reflect the beliefs and training of the dominant culture. In accordance with their easygoing lifestyle and attitude toward child rearing, Native American Indian parents do not strike their children. As a child grows, he or she learns to conform to the ideals and beliefs of the tribe; shame and fear become the primary agents in the educational process (More, 1987).

Native American Indian attitudes toward sex are likewise liberal; sex is treated as a part of the natural process of life. Sexual intercourse and facts surrounding it are understood at very early ages. Premarital sexual experiences are common in most Indian villages; in fact, they are so common that they are sometimes thought to be a normal part of the courtship period. When a birth does occur out of wedlock, the tribal community is very protective of the mother, even to the point of finding a husband for her, whether it is the biological father or not. No stigma is attached to the child, who is loved and cherished along with other children in the tribe (Harrington, 1984).

Religious Practices

To Native American Indians, religion is the universe. They believe that almost every act of life is regulated and determined by religion. Some early European settlers recognized the holistic quality of Native American Indian religion despite a general belief that Native American Indian religion was "crude"; some commented on the completeness and consistency in theory that was beautifully expressed through ceremony and everyday life (Rights, 1947). This holistic view is represented through the inseparability of person, nature, and the spirit.

Bryde (1971) identified four valued objects in Native American Indians' conceptualization of the universe: God, self, others, and world. All values and value-oriented actions are related to these four objects, and from this value system comes a way of life that encompasses ideas, beliefs, views, behaviors, traditions, and customs. *God* is positive, benevolent, and part of daily living for Native American Indians. *Self* is part of nature where people learn about their own nature from nature itself. Interpersonal relationships (*others*) are explained in the value of sharing and generosity. The *world* is interconnected, and everything lives according to the same process.

The spiritual beliefs of Native American Indians are still reflected in, and inseparable from, their daily lives. Medicine men or shamans are religious men and, commonly, the priests for the tribes. Historically, these men have been quite powerful within a tribe; they have been believed to have special powers not possessed by others. Dance, art, and ceremonial festivals are linked with religious beliefs. In Native American Indian government, councils that cannot reach a consensus are not concerned about not making a decision; they believe that such a failure indicates the time was not right (Brewington, 1959; South, 1980).

Native American Indians believe in many gods or spirits, usually with one chief god or Great Spirit. They worship the forces of nature, such as the sun, wind, water, fire, thunder, and lightning, as well as animals. They believe that, after death, their spirits live on or are reborn into new babies. Although to non-Native American Indians it sometimes seems contradictory, Native American Indians have easily accepted and adopted Christianity along with their own beliefs. This acceptance is understandable from the viewpoint of Native American Indian culture, which accepts all religions as part of the universe or Indian Hoop of Life (Rights, 1947; Sue, 1981; Sue & Sue, 1990).

Spencer and Jennings (1977) reported that the most widespread religion among Native American Indians is the "Peyote Cult, whose adherents have been brought together in the Native American Indian Church, which is now the principal religion of the majority of Indians between the Mississippi River and the Rocky Mountains, and is also represented in parts of the Great Basin, southern Canada, and east-central California" (p. 518). The cult combines social ethics and old Indian practices and beliefs. In the ceremonies,

> Members consume the nonnarcotic dried buttons of the peyote cactus, which induce visions and hallucinations of varied colors. Although the native components seem to be dominant in the Peyote Cult, it includes also various elements of Christian derivation, such as baptism, the Trinity, the Cross, and other Christian symbolism. At meetings of the cult, there is singing, prayers, and testimonials. (Spencer & Jennings, 1977, p. 518)

The popularity of the cult seems to spring from the Pan-Indian movement spreading throughout the United States that promotes and extols Native American Indian nationalism and identity through various national organizations. By returning to ancient religious practices, Native American Indians affirm their importance.

Family Structure and Dynamics

The traditional family form among Native American Indians is the extended family. In fact, it is probably more appropriate to speak in terms of the clan as the basic family unit. A *clan* consists of a "group of families or households which traces its descent through the head of the house from a common ancestor" (Wetmore, 1975, p. 116). Many clans trace their ancestry through matrilineal descent. In clans, the female has traditionally been responsible for and performed the duties necessary to preserve the "social organization," usually regulating such matters as punishment, adoption, and marriage (Johnson, 1967; Wetmore, 1975). Clans are often quite large and the birthrate quite high (Beuf, 1977).

Unlike the dominant culture of the United States, which emphasizes youth, Native American Indian culture values and respects the wisdom and experience of age. Thus, the elders are responsible for the education of the children and the leadership in the tribe. Usually, the elders fill positions on tribal councils, where they often serve until their deaths (Wetmore, 1975). The traditional family lifestyle focuses on cultural activities such as feasts, religions, and powwows. Sex roles are clearly defined, and the contributions of both genders are appreciated.

Exact genealogy is not important to Native American Indians. Ancestry may be actual or legendary and might be traced matrilineally or patrilineally. Authority and discipline have had a traditional structure as well. According to Olson and Wilson (1984),

> In a patrilineal family, for example, "grandfather" offered wisdom to everyone; "father" offered authority and responsibility; "uncle" offered assistance; "children" offered obedience; and "brother" offered equality. Since everyone understood the behavior associated with these roles, and most people occupied several roles simultaneously, family values actually governed society, providing direct moral restraints on individual deviancy. (p. 21)

Although the characteristics of Native American Indian family structure described above may suggest homogeneity, it is important to recall the diversity among Native American Indian families. Just as there is heterogeneity among individual Native American Indians in general, so is there diversity among families, in terms of both structure and function.

Cultural Values and Attitudes

Many values and attitudes of Native American Indians have already been discussed or alluded to in this chapter. Trimble, Fleming, Beauvais, and Jumper-Thurman (1996) identified Native American values as including a strong present-time orientation; a time consciousness defined socially, rather than by the clock; a sharing that is combined with avoidance of personal acquisitiveness; a respect for age and for elders; a preference for cooperation over competition; and an ethical concern for the natural world. To Native

American Indians, time is not an entity; it just "is." Therefore, they do not worry about or value time, and time is not structured in their everyday lives. Native American Indians live in the present. Their belief in immortality—in a soul that lives on or is reborn—and their belief in some individuals' ability to foretell the future while still living in the present (found in some, but not all, tribes) reflects the interconnectedness of all things and the never-ending cycle of time (Johnson, 1967; Osborne, 1985). Time consciousness is measured in terms of natural phenomena, such as days, nights, moons, and seasons. Time is cyclical, rather than linear.

Easily following from the Native American Indian sense of time and holistic culture is the dimension of human activity. The focus of Native American Indians is on "being," or existing. They do not worry about obtaining or losing material possessions. Everything that happens is part of the whole and is as it should be. Native American Indians will work for a purpose related to being, and once they fulfill that immediate purpose, they will continue to enjoy life as it is (Rights, 1947; Sue, 1981; Sue & Sue, 1990).

The relationship between the individual and nature is one of harmony. Although the supernatural, in the form of spirits, controls the natural world, Native American Indians consider that person, nature, and spirit are all one; all are part of the universe, and all are to live in harmony with each other (Johnson, 1967). Native American Indians understand nature as the essence of God. If there were no God, there could be no nature. Having the right relationship with nature gives the right relationship with God, which gives the right relationship with self. Sin is not represented by offending God, but in effecting an imbalance in nature. Living in ignorance of one's relationship to nature is more likely than moral sin to cause destruction (Axelson, 1993).

Social relationships are basically collateral. Everett et al. (1983) reported that although in the dominant culture a firm handshake generally means a person may be trusted, many Native American Indians view a firm handshake as aggressive and disrespectful. Social relationships exist in the here and now. Many Native American Indians value humility and modesty and view it as ill-mannered to talk about one's accomplishments. Although Native American Indians do communicate and have relationships with the dead, it is in the form of communicating with spirits of the dead that exist in the present. Often, these spirits coexist in the bodies of children (Badwound & Tierney, 1988; Wetmore, 1975).

Native American Indians consider human nature to be basically good (although their experiences with the dominant culture may be changing that belief); they act on this belief through their custom of welcoming strangers, sharing with each other, and helping others before self. Many believe that the one who gives the most is the most respected. People who do bad things are seen as inhabited by bad spirits or perhaps having had a spell put on them.

Overall, Native American Indians see all people as part of the universe, which should be harmonious as a whole (Johnson, 1967; Matijasic, 1987; Sue, 1981).

Implications

It is clear that educators or counselors wishing to work with Native American Indians need preparation beyond the typical classroom experiences offered in colleges and universities. By learning about the Native American Indian culture, one must come to appreciate it and even to revere it. Oswalt (1978) had this to say about Native American Indians:

> Indians themselves are increasingly aware that their cultural identity is important to them, no matter how different it may be from life when Whites first arrived. Many Indians seek not just tolerance of their ways but meaningful moral and financial support in order that their identity may endure so long as the waters shall flow and the sun shall shine. This is their clear right and our abiding obligation because this land indeed was theirs. (p. 549)

Johnson and Lashley (1989) found that the degree of commitment to Native American Indian culture affects preferences for counselors from a particular ethnic group. Those with strong cultural commitments expect more "nurturance, faciliative conditions, and counselor expertise than those with a weak commitment" (p. 120).

According to Hodge (1981), Native American Indians have three reactions to White-dominated society. His typology defines these three groups (bicultural, traditional, and marginal) in terms of Indian identity development. Sue and Sue (1990) used a worldview orientation that involved personal control and responsibility. These two perspectives can be combined to promote greater understanding of Native American Indians.

Bicultural Native American Indians emulate many White pursuits, such as wealth, formal education, and recreation. They attempt to obtain these material benefits through hard work and through manipulating politics and industry. These Native American Indians compete in economic and political affairs of the dominant culture while maintaining their cultural heritage. They believe that their efforts can effect change. They are self-reliant, possess a strong desire to overcome racial barriers, and value achievement.

Traditional Native American Indians distrust Whites in the dominant culture. This results from past conflicts and value differences between the two cultures. They use their "Indian-ness" to avoid Whites and the White lifestyle. Such Native American Indians pursue wealth only as a means of escaping White domination. They want to perpetuate their native culture. They realistically perceive barriers of discrimination. These individuals believe in their ability to improve their current conditions, yet they wish to maintain their identity, and sometimes their actions are militant.

Marginal Native American Indians do not attempt to compete with the dominant culture. They employ an internal exchange system involving goods, rights, obligations, and emotional support. They accept the dominant culture, believing that they are unable to have any impact on the established order. They expect the government to provide housing and financial assistance. Many resemble the external control-external responsibility worldview. They maintain a low profile and expect the dominant culture to provide for their needs and may be said to have developed a "learned helplessness."

After gaining awareness of Native American Indian culture, educators and counselors can incorporate this awareness into educational and counseling theory and practice. Theorists have concluded that Native American Indians value trustworthiness and understanding within the counseling relationship. Thomason (1991) suggested strategies for those who anticipate counseling interventions with Native American Indians, including the following:

- Become familiar with Native American Indian ideas about healing.
- Learn as much as possible about the client's specific tribe and tribal beliefs.
- Meet the client as a person, rather than as a case.
- Follow the client's lead in regard to nonverbal behavior.
- Use a fairly active and directive problem-solving approach with many clients, but other approaches may be useful as well.
- Maintain the options of involving the family of the client, visiting the home of the client, or involving a traditional healer in the counseling process.

Choney, Berryhill-Paapke, and Robbins (1995) made the following recommendations for work with Native American Indian clients:

- Consider use of traditional healers as adjuncts to traditional counseling.
- Consider the role and function of the extended family and its impact on location for counseling and the degree of motivation of clients to engage in therapy.
- Give careful consideration to differences in communication styles, perceptions of trustworthiness, gender role definitions, and social support networks.
- Exercise caution in the use of standardized tests.

Educators must be honest and accepting and must respect both the individual Native American Indian and the Native American Indian culture. It is not enough merely to assert that one is culturally sensitive and aware of Native American Indian values. Rather, educators and counselors must develop approaches that have demonstrated utility with Native American Indians in a variety of settings.

Questions for Review and Reflection

1. What has been the major impact of Native American Indian culture on the dominant culture of the United States?

2. What Native American Indian cultural trait is most similar to a trait in the dominant culture? Which is most different? How do this similarity and difference promote or hinder interactions between Native American Indians and the dominant culture?

3. What image comes to your mind when you think of "Native American Indian"? How does (or can) this image influence your interactions with Native American Indians? How does W. H. Hodge's (1981) three-group typology of Native American Indian worldviews help educators or counselors understand specific individuals in the culture?

4. What is the relationship between the attempts at forced acculturation for Native American Indians and the subsequent treatment of Native American Indians living on reservations?

5. What similarities and differences are likely to be evident between reserved and nonreserved Native American Indians? How can these similarities and differences be used in working with Native American Indian students or clients?

6. What impact does "Indian time" have on Native American Indians in the dominant culture? How can educators or counselors use the concept of Indian time in working with Native American Indian students or clients?

7. What impact does traditional body language of Native American Indians have on their interactions with the dominant culture? How can educators or counselors prevent miscommunication in these encounters?

8. Describe the cultural value that influences Native American Indian art. How does this view toward art affect other Native American Indian cultural values?

9. What is the meaning of the term *Indian giver*? In what ways do you think use of the term influences Native American Indian interactions with the dominant culture?

10. How do Native American Indian views of relation and respect for the elderly influence the way they interact with nature and with other people?

References

Axelson, J. A. (1993). *Counseling and development in a multicultural society.* Pacific Grove, CA: Brooks/Cole.

Badwound, E., & Tierney, W. G. (1988). Leadership and American Indian values: The tribal college dilemma. *Journal of American Indian Education, 28,* 9-15.

Berkhofer, R. R. (1978). *White man's Indian.* New York: Knopf.

Beuf, A. H. (1977). *Red children in White America.* University Park: University of Pennsylvania Press.

Blum, R. W., Harmon, B., Harris, L., Bergeisen, L., & Resnick, M. D. (1992). American Indian-Alaska Native youth health. *Journal of the American Medical Association, 266*(12), 1637-1644.

Brewington, C. D. (1959). *The five civilized Indian tribes of eastern North Carolina.* Clinton, NC: Bass.

Bryde, S. F. (1971). *Modern Indian psychology.* Vermillion: University of South Dakota.

Bureau of Indian Affairs (BIA). (1988). *American Indians today.* Washington, DC: Author.

Choney, S. K., Berryhill-Paapke, E., & Robbins, R. R. (1995). The acculturation of American Indians. In J. G. Ponterotto, J. M. Casas, L. A. Suzuki, & C. M. Alexander (Eds.), *Handbook of multicultural counseling* (pp. 73-92). Thousand Oaks, CA: Sage.

Dobyns, H. F. (1983). *Their numbers become thinned.* Knoxville: University of Tennessee Press.

Everett, F., Proctor, N., & Cartnell, B. (1983). Providing psychological services to American Indian children and families. *Professional Psychology, 14,* 588-603.

Foreman, L. D. (1987). Curricular choice in the age of self-determination. *Journal of American Indian Education, 26,* 1-6.

Harrington, M. (1984). *The new American poverty.* New York: Holt, Rinehart & Winston.

Hirschfelder, A. (1982). *Happily may I walk: American Indians and Alaska natives today.* New York: Scribner.

Hodge, W. H. (1981). *The first Americans.* New York: Holt, Rinehart & Winston.

Hodgkinson, H. L. (1990). *The demographics of American Indians: One percent of the people, fifty percent of the diversity.* Washington, DC: Center for Demographic Policy, Institute for Educational Leadership.

John, R. (1985). Service needs and support networks of elderly Native Americans: Family, friends, and social service agencies. In W. A. Peterson & J. Quadagno (Eds.), *Social bonds in later life: Aging and independence* (pp. 229-250). Beverly Hills, CA: Sage.

Johnson, F. R. (1967). *The Tuscaroras: Mythology-medicine-culture.* Murfreesboro, NC: Johnson.

Johnson, M. E., & Lashley, K. H. (1989). Influence of Native-Americans' cultural commitment on preferences for counselor ethnicity and expectations about counseling. *Journal of Multicultural Counseling and Development, 17,* 115-122.

Lomawaima, K. T. (1993). Domesticity in the federal Indian schools: The power of authority over mind and body. *American Ethnologist, 20,* 227-240.

Matijasic, T. D. (1987). Reflected values: Sixteenth-century Europeans view the Indians of North America. *American Indian Culture and Research Journal, 11,* 31-50.

More, A. J. (1987). Native Indian learning styles: A review for researchers and teachers. *Journal of American Indian Education, 27,* 17-28.

Nagel, J., & Snipp, M. (1993). Ethnic reorganization: American Indian social, economic, political, and cultural strategies for survival. *Ethnic and Racial Studies, 16,* 203-235.

Neumann, A. K., Mason, V., Chase, E., & Albaugh, B. (1991). Factors associated with success among southern Cheyenne and Arapaho. *Journal of Community Mental Health, 16,* 103-115.

O'Connell, J. C. (1985). A family systems approach for serving rural, reservation Native American communities. *Journal of American Indian Education, 24,* 1-6.

Olson, J. S., & Wilson, R. (1984). *Native Americans in the twentieth century.* Provo, UT: Brigham Young University Press.

Osborne, B. (1985). Research into Native Americans' cognition: 1973-1982. *Journal of American Indian Education, 24,* 9-24.

Oswalt, W. H. (1978). *This land was theirs: A study of North American Indians.* New York: John Wiley.

Pang, V. O. (1991). Teaching children about social issues: Kidpower. In C. L. Sleeter (Ed.), *Empowerment through multicultural education* (pp. 179-197). Albany: State University of New York Press.

Pertusati, L. (1988). Beyond segregation or integration: A case study from effective Native American education. *Journal of American Indian Education, 27,* 11-20.

Rickard, C. C. (1973). *Fighting Tuscarora: Autobiography of Chief Clinton Rickard.* New York: York State Press.

Rights, D. L. (1947). *The American Indian in North Carolina.* Durham, NC: Duke University Press.

Senate Select Committee on Indian Affairs. (1985). *Indian juvenile alcoholism and eligibility for BIA schools* (Senate Hearing 99-286). Washington, DC: Government Printing Office.

Shomaker, D. J. (1989). Transfer of children and the importance of grandmothers among Navaho Indians. *Journal of Cross-Cultural Gerontology, 4,* 1-18.

Snow, D. R. (1979). *Native American prehistory.* Bloomington: Indiana University Press.

South, S. A. (1980). *Indians in North Carolina.* Raleigh: North Carolina Department of Cultural Resources, Division of Archives and History.

Spencer, R. R., & Jennings, J. D. (1977). *The Native Americans: Ethnology and backgrounds of American Indians.* New York: Harper & Row.

Stock, L. (1987). Native Americans: A brief profile. *Journal of Visual Impairment and Blindness, 81,* 152.

Sue, D. W. (1981). *Counseling the culturally different: Theory and practice.* New York: John Wiley.

Sue, D. W., & Sue, D. (1990). *Counseling the culturally different: Theory and practice.* New York: John Wiley.

Thomason, T. C. (1991). Counseling Native Americans: An introduction for non-Native American counselors. *Journal of Counseling and Development, 69,* 321-327.

Trimble, J. E., Fleming, C. M., Beauvais, F., & Jumper-Thurman, P. (1996). Essential cultural and social strategies for counseling Native American Indians. In P. Pedersen, J. G. Draguns, W. J. Lonner, & J. E. Trimble (Eds.), *Counseling across cultures* (pp. 177-209). Thousand Oaks, CA: Sage.

U.S. Bureau of the Census. (1991). *Statistical abstract of the United States.* Washington, DC: Government Printing Office.

Wade, E. L., & Strickland, R. (1981). *Magic images.* Norman: University of Oklahoma Press.

Washburn, W. E. (1975). *The Indian in America.* New York: Harper & Row.

Wetmore, R. Y. (1975). *First on the land: The North Carolina Indians.* Winston-Salem, NC: John F. Blair.

Yates, A. (1987). Current status and future directions of research on the American Indian child. *American Journal of Psychiatry, 9,* 1135-1142.

5

Chinese Americans

The first Chinese came to the United States in search of wealth. California offered a chance to those who could not succeed in their home country and who were able to find passage across the Pacific. The Chinese who came to the United States were viewed by other Americans as a mass of contradictions. They were seen as "clean" because of personal appearance, yet "filthy" because they lived in cramped living quarters. They were viewed as "thrifty" because they spent little on food or clothing, yet "extravagant" because of the money they put into traditional feasts. They were labeled as "bright" because they learned quickly and succeeded in several industries, yet "stupid" because they would not adopt American customs. They were treated with both admiration and curiosity. Clearly, the Chinese were judged by a standard other than their own.

This immigration of Chinese to the United States began about 1840. As Sue (1981) noted, the Chinese were the first Asian group to arrive in the United States in large numbers. The discovery of gold in California served as a magnet, drawing the people of southern China and those of the eastern United States together in Sacramento Valley. The demand for cheap labor to build the transcontinental railroad was high because the gold seekers had no intention of performing those menial tasks. Under those circumstances, the Chinese were sought. The demand for laborers, coupled with political unrest and overpopulation in certain provinces in China, brought a steady stream of Chinese to the United States. By the 1860s, nearly all Chinese immigrants had settled on the West Coast, with the heaviest concentrations in California.

When the Chinese first arrived in California, their presence filled a void in the labor market. A series of business recessions, however, coupled with the completion of the Union Pacific Railroad in 1869, made competition for jobs fierce. When working men began to see the Chinese as an economic threat, labor organizations began to agitate against them.

Oppression of the Chinese began in the mining districts. A law was passed (later declared unconstitutional) that taxed Chinese miners. In 1852, the Miner's Convention banned all Chinese, and hatred of the Chinese grew in cities and mining camps. Because the Chinese rarely defended themselves, they became easy targets for the rowdy miners. They were robbed, beaten, and tortured, often for no reason (Wood, 1974).

In San Francisco, where many Chinese lived, the police and the courts were quite severe in arresting and sentencing the Chinese for crimes such as gambling, prostitution, theft, and disturbing the peace. Fines and jail sentences were usually stiff and not comparable with those imposed on non-Chinese defendants. Ordinances aimed directly at the Chinese were passed, such as those requiring laundries to be constructed with stone or brick walls, and the Cubic Air Ordinance, which required that every lodging house provide at least 500 cubic feet of air space for every lodger. Eventually, the great rise of anti-Chinese sentiment resulted in the first U.S. law restricting the immigration of an entire race of people. Beginning with the Chinese Exclusion Act of 1882, at least 14 pieces of discriminatory legislation were passed by the U.S. Congress over the years. The Exclusion Act was not repealed until 1943 (Sandmeyer, 1973).

The census of 1990 reported 1,645,472 Chinese Americans, making them the largest Asian population in the United States. States with the largest percentages of Chinese Americans are California (40%), New York (18%), Hawaii (6.9%), Illinois (3.6%), and Texas (3.3%) (U.S. Bureau of the Census, 1990).

Acculturation

The Chinese, like other groups, have found that coexistence of their culture with the dominant culture of the United States has created problems they otherwise would not have encountered. The process of acculturation takes place on two levels—externally and internally. *External acculturation* is behavioral; individuals acquire the material trappings, common language, and secular roles of the dominant culture. *Internal acculturation* is the acquisition of the dominant culture's attitudes (Zanden, 1983).

The first Chinese to arrive in the United States found themselves in a new land among new people with new ways. To ease their fears and sense of loneliness and to find comfort in the familiar, the Chinese clung together. They ate their own food, wore the clothing they were accustomed to wearing in China, and followed their own customs and traditions. When they settled in the United States, they brought with them ideas, customs, institutions, and practices that became the bases for communities they established, known as "Chinatowns."

Despite more than a century of migration, the Chinese have not fully adopted the culture, language, and behavior of the United States. Although no people from outside cultures seem ever to have been fully absorbed by a host culture, the forms and techniques by which the Chinese have maintained their traditions are unique. Their cultural and social exclusiveness within the cities of the host cultures is a phenomenon of worldwide historical significance.

Like any other group, the Chinese in the United States are not all alike; different segments of the Chinese American population have different attitudes toward the mainstream culture. The *Lo Wah Kiu* (older immigrants who came to the United States before 1965) cling to the Chinese mode of living, and many are convinced that they will never be treated equally by the dominant culture. They live in Chinatowns in larger cities, read only Chinese newspapers, listen to Chinese music, eat Chinese foods, and socialize only with other Chinese. These old immigrants (some of whom are successful entrepreneurs) also stay in Chinatowns for economic and political reasons because they can find cheap labor there and have more influence within their own ethnic neighborhoods (Wong, 1982). The "Gucci" Chinese are wealthy industrialists and entrepreneurs from Hong Kong seeking safe haven following the transfer of Hong Kong from the British to the Chinese in 1997.

Native-born Chinese Americans and foreign-born Chinese who are citizens of the United States (*Wa Yeoy*) constitute a solid professional group with similar aspirations. They tend to desire total acceptance by the dominant culture and are willing to fight for equal treatment. They often work as professionals. Interracial marriage is high among this group. These Chinese Americans work hard to bring more social agencies and community organizations to the various Chinatowns.

The term *new immigrants* refers to the group of Chinese Americans who settled after 1965. They tend to be more educated than the old immigrants and to come from urban areas of China. Their primary goal in coming to the United States is economic betterment. These new immigrants aim to transmit their cultural heritage to their children, as well as to blend in certain aspects of the dominant culture of the United States.

Within the Chinese American culture is also a group of disenchanted youths who have been recruited as "muscle men" for the Chinese gambling rooms. These youth gangs practice Chinese martial arts and flaunt their "ethnic chauvinism" when confronted by other ethnic gangs (Wong, 1982).

It should be noted that many Chinese immigrants to the United States had no intention of remaining here, and this is the reason they held on to their own culture. In their traditional culture, the set of mores defined a strong obligation of the individual to the family and to those of superior class. These obligations include group loyalty and obedience; avoidance of embarrassing situations; modesty, humility, and respect in the presence of superiors; and the absence of complaining in the face of hardship. Because they created their own communities, they were able to retain these cultural values. By forming their own communities and exhibiting nonthreatening qualities, they were able to resist acculturation without arousing the concern of the dominant group.

Poverty and Economic Concerns

In contrast with many other cultural groups, Chinese Americans have a contemporary image as a highly successful minority that has made it economically. Sue (1981) reported the general perception that Chinese Americans exceed the national median income and complete a higher median number of grades in school than members of other cultural groups. It needs to be taken into account, however, that an Asian family often has more than one wage earner. Also, although Asian wage earners may have higher levels of education, their wages are not commensurate with their training.

Owing to laws not changed until as late as 1940, some states that forbade Chinese to go into many occupations (e.g., dentist, chauffeur, pilot, architect, teacher) carved out an economic niche for Chinese Americans. They became laundry operators and restaurateurs; they opened garment factories, novelty shops, and grocery stores. Because many jobs demand a good command of Standard English, Chinese Americans have often been excluded (Wong, 1982).

Kinship plays a decisive role in the activities of many Chinese businesspersons. To start a small-scale family firm is the dream of many Chinese immigrants. Independence, profit, and being in control of one's employment are aspirations of many Chinese Americans. By accumulating capital from many years of hard work and pooling all the savings from all family members, quite a few small-scale businesses have been started. All family members who are able usually work in the family firm, but major decisions are typically made by the head of the family. Family members are expected to work harder than outsiders and are often underpaid because it is the family's business. Thus, low pay, hard work, and long hours are part of the economic reality for many Chinese Americans (Wong, 1982).

History of Oppression

The Chinese were subject to oppression even before they arrived in the United States. U.S. interest in China dated from the colonial commerce with Canton. Interest in Chinese material culture was not matched by a sympathy for the Chinese people, however. According to Miller (1969), U.S. traders in China reported that the Chinese were "ridiculously clad, superstitious ridden, dishonest, crafty, cruel, and marginal members of the human race who lacked the courage, intelligence, skill, and will to do anything about the oppressive despotism under which they lived or the stagnating social conditions that surrounded them" (p. 36).

Although trader prejudices were limited, for the most part, to commentaries arising out of experiences with Chinese merchants, American Protestant missionaries, ruled by a passion for their divine mission, tended to impugn the morality of the whole Chinese nation. To missionaries bent on conversion, the ordinary Chinese were debased heathens awaiting divine rescue from their unholy condition of "lechery, dishonesty, cruelty, filth, and intellectual inferiority" (Miller, 1969, p. 37). Thus, by the time the Chinese made their appearance in the United States, they had been preceded by an almost entirely negative stereotype.

Although a national feeling against the Chinese had been aroused even before the first immigrants arrived, their presence in California mines and in other primary laboring occupations and the prediction that they would flood the whole country triggered oppressive action.

A series of business setbacks and the completion of the Union Central Pacific Railroad in 1869 made jobs scarce. Because the Chinese represented a large percentage of that working force, the White workers began to see them as an economic threat. Thus, much of the Chinese oppression from the dominant group emerged when the market fell through in Comstock Lode mining stocks in 1876 and a depression resulted. Many were affected by this depression, and discontent and unrest were widespread. In this setting, Whites looked for a scapegoat, and the presence of the Chinese changed from a blessing to a curse (McClellan, 1971).

The Chinese, with their different dress, clannish ways, pigtails, and docile manner, were a perfect target. It was of no consequence that the jobs filled by the Chinese were scorned by White men when White laborers started rallying against the Chinese. Daniels (1971) noted that "the movement soon developed an ideology of White supremacy and Oriental inferiority that was wholly compatible with the mainstream of American racism" (p. 43).

Language and the Arts

The values embodied in traditional Chinese painting are those of the Confucian scholar or Taoist recluse—searching for truth in nature. Nature is seen by the Chinese as a partner in a harmonious productive relationship with humankind. This attitude has permeated Chinese culture and art over the centuries. China has the world's longest continuous cultural history, and the last 8,000 years have left an abundance of paintings, calligraphy, sculptures, ceramics, jades, bronzes, tombs, gardens, and architecture. Many of these treasures pay homage to the long and varied history of religion in China, the folk spirits, the tranquil Taoist contemplation of nature, and the monumental Buddhist cave temples (Juliano, 1981).

For thousands of years, the Chinese have been obsessed with the links between generations—past, present, and future. Ancestor worship is a major part of Chinese culture, stimulating art and ritual. Reverence for the past is demonstrated in the enormous energies devoted to tombs, rituals, and burial customs.

Because the Chinese still use the past as a standard by which to gauge the present, the subjects and purposes of most ancient and modern art have a great deal in common. Whether the art is Confucian (social) or Taoist (individualistic), a moral philosophical or religious message is behind every painting. Unlike many Western artists, Chinese artists do not attempt to depict exactly what is seen, but rather to capture the essence (or essential nature) of the subject. Hence, Chinese art is characterized by a lack of realism. Instead, Chinese art reaffirms a personal, harmonious relationship with nature in providing a "visible manifestation of the life-giving spirit that animates nature" (Terrill, 1979, p. 309).

There is no single "Chinese language." The major dialects are Cantonese and Mandarin. Chinatowns were formed by early Chinese settlers from Guangdong, and the Cantonese dialect is the predominant dialect spoken in the United States. Other dialects, such as Shanghainese and Fukienese, may also be heard around Chinatowns in the United States (Wong, 1985). Because the language has a different symbol for each word (about 25,000 Chinese characters exist), the written language is difficult to learn. Chinese children must study much longer than their American counterparts. Chang and Chang (1978) reported that "dictionaries and telephone books are clumsy servants" when written in Chinese (p. 13). The language is structured to emphasize indirect communication.

Although written Chinese is standardized and is read by educated Chinese throughout the world, the spoken language is extremely varied. The many Chinese dialects can be as different from each other as English is from German. It is not uncommon for a single family, separated by civil strife, to share several dialects.

The heavy emphasis on language memorization is partially responsible for the selection of applied and natural sciences as majors for many Chinese students in the United States. Well-developed memorization skills are part of the reason so many Chinese students excel in the sciences. This contributes to Chinese Americans taking the courses.

Racism and Prejudice

The Chinese, easily identifiable racially and culturally, became the unwilling victims of derogatory stereotyping in the United States. In addition to racial and cultural distinctiveness, the mutually reinforcing factors of spatial and social isolation provided ingredients for discrimination and prejudice. Laws were passed forbidding the Chinese from owning property, voting, or testifying against White people (Lyman, 1974).

Kagiwada and Fujimoto (1973) pointed out that the first Chinese coming to the United States found conditions little better than slavery. The first immigrants were males because the only females allowed to immigrate were prostitutes. Chinese men were prohibited from marrying White women. The phrase "not a Chinaman's chance" describes the conditions faced by these early Chinese immigrants. The pervasive attitude of the dominant culture culminated in the passage of the Chinese Exclusion Act of 1882, the only federal statute to deny citizenship to a people because they were considered undesirable.

Sue and Sue (1973) characterized the success myth directed toward Asians as a continuation of racist and prejudicial thinking. The myth holds that the Chinese are not experiencing adjustment problems, but rather have been successful in the dominant culture. This kind of faulty thinking suggests that, in this culture, individuals can succeed if they work hard enough. Therefore, if one does not succeed, it is not because of forces operating in society, but rather because of other factors such as racial inferiority or inappropriate values. A close examination of the plight of Chinese Americans does not support the success myth. Yee (1992) reported that not all Asian students excel in science and mathematics, not all are hardworking, and not all are passive. Although many Chinese have obtained high educational status, evidence still suggests that racism is practiced against Chinese Americans.

Sociopolitical Factors

In the home communities of Chinese Americans, kinship relations were used to organize social and economic life. Many villages consisted of single lineages, which were patrilineal and exogamous. The group shared a common ancestor associated with a locality. The males were members of the lineage, and the females joined their husbands' lineage through marriage. In the United States, the Chinese may or may not share common blood or locality ties, but they often group together under common surnames such as Lee or Chan. This practice arose from the needs of early immigrant married adult males who had left their wives behind in China and thus lacked family life.

Within the family name associations are smaller groups called *fongs* that share both a common surname and a common village of origin. The fongs and family name associations perform functions similar to those in the homeland—social, ritual, dispute settlement, and welfare. Some surname groups originally were small, so they united with other groups according to traditional family alliances to form larger multifamily name associations according to neighboring home districts in China.

Next to family and kinship, common geographic origin provides an important basis for voluntary associations in traditional China. In the United States, the Chinese have used this idea to form regional organizations. These district associations act as credit clubs and have their own credit unions. They also elect officials for spring and autumn sacrifices; these sacrifices involve the burning of incense and reverential bowing in front of a symbol of the spirit being honored. To get elected, candidates donate thousands of dollars to community activities. The elected leaders enjoy prestige in the business community and will often be invited to join in economic partnerships and other gainful pursuits (Wong, 1982).

Because of attacks by members of the dominant culture on Chinese businesses, since 1933, Chinese business owners have regularly formed trade associations, such as the American-Chinese Restaurant Association and Chinese Chamber of Commerce. These associations often negotiate with the larger culture on matters of Chinese business. They provide information on taxes, sanitation, wages, and licenses and advise members about technical and legal details. They donate to cultural activities and to improving resources in the community.

In the early days of the family associations and district associations, merchants easily assumed positions of dominance because of their positions as brokers who extended credit and negotiated employment for peasants seeking passage to the United States. Later, these merchants received additional status by assuming positions as spokespersons who represented Chinatown communities on the outside.

Resentment against merchant domination of early Chinese society, coupled with the anti-Chinese climate in the late 19th and early 20th centuries in the United States, contributed to the formation of *tongs*. Tongs were patterned after secret societies in China and attracted the discontented elements of society. In most cases, they were formed to deal with some local situation of oppression. The tongs were also involved in gambling and prostitution and financed youth gangs to police the streets and to protect gambling dens (Nee, 1974).

Child-Rearing Practices

Relationships between parents and children are based on the dual principles of filial piety and veneration of age. *Filial piety* demands absolute obedience and complete devotion to the parents. This is enhanced by genuine affection between parents and children and emotional bonds of mutual interdependence. The most important relationship in Chinese families is that of the father and son. Sons, and especially the oldest, have specific obligations to the family. They are controlled by their fathers, whom they call *yeh* ("dignity and sternness") in a patrilocal residence arrangement (Char, 1981). Children depend on their parents when young; parents depend on their sons for security in old age.

Wong (1988) reported that Chinese parents tend to be more indulgent with their young children than are White parents. Discipline is much stricter, and punishment "involves withdrawal from the social life of the family or the deprivation of special privileges or objects rather than physical punishment" (p. 249).

Chinese children tend to be very well behaved, especially in public. Parents use a combination of gentle admonition and encouragement for discipline and would consider it a loss of face if they had to become angry in public (Sidel, 1972). A permissive attitude pervades during the early years, and children are not expected to be toilet trained until about 4 years of age (Char, 1981). The primary means by which parents keep family members in line is through the use of guilt, shame, and appeals to obligation. Shame is the most powerful of these for motivating children because it provides a frame of reference by connecting the child to other Chinese. Guilt, in contrast, is a highly individualistic concept. If children attempt to act independently of their parents' wishes, they are labeled selfish, inconsiderate, and ungrateful (Sue, 1981).

Religious Practices

The religious roots of the Chinese are varied. Hu (1960) reported that ancestral cult worship is the oldest and most pervasive of all Chinese religions. It is based on the belief that the living can directly communicate with the dead. It is believed that the dead, though now living in a different world, can still influence and be influenced by events in this world.

The scholar gentry class practiced Confucianism, which was considered more a philosophy than a religion. *Confucianism* is directed toward solving the practical concerns of everyday life: social relationships, government, and ethical concerns. It teaches respect for education and encourages education throughout one's life. Heaven is thought of as a universal moral law, a cosmic order. Just as nature should move in accord with this ultimate law, so should people. If they do, good things will happen to them. Unlike Western religions, there is no sense of sin in Confucianism. Human nature is basically good, and the evils of human society are a result of the example of immoral leaders. Morality does not rest on religious faith. Having no religious authority, the Chinese used the behaviors of good and wise men from the past as the chief source of values (Terrill, 1979). Confucianism deals with visible facts, is formal, values self-restraint and order, and cultivates deportment.

In traditional Chinese thinking, the family was the center of society, so if China was to be a moral society, living in harmony with Heaven's way, the place to begin was in family relationships. A hierarchical, class-stratified society was created in which each person knew his or her role and was expected to accept the inequalities of the system for the larger good. Sacrifices were offered to one's ancestors because it was believed that the spirits of the ancestors would punish moral offenders and see that good behavior was rewarded. Belief in life after death was also strengthened by the building of altars to one's ancestors and the placing of spirit tablets on them (Orr, 1980).

Although the scholars embraced the intellectual aspects of Confucianism, the common people developed a folk religion that was supplemented over the centuries by the two other major Chinese religions—Buddhism and Taoism. Orr (1980) reported that very few Chinese, educated or not, found any great difficulty in following all of these religious traditions. Each was regarded as "a different road to the same destination" (p. 86). Folk religion assumes that the world is alive with spirits and gods, such as kitchen gods and earth gods. These deities have magical power and are feared. Many local gods were later interwoven with the gods of Buddhism and Taoism. Folk religion was closely tied to festivals, such as New Year's, when family members returned to their ancestral villages. A wide variety of practices, such as divination, astrology, reading of palms, and dream interpretation, were used to determine what the gods intended and how to influence the unseen forces that controlled human life.

Taoism, another important Chinese religion, developed out of the life and writings of Lao-tse. The central concept is that great inner peace and power come to persons who can center their lives on the way of the universe, or the *dao.* Taoism is closely identified with divination, witchcraft, fortune-telling, astrology, and communication with the dead. Through contemplation of nature, one's deepest and most human part can surface from the artificial expectations of society. Taoist priests used a variety of elixirs to delay or prevent death, taught breath control exercises similar to Hatha yoga, and produced herbal medicines to heal and prolong life that are still used in traditional Chinese medicine.

Buddhism was established in China by missionary monks from Central Asia and was adapted to the Chinese culture. One great desire of the Chinese is assurance of life after death. Buddhism, with its teaching of reincarnation, is attractive to the Chinese. The most popular form of Buddhism became the Pure Land Sect, which holds that all people are capable of salvation in one life if they achieve devotion to the Buddha through meritorious deeds and faith, kindness, and compassion (Orr, 1980). Buddhism seeks enlightenment and avoidance of earthly or blind desires of ignorance. It teaches the eternity of life and that one's conduct and deportment in this world can influence the eventual form of existence in the next world.

The varied religious traditions among Chinese Americans are celebrated in festivals such as the Chinese New Year, "Sweeping of the Grave Festivals" dedicated to remembering the dead, and the Mid-Autumn Festival, which is rooted in many ancient legends and celebrates fertility and longevity (Wong, 1982). Although the Chinese have mingled some ideas of Christianity with their own religions, most Chinese people have failed to convert to Christianity (Bonavia, 1980).

Family Structure and Dynamics

In the traditional Chinese family, age, gender, and generational status are the primary determinants of role behavior. Ancestors and elders are viewed with great reverence and respect. The father is the head of the household, and his authority is unquestioned. The primary duty of the male is to be a good son; his obligations to be a good husband or a good father are secondary. For this reason, the primary allegiance of a son is to the family into which he is born. Females are subservient to males and perform all domestic duties, although in many Chinese American families, both the husband and the wife work outside the home, often in the family business (Sue, 1981).

A common family type in many Chinatowns is the nonresidential extended family, consisting of several nuclear families related to each other who live in separate homes but in close proximity. Many first-generation Chinese who arrived in the United States prior to 1965 have retained traditional family values. New immigrant families who arrived after 1965 tend to be less traditional, preferring the nuclear family model and that their children be bicultural (Wong, 1985).

The Chinese American family is, for the individual members, a reference group and source of personal identity and emotional security. It exerts control over interpersonal conduct, social relations, and the selection of occupation and marital partner.

In Chinese American culture, a subtle and indirect approach to problems is valued over an open and straightforward one; the avoidance of offending others is emphasized. Family members are encouraged to restrain feelings that may disrupt family harmony. Because the culture is so homogeneous, much of the communication is contextually determined, leaving little need to be verbally confrontational. Dependence, conformity, and restraint of disruptive emotions are valued in the development of character.

The welfare and integrity of the family are of the utmost importance. Individual family members are expected to put the welfare of the family and its reputation before their own individual needs. The behavior of each family member is considered a reflection on the entire family. Therefore, there is much cultural pressure to behave in a way that will not embarrass or shame one's family and cause them to "lose face." So important is the reputation of the family that problems such as failure in school or juvenile delinquency are handled as much as possible within the family, and public admission of these problems is suppressed (Sue, 1981). When irreconcilable problems do arise, face is restored by formally disowning the child.

Because of the cultural pressure to maintain family integrity and because Chinese youths identify more with their families than with their peers, sexual intercourse before marriage is not common. Out-of-wedlock births, abortion, and divorce are also rare (Sidel, 1972).

Cultural Values and Attitudes

Chinese values are reflected in all aspects of the Chinese lifestyle. Selflessness is one of the oldest values in China. The selfless person is always willing to subordinate his or her own interest or the interest of a small group to the interest of a larger social group. This value grew out of the beliefs of the Confucians, who perceived the individual as part of a network of related social positions. Obedience to authority is taken as a sign of selflessness because the leaders of an organization are understood to be working on behalf of the interests of the larger whole. This value of selflessness, or deference to the collective unit, is quite different from the value of individualism and individual rights of the dominant culture of the United States.

A second contemporary value rooted in Confucianism is "knowing the meaning of your work" and understanding the interrelatedness of tasks (doing vs. being). This value involves understanding how subordinate tasks are related to a greater goal and is instrumental in fostering the cheerful approach of the Chinese toward all kinds of work.

Harmony, or the avoidance of conflict, especially in the area of social relations, is valued in the Chinese culture. The idea of harmony also applies to the relationship between people and nature and to a person's inner psyche, for which breath control and meditation are employed to help foster tranquillity.

Another value is related to the concept of peer respect and the avoidance of disrespect to enforce compliance with rules or to motivate toward education. One interesting practice in many rural Chinese villages is for the entire village to laugh at someone who has violated a social norm. This method of societal control over its members contrasts sharply with the fear of arrest and punishment used in the United States (Terrill, 1979).

Chinese Americans still hold to many cultural values and attitudes that are deeply rooted in their native culture. Rawl (1992) identified significant personality traits among Chinese Americans to include familism, collective responsibility between kinship members, group solidarity, conformity, and suppression of individuality. Some Chinese have been found to be strongly past-oriented and may experience rigidity in role and status. With the process of acculturation, many Chinese Americans have adapted while maintaining traditional values such as the belief in the family structure and a strong system of discipline.

Implications

Chinese Americans practice a system of balance and harmony of energy fields. *Yin* and *yang* are polar terms that describe the contrasting yet complementary elements of the universe. A yin-yang imbalance results in dysfunction. Yin represents the female, negative energy—passive, unassertive, inhibited, vague, internal, and concrete human factors. Yin stores the vital strength of life. Winter and spring illnesses are Yin. Yang represents male, positive energy—active, excited, aggressive, external, bright and abstract human factors. Yang protects the body from outside forces. Summer and fall illnesses are yang (Spector, 1991).

Chinese Americans appear to be more acculturated than other groups. This may be because of their own cultural tendencies to conform, obey authority, and restrain strong feelings. Furthermore, family honor is so important to many Chinese Americans that they suppress any admission of personal problems. For this reason, Chinese Americans may first present personal problems in the form of physical or vocational complaints. Counselors must initially respond to these "superficial" problems in an effort to establish a relationship of trust (Sue, 1981; Sue & Sue, 1990).

Lee (1996) identified popular explanations, influenced by both religion and concepts of health in traditional medicine, that outline the development of emotional problems:

- Imbalance of yin and yang and disharmony in the flow of *chi* (energy)
- Supernatural intervention by a "ghost" or vengeful spirit as punishment
- Religious beliefs that problems are caused by deeds from past lives or as punishment from God
- Genetic vulnerability or hereditary defects
- Physical and emotional strain and exhaustion caused by external stresses
- Organic disorders such as brain disorders, diseases of the liver, and hormonal imbalance
- Character weaknesses that make a person vulnerable to emotional problems

Huang (1991) suggested principles useful in working with Chinese American clients:

- Both intrusive and indirect questions may be resisted because the client expects a rapid diagnosis and prompt intervention.
- Competence is displayed when the helper reveals a firm but comfortable sense of authority.
- Many Chinese American clients see the need to ask for professional advice on personal problems as potentially shameful, and their concern about this should be addressed early.
- Personal questions made to the counselor are not out of place, and an honest, straightforward response is a sign that the relationship is a positive one.
- Fathers, physicians, and teachers occupy positions of respect, so communicating unpleasant things to them is considered inappropriate.

An educator working with a Chinese American must first determine whether he or she is traditional, acculturated, marginal, or bicultural; interactions with the dominant culture will often hinge on the Chinese American's view of his or her own culture. For example, if a Chinese American is *traditional,* the educator needs to offer a logical, rational, structured approach over an affective, reflective, ambiguous one. If the Chinese American is *marginal,* he or she must be helped to distinguish between negative rejection of his or her own culture and positive attempts to acculturate. This process requires a great deal of cultural knowledge and flexibility with regard to both theory and technique on the part of the educator (Sue, 1981; Sue & Sue, 1990).

Only through an awareness and acceptance of all aspects of the Chinese American culture can educators truly understand the complexity of human behaviors of Chinese Americans. Chinese Americans continue to be both Chinese and American, and they must do so without sacrificing the security provided by their ethnic identity or the challenge offered by the dominant culture.

Questions for Review and Reflection

1. What differences in degree of acculturation are likely to exist between the Lo Wah Kiu and the Wa Yeoy? How can educators and counselors use the knowledge of these differences in working with Chinese Americans?

2. How does the Chinese view of nature influence Chinese American interactions with other people?

3. How does the Chinese reverence for the past affect Chinese Americans?

4. What factors appear to be primarily responsible for Chinese American success in science and engineering? How can educators or counselors determine whether a Chinese American student should be directed toward science or engineering or to some other career path?

5. What is meant by the phrase "not a Chinaman's chance"? In what ways do you think use of the phrase influences Chinese American interactions with the dominant culture?

6. What misperceptions exist within the success myth associated with Chinese Americans?

7. What are fongs? What is the role of family and kinship to business and economic concerns for Chinese Americans?

8. How can educators or counselors help Chinese American children develop positive self-esteem when Chinese parents use guilt and shame in the discipline of their children?

9. How can educators or counselors work with traditional Chinese American females, whose culture prescribes a different role from female assertiveness found in the dominant culture?

10. How does the traditional Chinese American subtle and indirect approach to problems affect the open, direct, and honest approach of the dominant culture?

References

Bonavia, D. (1980). *The Chinese*. New York: Lippincott & Crowell.

Chang, R., & Chang, M. S. (1978). *Speaking of Chinese*. New York: Norton.

Char, E. L. (1981). The Chinese American. In A. L. Clark (Ed.), *Culture and child rearing* (pp. 140-164). Philadelphia: Davis.

Daniels, R. (1971). *Concentration camps USA: Japanese Americans and World War II*. New York: Holt, Rinehart & Winston.

Hu, C. (1960). *China*. New Haven, CT: Human Relations Area Files Press.

Huang, K. (1991). Chinese Americans. In N. Mokuau (Ed.), *Handbook of social services for Asian and Pacific Islanders*. Westport, CT: Greenwood.

Juliano, A. (1981). *Treasures of China*. New York: Richard Marek.

Kagiwada, G., & Fujimoto, I. (1973). Asian American studies: Implications for education. *Personnel and Guidance Journal, 51*, 400-405.

Lee, E. (1996). Chinese families. In M. McGoldrick, J. Giordano, & J. K. Pearce (Eds.), *Ethnicity and family therapy* (pp. 249-267). New York: Guilford.

Lyman, S. M. (1974). *Chinese Americans*. New York: Random House.

McClellan, R. (1971). *The heathen Chinese*. Athens: Ohio University Press.

Miller, S. C. (1969). *The unwelcome immigrant: The American image of the Chinese, 1785-1882*. Los Angeles: University of California Press.

Nee, B. D. (1974). *Longtime Californian: A documentary study of an American Chinatown*. Boston: Houghton Mifflin.

Orr, R. G. (1980). *Religion in China*. New York: Friendship.

Rawl, S. M. (1992). Perspectives on nursing care of Chinese Americans. *Journal of Holistic Nursing, 10*(1), 6-17.

Sandmeyer, E. C. (1973). *The anti-Chinese movement in California*. Urbana: University of Illinois Press.

Sidel, R. (1972). *Women and child care in China*. New York: Hill and Wang.

Spector, R. E. (1991). *Cultural diversity in health and illness*. New York: Appleton-Century-Crofts.

Sue, D. W. (1981). *Counseling the culturally different*. New York: John Wiley.

Sue, D. W., & Sue, D. (1973). Asian Americans: The neglected minority. *Personnel and Guidance Journal, 51*, 386-389.

Sue, D. W., & Sue, D. (1990). *Counseling the culturally different*. New York: John Wiley.

Terrill, R. (Ed.). (1979). *The China difference*. New York: Harper & Row.

U.S. Bureau of the Census. (1990). *Statistical abstract of the United States*. Washington, DC: Government Printing Office.

Wong, B. P. (1982). *Chinatown: Economic adaptation and ethnic identity of the Chinese*. New York: Holt, Rinehart & Winston.

Wong, B. P. (1985). Family, kinship, and ethnic identity of the Chinese in New York City, with comparative remarks on the Chinese in Lima, Peru and Manila, Philippines. *Journal of Comparative Family Studies, 16*(2), 231-253.

Wong, M. G. (1988). The Chinese American family. In C. H. Mindel, R. W. Haberstein, & R. Wright, Jr. (Eds.), *Ethnic families in America: Patterns and variations* (pp. 230-257). New York: Elsevier.

Wood, E. R. (1974). *Californians and Chinese: The first decade.* San Francisco: R and E Research Associates.

Yee, A. H. (1992). Asians as stereotypes and students: Misperceptions that persist. *Educational Psychology Review, 4*, 95-132.

Zanden, J. W. (1983). *American minority relations.* New York: Knopf.

6

Japanese Americans

Japanese Americans comprise the third largest Asian group (after Chinese Americans and Pilipinos) in the United States, numbering about 850,000. Approximately 72% of Japanese Americans reside on the West Coast (U.S. Bureau of the Census, 1991).

As Japan moves into a position to dominate the world economy in the 21st century, it is imperative that we look carefully at how the Japanese and Japanese Americans influence the dominant culture of the United States. An advertiser's campaign to buy only products "made in the U.S.A." supports the contention that many in the dominant culture of the United States feel threatened, resentful, and suspicious of the Japanese. Japanese technology has outstripped that of the United States, causing negative feelings to persist. The Japanese economy is highly industrialized, and technologically, they are giving industries in the United States fierce competition. In its February 4, 1988, issue, *Newsweek* reported on a Gallup Poll that showed 50% of Americans favored trade barriers in certain industries that would make it difficult or expensive to sell foreign imports here; 46% thought Asian American students were winning an increasing number of academic awards and scholarships (Powell & Martin, 1988).

Given this impact on the dominant culture of the United States, we need to be aware of the Japanese not only in economic terms but in cultural terms as well. In analyzing the Japanese community in the United States, one must review the changes throughout history from generation to generation. The first Japanese to migrate to the United States, whether they settled in cities or in rural areas, sought out other Japanese. This caused them to fashion a unique mode of community life in their efforts to adjust to the conditions in a new environment, as well as to maintain traditional values. One may describe the picture of the Japanese American family and community prior to World War II as an immigrant group trying to establish itself in the new country.

Acculturation

The degrees of acculturation to the dominant culture range from scant to full acculturation. Marsella (1993) asserted that ethnic identity among Japanese Americans is not a linear process of movement from traditional-minded immigrants to full acculturation. Each succeeding generation of Japanese Americans has been known by the Japanese word for that generation, a unique practice among immigrant groups. The naming of generations is the Japanese way of honoring those who came to the United States. Mass (1976) noted that Japanese immigrants are the only ethnic community in the United States who name their generations and that it is virtually impossible to discuss their history without knowledge of this practice. To describe the differences between generations as simply differences in acculturation is to miss much of the importance of the naming process.

First-generation Japanese, the generation that immigrated to the United States between 1885 and 1924, are known as *Issei* (literally "first generation"). These immigrants were tightly bound to the traditions of their homeland, tended to live in segregated communities, and upheld their Japanese identity. Kitano (1988) described the Issei as patriarchal with emphasis on obedience to elders and women subordinate to men. Interestingly, the Issei experienced more psychological stress and were more externally controlled than subsequent generations. They also had lower self-esteem than later-generation Japanese Americans (Padilla, Wagatsuma, & Lindholm, 1985). The Issei essentially resisted acculturation.

Second-generation Japanese, or *Nisei,* were more acculturated than the Issei. They were less psychologically stressed and more internally controlled than the Issei but had lower self-esteem. This might be a result of being taught through the media and schools about individuality, freedom, and other dominant-culture values but being infused at home with quite different traditional Japanese values of their Issei parents. Yanagisako (1985) described the Nisei, whose emphasis is on upward socioeconomic mobility, as having greater flexibility of sex roles and the bond between husbands and wives (conjugal bonds) taking priority over the bond between parents and children (filial bonds). Montero (1981) found that, on every indicator of assimilation (visiting patterns with relatives, ethnicity of two closest friends, ethnicity of favorite organization, and ethnicity of spouse), the socio-economically successful Nisei are most assimilated and cut off from the ethnic community. According to Tomine (1991), this intensified urgency toward acculturation was the result of "questioned loyalty" and "wartime hysteria."

The *Kibei* (who are technically Nisei) find themselves in a unique position of being outside both the Japanese and the dominant cultures. They are the midgeneration Japanese whose Nisei parents sent them to Japan to school between their 8th and 14th years and then brought them back to the United States as young adults. They were ostracized by the Japanese and rejected by the dominant culture of the United States.

Wilson and Hosokawa (1980) found that the dilemma in which the Kibei found themselves was dependent on the age at which they were sent to Japan, the length of time they remained there, and the educational practices in place at the time they were there. Some returned to the United States with anti-American attitudes; others returned and adjusted easily. Both groups were less proficient in English than the Nisei who had remained in the United States. During World War II, according to Wilson and Hosokawa, "hundreds of Kibei provided an invaluable service as instructors in military language-training programs, as interpreters and translators in the Pacific theater, and psychological warfare specialists" (p. 167).

Third-generation Japanese, or *Sansei* youths, have the highest degree of acculturation. Reared by the assimilation-oriented Nisei, they are driven to prove themselves, to succeed and excel in the dominant culture. Padilla et al. (1985) found the Sansei to have higher self-esteem, lower stress, and higher internality than the two previous generations. It may be assumed that many Sansei are affected by what is called the *Hansen effect.* Hansen (1952) pointed out that although some might view third-generation persons as acculturated, many have retained their ethnic identity and express an intense interest in their families' backgrounds and histories. It seems reasonable to expect the fourth generation (*Yonsei*) and the fifth generation (*Gosei*) to have even higher degrees of acculturation than previous generations. What might be viewed as acculturation of these groups may actually be biculturalism, or the ability to select a particular value system, depending on the situation.

In Los Angeles is an area called Little Tokyo. Japanese nationals who reside there are able to interact almost exclusively with other Japanese, speak only Japanese, and have all the other experiences of being in Japan.

Although initially it was said that the Japanese could not be assimilated because of their "vile habits, low standard of living, extremely high birthrate, and so on" (Chuman, 1976, p. 74), very little opposition to acculturation by Japanese Americans has been expressed. Certainly, no militant or blatant opposition has occurred. Atkinson and Matsushita (1991) found that Japanese Americans who were identified as bicultural found counselors to be more attractive sources of help than did those who were identified as either acculturated or traditional. In keeping with the Japanese emphasis on education and social status, acculturation has been "rewarded" by the dominant culture.

Poverty and Economic Concerns

In Japan, schools at the primary and secondary level have assumed such importance in determining a person's future that chances of acquiring higher status are virtually decided before one is barely out of the teenage years. Schooling is critical because social advancement for most Japanese means joining the ranks of white-collar workers in one of the country's giant corporations. Nakane (1972) reported that, once a man gets such a job—known in Japan as becoming a "salary man"—he can generally count on remaining with the company for life. During his career, promotions come regularly; he can usually predict when he will become the head of a department or assistant to a manager. Except during periods of unusual economic turmoil, employees are seldom discharged or laid off.

To obtain a corporate job that will set him up for life, however, the aspirant must be a graduate of one of the better universities. The difficult stage in the man's career is passing the examinations that qualify him for the limited positions open in the universities. The psychological toll of such early status competition is marked by an alarming number of suicides among children who despair over their academic prospects.

Jenkins (1973) conducted a study on blue- and white-collar democracy in other countries and found that, in Japan, a man is known by the company that keeps him. Joining a large corporation after leaving school, the Japanese man expects to stay with the firm for his entire working life, never to be fired except for criminal acts or on grounds of insanity. In return, he is expected to work loyally, identify with the corporation, follow the rules, and wait his turn for promotion. The Japanese workman derives not only his livelihood and security but also his health care, further education, and social life from his place in the corporation. Every large corporation also has a semiformal system to ensure that the male employee's assignments match his personal needs and career desires as much as possible. If he is a young man seeking to marry, the company stands ready to help him find a bride and to provide a priest and a hall for the wedding ceremony.

This kind of lifelong dependency on a single organization clearly does not fit Western traditions of mobility and diversity. In the United States, one finds a somewhat different educational and occupational pattern of development among Japanese Americans. Although the "model minority" label often attached to them is considered to be inaccurate by some experts, Japanese Americans do constitute a group that seems to have "made it" as far as educational attainment is concerned. Ohnuki-Tierney (1993) reported that, in the Japanese cosmology, wealth is not understood as a function of hard work, but rather as a reward for good nature and conduct.

A study by Chu (1971) found that 68.2% of Japanese American males studied engineering or the physical sciences. Lack of English-language skills may lead some Japanese Americans into disciplines requiring a minimum of self-expression. Several possible reasons have been given for the movement of Japanese Americans into the physical sciences: deficiency in language skills (Kagiwada & Fujimote, 1973; Kaneshige, 1973; Sue & Kirk, 1972; Watanabe, 1973); cultural injunctions that restrict self-expression (Kagiwada & Fujimote, 1973; Sue & Kirk, 1972; Sue & Sue, 1973; Watanabe, 1973); pressure by Japanese American families that directs their children into areas where they have the best chance of succeeding; and educators and counselors who unthinkingly place Asian students into courses that minimize English and maximize mathematical skills (Watanabe, 1973). Sue and Sue (1973) addressed the issue of this success myth about Asians, pointing out that it seems to serve three purposes:

1. It represents an attempt to reaffirm the belief that any group, regardless of race, creed, or color, can succeed in a "democratic" society if they work hard enough.
2. The success myth has created friction between Asians and other minority groups.
3. The belief that Asian Americans are problem-free has shortchanged them from obtaining needed moral and financial assistance from education, business, government, and industry.

History of Oppression

Japanese immigrants began coming to the United States in large numbers around 1890. They were at once subjected to the punishment and harassment already known to the Chinese. This "anti-Oriental" atmosphere was the result of the fear and ignorance summed up in the phrase "the Yellow Peril." Chuman (1976) described the propaganda against the Japanese:

Through exaggerated reports of the number of Japanese entering America and their control or use of agricultural lands or through outright expressions of hatred for them, the agitators made a case that the apparently peaceful

Japanese immigrants were in truth the sinister vanguard of an invading horde, bent solely on the conquest of the country. (p. 74)

Sue and Sue (1990) concluded that because Japan was a rising international power, the anti-Japanese feeling did not manifest itself directly in legislation to restrict immigration, but rather led to a "gentlemen's agreement" to seal the flow of Asians to the United States. To harass the Japanese further, California in 1913 passed the Alien Land Law, which forbade immigrants from owning land. The Alien Land Law was an emotional warning to the public that Japanese farmers were going to take over agricultural land. In fact, the Japanese owned only 12,726 farm acres out of 11,000,000 acres in California in 1912 (Chuman, 1976).

After the devastating attack on Pearl Harbor on December 7, 1941, all Japanese living in the United States came under suspicion. Thousands of Japanese Americans were rounded up, and "contraband" such as cameras, flashlights, and hunting rifles were confiscated. These events were reported prominently by the news media, but the fact that none of those apprehended had done anything to harm the national interest was largely ignored. Executive Order 9066, signed by President Franklin Roosevelt in February 1942, created internment camps. They were in remote desert camps in Nevada, Utah, and as far away from the West Coast as Arkansas. Farm homes and personal property were stolen, lost, or sold at such deflated values that even their sale was virtually theft. An estimated 110,000 Japanese Americans were sent to these camps. They accepted their internment with virtually no resistance; imprisoned for no crime but their ethnicity, they met their fate with resignation, a primary characteristic of Japanese culture.

Even though at least 50% of the citizens of the United States viewed the average Japanese American as loyal, after their release it was an uphill battle for Japanese Americans to readjust and readapt to the environment after the war. Prewar competitors of Japanese American produce wholesalers had founded the American League of California, which urged Japanese Americans to demonstrate their patriotism by "remaining away from the Pacific Coast" (Petersen, 1971). Bumper stickers proclaiming "No Japs Wanted in California" were popular. Until the beginning of 1946, the Teamsters boycotted Japanese produce. The California Board of Equalization issued no commercial licenses to Japanese until the War Relocation Authority threatened to initiate legal action.

According to Kitano (1976), elderly Japanese Americans were beaten down and afraid. Most settled in trailer parks off the beaten path. For a decade after World War II, Japanese Americans found housing to be the most significant area of discrimination against them. Japanese Americans were often underemployed in terms of their educational background, occupational skills, potential, and economic aspirations. It was common for Nisei with degrees from U.S. colleges and universities to be found in underpaid, menial, unskilled work because they were denied employment in fields for which they had been trained.

Language and the Arts

Many Japanese American families still speak Japanese at home but communicate well in English outside the home. Schoonmaker (1989) reported that the Japanese language may have about a dozen ways of saying "you." One must know the age, status, and background of a person before selecting a form of address. Many other differences in styles of communication between Japanese culture and the dominant culture in the United States are nonverbal. For instance, very little eye contact is made among the Japanese. Direct eye contact is considered impolite and even disrespectful toward seniors. Minimal eye contact takes place only among families and peers.

In Japan, there is a maximum amount of body contact between mother and child, including sleeping together. Dating teenagers might hold hands, but hugging and kissing are considered to be in poor taste. After childhood, there is no body contact with others except husband and wife, which occurs only in total privacy.

Instead of hand shaking, the Japanese traditionally bow. The depth of the bow indicates the social position of the person being greeted. A complete bow is made when looking at a shrine. On encountering an old friend or relative who has not been seen in a long time, a Japanese person bows many times.

Because physical space is limited in Japan, the amount of "personal space" that individuals are comfortable with is smaller than in the United States. Taking up a large personal space is interpreted as rude and hostile.

For the Japanese, earth and Heaven meet through people to form art. Art is elegant and even reverent, yet simple and easily handled. It is usually linear and nonrepetitive; it has one theme and definite closure. Often, art in the form of painting, screens, scrolls, and clothing are characterized by bright colors or subjects of nature or people or both. The cultural emphasis on silence and reservation of verbal communication can be seen in the classical dance-drama form known as *Noh,* in which actors wearing masks exchange little or no verbal dialogue. The martial arts stress relaxation, deflection, and the interaction of mind and body as sources of inner strength in defending against an outside aggressor. Other important Japanese art forms that combine a spiritual and aesthetic experience are *ikebana* (flower arranging), gardening, and the intense and highly stylized tea ceremony.

Racism and Prejudice

Japanese Americans have experienced intense racism, discrimination, and prejudice in the United States. Early Japanese Americans were ambitious and industrious, expecting upward mobility and the American Dream. Kitano (1976) pointed out that even though their ideals were similar to those found in the dominant culture, the ambition and striving of Japanese Americans drew suspicion and resentment from the dominant culture.

Prejudice and discrimination left over from the "Chinese problem" created an anti-Asian atmosphere. During World War II, the print media incited racial violence against the Japanese by alleging espionage and sabotage (Okihiro & Sly, 1983). The press fostered the notion of the Yellow Peril, creating a climate of intolerance and racism. Sue and Sue (1990) characterized the wartime relocation of Japanese Americans into internment camps as the most blatant evidence of prejudice and discrimination.

Okihiro and Sly (1983) suggested that very few Sansei have felt the demoralizing agony of anti-Japanese prejudice and racism. Most Sansei have grown up in homes unmarked by a noticeable cultural division between Japan and the United States. They have benefited from the material success of their parents and the physical labor of their grandparents. They have received parental support for their educational pursuits without difficulty. Henkin (1985) described the subtle forms of racism and prejudice that are felt by the Sansei:

> Outside the home, the Sansei live very much in the heart of American culture. They may feel American, speak American, act American, and think American. But unlike their friends in the cultural mainstream, they can never look American, and as far as America is concerned, then, there is some important way in which they can never be American. The tacit prejudice that is often unacknowledged and even unperceived dogs their steps and generates confusion about the Sansei's identity. (p. 502)

According to Kitano (1976), there are elements of a "schizophrenic adaptation" on the part of Japanese Americans to life in the United States. He added that this is true of most other physically identifiable groups as well. The dilemma of how to behave when interacting with the dominant culture and how to behave when interacting with one's own group is a major concern for culturally different group members. The fact is that Japanese Americans are trying to achieve acceptance in a culture where the terms of citizenship, social status, and economic well-being are often racially or ethnically determined.

Sociopolitical Factors

The Japanese American social structure has often been described as vertical rather than horizontal, meaning that relations with those above or below in the social hierarchy are clearly defined. The lack of political activity among Japanese Americans can be explained by a close examination of these values. Japanese Americans value maintaining low visibility and conformity so as not to bring negative attention to themselves. A model Japanese leader is one who is informed, possesses thorough knowledge, and yet avoids the spotlight.

The Japanese American Citizen's League (JACL), the only national organization for the Japanese, began in the early 1920s in response to the special interests and problems of Japanese Americans. Given little choice, the organization cooperated with the evacuation orders of World War II. The JACL reorganized after the war and redefined its goals and functions. The organization maintains lobbies in Washington, lodges legal protests, and generally protects and assists Japanese Americans. The JACL spearheaded the successful movement to gain reparations for those interned during World War II.

Japanese Americans formed voluntary associations that promoted economic survival and success. Some of these associations provided financial and burial assistance, and members frequently pooled resources for starting businesses. The *tandmoshi* was akin to a small band in which money was pooled and then extended, with credit, for business start-up costs.

The Japanese American community has served to hold the Japanese Americans together by reinforcing values, customs, behaviors, and social control. According to Kitano (1976):

> The most pressing reason of the Japanese Americans for maintaining their own social groups revolves around the problem of dating and marriage. "Do you want your daughter to marry one?" is a question that is asked not only by the majority group but also by ethnic parents. This concern has led to the development and maintenance of many Japanese organizations. (p. 113)

In general, Japanese Americans have achieved high socioeconomic mobility despite the discrimination against them. The most common Japanese American employment categories are technical, sales, and administrative support (32%), followed by managerial and professional specialty occupations (29%). Kitano (1988) characterized Japanese Americans as one of the most economically successful ethnic groups in the United States. The value system of the Japanese encouraged economic success and educational opportunity and further opened the door to higher occupational status.

To work effectively with Japanese Americans, educators or counselors must be aware of and understand Japanese customs and values and must comprehend several aspects of the Japanese personality. A Judo Shinto priest attests to the enigmatic nature of the Japanese personality when he states that "it takes 20 generations to mold a Japanese, i.e., to inculcate the essence of order, obedience, and conformity" (Masuda, Matsumoto, & Meredith, 1970).

Child-Rearing Practices

In Japan, as well as among Japanese Americans, the elders are viewed with great respect, and a strong family system is very important. According to Garfinkle (1983), the dominant orientation of the Japanese family begins with the constant interest and pressure that Japanese mothers provide for their children. The Japanese mother devotes herself to the rearing of her children and pushes them to excel academically. The intensely close relationship between mother and child shows the most pervasive values of Japanese society: the work ethic, selflessness, and group endeavor. When it comes to the discipline of children, the Japanese mother is more inclined than the American mother to appeal to feelings as a coercive tool by simply expressing her displeasure. Japanese writers on child rearing recommend mildness in the direct verbal teaching of children. They believe that children should be admonished in a firm but calm manner and that adults should not use abusive language or show anger and impatience. A study by Kurokawa (1968) with Japanese American families showed that the Japanese mother rocks her child more and talks less, whereas the American mother talks to her child more and touches less. The mean age for independence training was 8.9 years for Sanseis and 6.8 for Whites. According to Nancy Shand, an anthropologist at the Menninger Foundation, an expression used to describe Japanese mothers is *Kyoiku-Mama,* which translates to "education mommy." Perhaps the social prestige of motherhood among the Japanese is one reason for the critical difference in child-rearing patterns ("The Drive to Excel," 1984).

According to anthropologist Ruth Benedict (1945), the Japanese father is less of a disciplinarian than are fathers in almost any Western nation. To the Japanese father, the child may show only respect. The father is the great exemplar to the child, of high hierarchical position, and the child must learn to express the proper respect to him. Sue and Sue (1990) and Watanabe (1973) also described the family system as patriarchal, with the father's authority unquestioned. The primary duty of a son is allegiance to his father, before his obligations to be a good husband and father to his own children.

Subservience to males is the female role in the family, along with the performance of domestic duties and education of the children.

Religious Practices

Japanese churches have played a significant role in the development of community solidarity and cohesion. Most first Japanese who came to the United States were Buddhists. Buddhism is closely tied with the family system so revered in Japanese culture. Many sacred rites are performed at a family shrine. Faith is renewed on a day-to-day basis, with observances conducted within the family. *Buddhism* encourages the awareness of Japanese values and heritage. From *Confucianism* came the standard of social behavior that dictates respect and obedience for authority and for elders. *Shintoism* embraces the devotion to deities representing natural forces. It is characterized by various ceremonies, including those to honor ancestors, to request blessings for the Japanese nation, and to request protection from evil. Henkin (1985) explained how the Buddhist/Confucian/Shintoist background of the Japanese culture in Japan established a perceptual, conceptual, and behavioral ground of being that advocates inner discipline and encourages people to conceal frustrations and disappointments. Also, they are expected to submerge individual concerns, to recognize filial piety and moral obligations to others as superior to personal desires, and to persist in their tasks in the face of unhappiness despite the probability of failure or defeat.

Christian churches in the United States attracted many immigrants who were seeking cultural belonging and economic advancement. The structure of the Japanese Christian church was fitted to the needs of the Japanese family. Variation in religious practices, however, reflected age and generational differences among the Japanese Americans. The concerns of the Issei are geared to the needs of the aged. The majority of Issei attend Buddhist and Christian churches in large numbers and appear to be seeking comfort and reassurance in the face of old age and death. The Nisei, in contrast, have very different concerns. Their social status is likely to influence their pattern of church attendance. Thus, there seems to be no universal concern with religion among Japanese Americans. Loyalties are instead to the home, the family, and related specific groups.

Cultural emphasis on money, education, and group conformity does not come from religion as much as from the geography and history of Japan. The standard of group cooperation grew out of Japan's being a rice-growing country. During the days of the feudal system and afterward, neighbors had to work together because survival depended on it. Even though Japan now has a large urban population, these values are still upheld. Also, because

Japan is so small, competition for jobs is fierce. Thus, the geography of the land dictates the almost obsessive value the culture places on education and money—not religion. The values of group conformity and social status via education and money are very much a part of life of Japanese Americans as well.

Family Structure and Dynamics

Consistent with the value of respect for authority and elders, one finds among Japanese Americans values of allegiance to the family and dependency versus individualism and self-reliance. Whether children are taught the reciprocal family obligation as shared family values or, as Watanabe (1973) asserted, because of racism in the United States that forces family members to rely on each other for personal security, the fact remains that Japanese Americans find themselves duty-bound and obligated to the family. According to Kaneshige (1973), internal conflicts involving any family members are resolved only within the family system. To display to outsiders that problems exist is to bring disgrace to the family name. Related to this concept of shame, or the avoidance of bringing disgrace to the family name, is the idea that the individual is of minimal importance. The belief that one exists only in relation to one's group seriously conflicts with the concept of reaching individual self-fulfillment. Reaching for self-fulfillment would be to display attributes of selfishness and exaggerated self-importance (Kaneshige, 1973). Sue and Sue (1973) stated that the Japanese tendency toward perseverance as role perfectionism is one prime motivator of Japanese children and their mothers. This type of motivator has the effect of exhorting the Japanese to endure experiences with a stoic attitude. The Japanese mother-child relationship may be summarized in one word, *amae,* an attitude toward people that is characterized by affection, feelings of dependency, and the expectation of an emotionally satisfying response. This means that love is combined with a strong sense of reciprocal obligation and dependence. Watanabe also identified the learned family trait of indirect communication versus direct communication. Clearly defined roles of dominance and deference virtually rule out arguments and debate. Communication flows one way: from parent to child. Direct messages predominate, and exchanges are generally brief and perfunctory.

One area of extreme contrast between the Japanese and Japanese Americans may be found in the institution of marriage. According to Ravich and Wyden (1974), in Japan, matchmakers hired by parents were still arranging more than one third of all marriages during the early 1970s. According to Benedict (1945), the Japanese set up no ideal, as do members of the dominant

U.S. culture, about love and marriage as one and the same thing. The Japanese regard the real aim of marriage as procreation and believe that love takes time to develop during the family life. The rate of divorce in Japan is low. If a divorce does occur, the wife usually loses everything, including her children, and returns to her own family in shame. If a Japanese husband can afford it, he often will keep a mistress. The mistress is not added to his family but is set up in her own home. Only in exceptional cases—for instance, when the mistress has a child—does he bring her into his home, and then she is usually treated as one of the servants. This practice crosses all class lines among the Japanese, with economics being the determining factor as to the status of the woman chosen for a mistress.

In Western cultures and among most Japanese Americans, marriage for love is the ideal. In a study by Nishio (1982) of characteristics of the Japanese and Japanese Americans, about one half of Japanese Americans sampled had been married to non-Japanese. He also found divorce rates higher among Japanese Americans than among the Japanese in Japan. Kikumura and Kitano (1973) and Tinker (1973) found that, for such areas as Los Angeles, San Francisco, and Fresno, California, the incidence of Japanese American interracial marriage had approached 50% as of the time of their studies. Presumably, this is a measure of the success of acculturation of the Japanese. Certainly, these interracial experiences present an arena for possible conflict for those of Japanese ancestry.

Cultural Values and Attitudes

Japanese Americans are traditionally influenced by strong values of filial piety, respect and obligation, harmony, and group cooperation. Avoidance of shame, indirect communication, self-effacement, and modesty appear to be maintained in recent generations. Japanese American values include *amae,* the emphasis on interdependence in preference to individualism; a marked sense of hierarchical order in personal relations; well-defined obligations that attach to one's position in the family and culture; and *enryo,* respect and modesty. Other concerns include controlling emotions, doing the best one can do in adverse circumstances, and appreciating one's limits in difficult situations (Fugita, Ito, Abe, & Takeuchi, 1991).

Conformity is another value that stresses conventional behavior and strict allegiance to rules and regulations (Kitano, 1976). This value often leads to the development of dependent personalities. Many Japanese believe that suffering and hard work are necessary ingredients of character building. Finally, the Japanese place great emphasis on status distinction, so gender,

class, age, caste, family, lineage, and other variables of social status are vital
to the culture.

Being future oriented and concerned about the welfare of their children,
the Japanese value education. In fact, the Japanese educational system may
be the most effective in the world. The estimated illiteracy rate is less than
1%. One of the most powerful forces for uniformity in education is derived
from the Japanese reluctance to stigmatize or embarrass anyone publicly.
Tracking is not done in Japanese elementary and secondary schools. Students
of varying abilities study in the same classes. Automatic promotion is the
unchallenged rule throughout the 9 years that Japanese children are required
to attend school. Academic competition is intense because a person's social
status depends heavily on which university she or he attends.

The Japanese values and norms most likely to endure are those that
intersect with the relative power position of the Japanese in the United States.
Many of those are consistent with the stereotypical traits associated with
Japanese Americans by those in the dominant culture: quiet, conforming,
loyal, diligent, good citizens, high achievers in education, group oriented,
indirect communicators, respectful of hierarchy, submissive (if female),
dependent on family, and having a high sense of family obligation. These
values are in contrast with the dominant-culture values of individual self-
realization, high verbal participation, female assertiveness, challenge of
authority, and a more egalitarian system of family dynamics.

Implications

Of special importance, as Motet (1981) pointed out, is to differentiate
between the Japanese resident who is returning to Japan and the Japanese
American citizen. How can we make for a good adjustment and yet not cause
reentry problems for the immigrant eventually returning to Japan? The
answer is to pursue a course of cultural enrichment, rather than cultural
change. To ask that the Japanese adopt dominant-culture values would be
inappropriate. The helper role in this case might be more as a translator of
differences between the two cultures, an informational resource. To help
Japanese students and their families function efficiently and to broaden their
perspective on both cultures, helping professionals need to have an understanding of areas such as the following:

- The differences in values and customs of the two cultures
- The Japanese values of respect for hierarchy and authority, elder orientation,
  submissive role of women, role of the Japanese mother in educating the

children, indirect rather than direct communication, and family dependence and dynamics

- The difficulties of the reentry of Japanese families to Japan—especially, the children who have become more acculturated
- The dependency of the family, when applicable, on the corporation where the father is employed
- The difficulties of the Japanese student and his or her family with the English language (referral of family to English language courses)
- The need of the educator or counselor to serve as an information source of Japanese values and customs
- The need to supply classroom teachers with materials on ethnic differences (use of classroom films on modern Japan)
- The need of the educator or counselor to serve as a sensitive and special support system as the child begins the adjustment process in the particular school setting
- The need of the educator or counselor to suggest environmental modifications for the Japanese child (e.g., tutors within the school setting, particular schools in the area that service foreign language children)
- The need of the educator or counselor to assist the family in securing outside community resources
- The need of the Japanese student to continue learning the Japanese language
- The needs of the family for information on customs of the dominant culture, along with social and psychological support for themselves
- The need of Japanese American cultural exchange enrichment programs to appreciate unique resources such as food, drama, dance, music, arts, and crafts (coordinate cultural exchange programs either in a classroom or for the whole school)

Keeping in mind the generational orientation of Japanese Americans (Issei, Nisei, or Sansei) and recognizing where they may be on a continuum of degree of assimilation and acculturation, it is important to note that Japanese Americans are still placed in situations of extreme cultural conflict. Two therapies unique to Japanese culture offer promise for those experiencing psychological difficulty.

Naikan therapy (Lebra, 1976) was developed by Ishin Yoshimoto in 1954. It involves a period of isolated introspection during which the client searches for the true self. Through reflection on relationships with significant others, the client reflects on the care received from others and how to repay this debt. Once this dependency is reconceptualized, the client acknowledges his or her social insensitivity and develops a sense of debt and gratitude toward others. Naikan therapy was originally developed to rehabilitate antisocial individuals into morally upright people.

Morita therapy (Lebra, 1976) is based on Zen Buddhism and aims at liberation of the client from excessive self-preoccupation and intellectualization, enabling him or her to accept things "as they are." The therapy encourages the client to submit to symptoms in defeat and resignation, to unite with the illness, and to enact or produce symptoms. Morita therapy was developed to transform clients with mental illness into healthy individuals.

Reynolds (1989) developed a system called *Constructive Living,* which combines Naikan and Morita therapies. Constructive Living Centers are located in Los Angeles, Hawaii, Salt Lake City, New York, San Francisco, Seattle, and Washington, D.C.

Nishio's (1982, pp. 10-11) findings suggest that U.S. clinicians and counselors take the following therapeutic and nontraditional approaches with Japanese American clients:

- Give advice (Tamura & Lau, 1992, suggested that the Japanese tend to view helpers as teachers and expect them to be active, even authoritarian).
- Offer environmental and practical help.
- Make home visits or be available at irregular hours or both.
- Deal with the issue of the client's being of Japanese descent.
- Use Japanese modes of psychotherapy (e.g., Naikan therapy, Morita therapy).
- Provide education and consciousness-raising.
- Offer telephone sessions.
- Make collateral contacts (work with other professionals, agencies, and parents).
- Use cultural knowledge and experience.
- Participate in social dialogue before working on problems.

A group-centered approach that might be used by educators and counselors is suggested by Kaneshige (1973):

- Provide a nonthreatening group climate to encourage more verbal participation.
- Verbalize to group members some of their cultural value differences.
- Minimize interruptions of other group members while the nonexpressive Asian is speaking.
- Assure confidentiality.
- Clarify and interpret the expressions of all group members.
- Challenge White Americans' critical statements to Asians.
- Recognize your role as an authority figure to the Asian student.
- Encourage listening skills of other group members.

- Encourage the Asian American student to change his or her pattern of behavior as an outcome of personal growth, rather than as a statement of denying his or her cultural identity.

Not only do educators or counselors working with Japanese American clients have responsibility to be aware of their clients' lifestyles, but they also have a responsibility to function as change agents in existing institutions to foster a helping environment that can truly benefit Japanese Americans. Included in the service delivery would be changes in mental health policies (personnel, as well as selection of techniques), community agencies to service the needs of Asian persons (financial, career counseling, and networking for social and psychological support), educational reevaluation (encouraging creativity among Japanese American students, rather than stereotyping them as suited only for the physical sciences), and advocacy for more governmental intervention to ensure Asians financial assistance for degrees in higher education.

Questions for Review and Reflection

1. What impact did the internment camp experience have on Japanese American culture? Why should or should not this event be prominent in a discussion of Japanese Americans?
2. How does the strong "caste" system culture of Japanese Americans influence their acculturation into the dominant culture?
3. What factors contribute to Japanese Americans being called a "model minority"? What danger, if any, exists in such a label? How does this label affect Japanese American relationships with other Asian Americans?
4. How does knowledge of the generation from which Japanese Americans come help establish educational or counseling goals for them? Identify a concern and describe how you might approach it on the basis of the generation of the Japanese student or client?
5. What Japanese American values are responsible for the relative success of Japanese Americans in the dominant culture of the United States? Are these values different from those of the dominant culture, or are Japanese Americans better than dominant culture members at living according to the values?
6. How does the allegiance of Japanese Americans to family influence educational or counseling practices?
7. How does the relationship between the governments of the United States and Japan affect Japanese Americans and their relationships with members of the dominant culture and other culturally different persons in the United States?

8. What unique problems might one expect the Kibei to experience that are different from problems experienced by other Japanese Americans?

9. What impact does the traditional body language of Japanese Americans have on their interactions with members of the dominant culture? How can educators or counselors prevent miscommunication in these encounters?

10. W. A. Henkin (1985) described a unique form of prejudice directed at the Sansei. How can educators or counselors explore this prejudice from the perspective of both dominant-cultural values and Japanese American values?

References

Atkinson, D., & Matsushita, Y. (1991). Japanese American acculturation, counseling style, counselor ethnicity, and perceived counselor credibility. *Journal of Counseling Psychology, 38,* 473-478.

Benedict, R. (1945). *The chrysanthemum and the sword: Patterns of Japanese culture.* New York: New American Library.

Chu, R. (1971). *Majors of Chinese and Japanese students at the University of California, Berkeley, for the past 20 years* (Project Report, AS150, Asian Studies Division). Berkeley: University of California.

Chuman, F. F. (1976). *The bamboo people: The law and Japanese Americans.* Chicago: Japanese American Citizens League.

Drive to excel. (April, 1984). *Newsweek on Campus.*

Fugita, S., Ito, K. L., Abe, J., & Takeuchi, D. T. (1991). Japanese Americans. In N. Mokuau (Ed.), *Handbook of social services for Asian and Pacific Islanders.* Westport, CT: Greenwood.

Garfinkle, P. (1983). The best "Jewish mother" in the world. *Psychology Today, 17,* 56-60.

Hansen, M. L. (1952). The problem of the third-generation immigrant. *Commentary, 14,* 492-500.

Henkin, W. A. (1985). Toward counseling the Japanese in America: A cross-cultural primer. *Journal of Counseling and Development, 63,* 500-503.

Jenkins, D. (1973). *Job power: Blue- and white-collar democracy.* Garden City, NY: Doubleday.

Kagiwada, G., & Fujimote, I. (1973). Asian American studies: Implications for education. *Personnel and Guidance Journal, 51,* 397-405.

Kaneshige, E. (1973). Cultural factors in group counseling and interaction. *Personnel and Guidance Journal, 51,* 407-412.

Kikumura, A., & Kitano, H. (1973). Interracial marriage: A picture of the Japanese Americans. *Journal of Social Issues, 29,* 67-81.

Kitano, H. H. L. (1976). *Japanese Americans.* Upper Saddle River, NJ: Prentice Hall.

Kitano, H. H. L. (1988). The Japanese American family. In C. H. Mindel, R. W. Haberstein, & R. Wright, Jr. (Eds.), *Ethnic families in America* (pp. 258-275). New York: Elsevier.

Kurokawa, N. (1968). Lineal orientation in child rearing among Japanese. *Journal of Marriage and Family, 30,* 129-135.

Lebra, T. S. (1976). *Japanese patterns of behavior.* Honolulu: University of Hawaii Press.

Marsella, A. J. (1993). Counseling and psychotherapy with Japanese Americans: Cross-cultural considerations. *American Journal of Orthopsychiatry, 63,* 200-208.

Mass, A. I. (1976). Asians as individuals: The Japanese community. *Social Casework, 57,* 160-164.

Masuda, M., Matsumoto, G. H., & Meredith, G. (1970). Ethnic identity in three generations of Japanese Americans. *Journal of Social Psychology, 81,* 199-207.

Montero, D. (1981). The Japanese Americans: Changing patterns of assimilation over three generations. *American Sociological Review, 46,* 829-839.

Motet, D. (1981, April). *Adjustment therapy with Japanese.* Paper presented at the annual meeting of the Western Psychological Association, Los Angeles.

Nakane, C. (1972). *Human relations in Japan.* Tokyo: Ministry of Foreign Affairs.

Nishio, K. (1982, August). *Characteristics of Japanese and Americans in psychotherapy in Japan and the United States.* Paper presented at the annual convention of the American Psychological Association, Washington, DC.

Ohnuki-Tierney, E. (1993). *Rice as self: Japanese identities through time.* Princeton, NJ: Princeton University Press.

Okihiro, G. Y., & Sly, J. (1983). The press, Japanese Americans, and the concentration camps. *Phylon, 44,* 66-83.

Padilla, A. M., Wagatsuma, Y., & Lindholm, K. J. (1985). Acculturation and personality as predictors of stress in Japanese and Japanese Americans. *Journal of Social Psychology, 125,* 295-305.

Petersen, W. (1971). *Japanese Americans.* New York: Random House.

Powell, B., & Martin, B. (1988, February 4). The Pacific century. *Newsweek,* pp. 42-58.

Ravich, R., & Wyden, B. (1974). *Predictable pairing.* New York: Wyden.

Reynolds, D. K. (1989). *Flowing bridges, quiet waters.* Albany: State University of New York Press.

Schoonmaker, A. N. (1989). *Negotiate to win: Gaining the psychological edge.* Upper Saddle River, NJ: Prentice Hall.

Sue, D. W., & Kirk, B. (1972). Psychological characteristics of Chinese American students. *Journal of Counseling Psychology, 2,* 11-17.

Sue, D. W., & Sue, D. (1973). Understanding Asian Americans: The neglected minority. *Personnel and Guidance Journal, 51,* 385-389.

Sue, D. W., & Sue, D. (1990). *Counseling the culturally different.* New York: John Wiley.

Tamura, T., & Lau, A. (1992). Connectedness versus separateness: Adaptability of family therapy to Japanese families. *Family Process, 31*(4), 319-340.

Tinker, J. (1973). Intermarriage and ethnic boundaries: The Japanese American case. *Journal of Social Issues, 29,* 49-66.

Tomine, S. I. (1991). Counseling Japanese Americans: From internment to reparation. In C. C. Lee & B. L. Richardson (Eds.), *Multicultural issues in counseling: New approaches to diversity* (pp. 91-105). Alexandria, VA: American Association for Counseling and Development.

U.S. Bureau of the Census. (1991). *Statistical abstract of the United States.* Washington, DC: Government Printing Office.

Watanabe, C. (1973). Self-expression and the Asian American experience. *Personnel and Guidance Journal, 51,* 390-396.

Wilson, R. A., & Hosokawa, B. (1980). *East to America: A history of the Japanese in the United States.* New York: William Morrow.

Yanagisako, S. J. (1985). *Transforming the past.* Stanford, CA: Stanford University Press.

7

Korean Americans

Korean Americans who live in the United States are among the most recent immigrants to this country. Most of them arrived after 1970 and are middle-class owners of businesses. These people are quite different from the first Koreans who arrived in Hawaii in 1903 to work the sugar and pineapple plantations.

The number of Korean Americans is rapidly increasing. In 1970, approximately 70,000 lived in the United States. By 1990, that number had increased to 800,000, primarily as a result of revised immigration laws (U.S. Bureau of the Census, 1991). Korean Americans represent one of the largest Asian American groups in the United States (Ramsey, 1987). It is estimated that, by the year 2000, nearly 1 million Koreans will reside in the United States. Korean Americans are geographically more dispersed than other Asian immigrants, but the heaviest concentration is in Los Angeles. Not much is known about Korean Americans because of their small number, which contributes to "general ignorance about [them] as a distinct ethnic group differing significantly from the Chinese and Japanese" (Hurh & Kim, 1984, p. 22).

Acculturation

Patterson (1979), who examined the acculturation process of Korean Americans in Hawaii, thought his analysis applicable to Koreans in the

United States because of the large concentration of Korean Americans in Hawaii. In his study, he equated upward social mobility with acculturation. The following points made by Patterson illustrate the rapid adjustment and upward mobility of the Koreans:

- The diet, dress, and habits of Korean immigrants changed quickly from Oriental to American.
- Koreans left plantation work faster than any other ethnic group in the history of Hawaii.
- Koreans recorded one of the highest rates of urbanization.
- Koreans generally spoke better English than the Japanese or Chinese.
- Second-generation Korean children were staying in school longer than any other ethnic group, including Chinese, Japanese, and Caucasian.
- Second-generation Koreans recorded one of the highest rates of professionalism.
- Second-generation Koreans exhibited more liberal and egalitarian attitudes toward social issues than Chinese Americans or Japanese Americans.
- By the early 1970s, the Koreans had achieved the highest per capita income and the lowest unemployment rate of any ethnic group in Hawaii, including Caucasians (p. 83).

Because of their small numbers, Koreans in Hawaii were forced to mingle with other ethnic groups. This is one factor in the explanation for their rapid acculturation. Other data reveal that Korean immigrants differed markedly from their countrymen in five areas.

1. *Religion:* In a country where traditional orthodoxy was based on Buddhism and Confucianism, the majority of Korean immigrants to Hawaii were connected in some way to Christianity.
2. *Demographics:* Most immigrants came from urbanized areas, yet the majority of Korea is rural.
3. *Occupation:* Most Koreans were peasant farmers, yet the majority of immigrants were government clerks, political refugees, students, policemen, miners, woodcutters, household servants, and Buddhist monks.
4. *Education:* The immigrants may have been better educated than their countrymen.
5. *Nontraditional value system:* Armed conflicts, drought, famine, and oppressive taxes forced people to abandon the countryside for the uncertainties of the city. In the cities, young refugees came to embrace cosmopolitan, modern, and antitraditional liberal influences. Forced to abandon the graves of their ancestors and therefore the required Confucian rituals, they became primary can-

didates for conversion to Christianity and other influences of the culture in the United States (Patterson, 1979).

Hurh and Kim (1988) described a model of the stages of adjustment following Korean migration:

1. *The exigency stage:* The first 1 or 2 years of resettling were the most stressful, and the immigrants were most vulnerable during this stage. The factors that contributed most to their difficulties were economic hardship, culture shock, language problems, lack of social support, and family conflict.

2. *The resolution and optimism stage:* The immigrants' mental health and life satisfaction improved the longer they stayed in the United States and the more confidence and mastery they gained in their new environment.

3. *The stagnation stage:* Their life satisfaction reached a plateau around the 15th year or thereabouts after immigration. The life-satisfaction index remained flat or slightly decreased thereafter.

One group that faces unique challenges of adjustment to the culture of the United States is the "1.5-generation Korean Americans" (Lee & Cynn, 1991). These Korean Americans were born in Korea but have spent most of their lives in the United States. Their adjustment difficulties center around differences in the rate of their acculturation and that of their immigrant parents. The 1.5-generation Korean Americans are young, mobile, and quick in adapting to values of the dominant culture in the United States. These characteristics place them in conflict with their parents and the traditional values of the Korean culture.

Hurh and Kim (1988) found that the ethnic attachment of Korean immigrants remained strong regardless of their stay in the United States and the degree of their education and acculturation. Their "adhesive adaptation pattern" of becoming acculturated indicates that they do not resist acculturation, but rather seek to adopt the new culture whenever possible without discarding or weakening the old. Korean Americans maintain a high level of ethnicity, probably higher than any other Asian ethnic group, partly because the vast majority are affiliated with ethnic churches.

Poverty and Economic Concerns

The first wave of Korean immigrants came to Hawaii to work on the sugar cane plantations. Economic improvement for these early Korean immigrants was difficult because they were exploited by plantation owners, whose main concern was obtaining profit. Although they were not contract laborers, the language barrier, racial discrimination, and cultural conflicts prevented them from obtaining more gainful employment consistent with their individual abilities and skills. The first generation worked hard and saved to ensure that their children would receive a good education. Many eventually opened their own businesses. By the 1970s, it was reported that Koreans in Hawaii had the highest per capita income of all groups, including Whites.

Koreans helped one another financially. Communities or groups of tradespeople would organize *qyes* (revolving credit unions) to look after their own. This helped improve the economic status of the group as a whole.

Although many Korean Americans today are underemployed as a result of language barriers and racial discrimination, few receive public assistance. The newer immigrants seem to be respecting the pattern of the first immigrants, establishing independent businesses.

Unlike in earlier immigration patterns, a different kind of Korean has been coming to the United States recently. The most recent group is composed primarily of extremely wealthy Koreans migrating from South Korea. They, of course, are not faced with economic hardship in the United States.

History of Oppression

Korea has a long history of oppression. The Korean peninsula is surrounded by three powerful countries—China, Russia, and Japan. Koreans have been subject to oppression both in their native country and in the United States, where they came to escape from oppression. A capsulized version of Korea's history illustrates this oppression.

The traditional view about the origin of the Korean people is based on legend. Tradition places the founding of the tribal state in the year 2333 B.C.E. with the descent of Tan'gun-wanggom, a spirit king of divine origin. His successors reigned for 1,200 years. Although no archaeological evidence supports this story, some Korean historians write about it nonetheless.

According to anthropologists, the Korean people are descended partly from the Mongolian race and partly from the Tungus and Proto-Caucasoids who arrived from the plains of Manchuria or Central Asia. Koreans suffered from almost unbearable exploitation and humiliation under the Mongols, and national strength and resources were gradually exhausted.

During the 17th and 18th centuries, considerable factionalism within the ruling class was based on southern versus northern provincialism, and fights over the division of land developed. The traditional Confucianists and the neo-Confucianists were also at odds. The ultimate struggle was for the monopoly of political power by one group. This factionalism weakened the government and hindered social and economic progress. The ruling class had developed a reliance on China as a safeguard for independence. They hoped China would provide a buffer from the outside world because China treated Korea as a tributary state. The Yi dynasty did not develop any foreign policy of its own and was ill-prepared to defend against the events during the last 25 years of the 19th century (Choy, 1979).

The French in 1866 and the United States in 1871 tried to open the doors to the "Hermit Kingdom" without success. Isolation ended, however, when Japan and Korea entered into a treaty of friendship and commercial trade. By 1882, Korea signed a similar treaty with the United States. Soon, European nations also entered into diplomatic relations with Korea. With the end of isolation, Korea became a battleground of political strife in the Far East. As its social, economic, and political feudal system disintegrated, revolts took place in 1882, 1884, and 1894. The last revolt led to a Japanese invasion, which in turn resulted in the Sino-Japanese War of 1894–95.

Following the end of World War II in 1945, the U.S. Army established a military government in South Korea while the Russians occupied the North. The Republic of Korea was formed in the south in 1948. By 1949, the People's Republic of Korea was formed. On June 25, 1950, hostilities broke out on the border at the 38th parallel, launching the Korean War.

The experience of Koreans in the United States was similar to that of Japanese and Chinese immigrants: They all faced economic hardships and were victimized by the anti-Asian movements on the West Coast. Their economic ventures were greatly limited by racial discrimination.

The National Origins Act of 1924 closed the door on Korean immigration for almost 40 years. The Immigration Act of 1965 once again allowed entry of Koreans who had close relatives in the United States or who possessed specific skills defined as contributing to the growth of the U.S. economy.

Language and the Arts

The Korean language is of the Ural-Altaic language family, which also includes Japanese, Turkish, Mongolian, and Manchu. Despite the official writing system of the Korean government for many years being that of the Chinese, the Koreans never adopted the Chinese language; they did, however, borrow some words from it. The dialect differences that exist between North and South Korean are not sufficiently large to provide a barrier to understanding. During the reign of King Sejong (1397–1450), a royal commission of scholars, after many years of study, developed a Korean alphabet. The Korean alphabet is phonetic and consists of 19 consonants, 8 vowels, and 2 semivowels. This phonetic system was credited to the personal leadership of the king and was called *hunmin jongum*. Today, it is named *Han'gul* and is the oldest known alphabet of its kind still in use. Considered an inferior system by the Confucian scholar-officials, Han'gul was little used until revived by missionaries in the 19th century. Suppressed by the Japanese during the years of Japanese occupation, Han'gul was adopted in 1945 as the official written language. Both North and South Korea have endorsed Han'gul to symbolize their nationalism. The invention of this alphabet has been held in such high regard that a national holiday celebrates the event.

In any language, spoken and unspoken ways express the speaker's attitude toward the person about whom or to whom the speech is addressed. Korean has grammatical devices specifically for this purpose. Use of an inappropriate sociolinguistic level of speech is socially unacceptable and is usually interpreted as having a special message, such as intended formality (e.g., use of the honorific level when familiar level is acceptable) or disrespect or contempt to a social superior (e.g., use of the familiar level when the honorific is appropriate). One sometimes may have to evaluate the degree of intimacy with the speech partner before choosing an appropriate level of formality from among the four levels of speech (higher honorific, simple honorific, simple familiar, and lower familiar). This speech level system is an important linguistic feature characterizing interpersonal relationships in the Korean culture.

By elementary school, children have acquired the basic rules of honorifics. If a child does not know how to choose an appropriate level of speech in a given situation, the child's parents are blamed for poor home education, and the child's speech is branded as "baby talk." Many Korean immigrant parents point out that if their children have not acquired the honorifics system, they avoid using Korean whenever possible.

Another aspect of Korean language is that of names. Koreans have only 232 surnames. Over 53% of the whole population has one of the five major surnames: Kim, Lee/Rhee/Yi, Park, Choi/Choe, and Chung/Jung.

Each individual name has two Chinese characters, one of which identifies the generation, and the other of which is the individual's personal name. For example, in a family, three children may be named Kim Sung Shik, Kim Sung Ja, and Kim Sung Chul. Kim is the surname, Sung is for the generation, and Shik, Ja, and Chul are the individuals' names. Sometimes the generation and individual names are reversed, but the surname always comes first. Because of the rule in English that surnames come last, Korean family names and personal names are often confused.

The art of Korea is reflected in its music and dance. Music is of two kinds: *Court ceremonial music* is solemn and dignified and is written; *folk music* is usually fast and lively. One traditional folk song is the farmer's song, which is basically a prayer for good harvest. Korean folk songs are different from those of other Asian countries. First, women are credited with the writing of many folk songs. The songs are an emotional outlet for them and express their feelings about being repressed by men. Second, humor is used to turn a sad occasion into a lighter event. Of all Korean folk songs, the best known is the "Arirang," which is the name of a mountain pass. It was very popular with Korean underground patriots when the Japanese dominated Korea. Japanese authorities banned the singing of the Korean national anthem, so freedom-loving Koreans expressed their patriotism by singing "Arirang."

A typical Korean musical instrument is the *kayaqeum,* which was invented during the Silla period. It is a 12-string harp-type instrument played with the fingers. Usually played by women, it produces a melancholy sound.

Korean dances are expressions of wishes for good luck, wealth, and rich harvests. Of the many kinds of dances, the drum dance is typical. It is performed by a woman who beats a drum that is slung across her shoulder. In another type of drum dance, several drums, sitting in two rows, are beaten by the dancer in various tempos and rhythms.

Racism and Prejudice

Most immigrant groups are discriminated against shortly after their arrival in the United States, yet with some groups prejudice tends to fade away. Overt prejudice appears to diminish as a group assimilates into the dominant culture of the United States. Korean Americans faced racism and prejudice on their arrival in this country, and they continue to face it at the covert level. Most American-born Koreans have achieved high levels of education and are able and qualified professionals, but racial discrimination sometimes prevents their finding jobs consistent with their abilities. Virtually no Korean American holds a position as a business executive in any large American corporation (those without Korean ties). Almost no Korean lawyers work in large American law firms. The most conspicuous areas of underemployment are in the field of medicine (doctors, dentists, nurses), architecture, and pharmacy. Choy estimated that, as of 1979, only 5% of Korean Americans were doing what they were trained for.

Although the United States gives preferential admission to persons of select professional classes, U.S. licensing agencies are discriminatory against foreign professionals. Consequently, the only option available for many Korean Americans is to start their own businesses.

Sociopolitical Factors

Most sociopolitical factors in Korean American culture are the result of the political turmoil in the homeland and efforts of the immigrants to aid in the movement for independence.

The National Origins Act of 1924, an effort to increase the number of European immigrants, prevented Koreans from entering the United States. The Immigration Act of 1965 and its 1976 amendment determined both the number and social characteristics of acceptable Korean immigrants—their gender, age, occupation, and educational level (Kim, 1981).

The church has become the primary social organization among Korean Americans. Kim (1981) reported that two anti-Park (South Korean President Park Chung-hee) associations, the Korean American Political Association, and the Korean American Chamber of Commerce were founded in New York City.

Child-Rearing Practices

Acceptable norms for behavior in the Korean family and society are strongly influenced by the teachings of Confucius, a Chinese philosopher. Much of Confucian teaching focuses on the need to maintain social order through nurturing and preserving the "five relationships": between parents and children, between older persons and younger persons, between husband and wife, between friends, and between ruler and subject (which includes the teacher-student relationship). Interest in preserving these relationships is quite prevalent among Korean Americans and should be noted by those involved with teaching and counseling this group. Each of these relationships is hierarchical and dictates appropriate behavior. Kim (1981) described these Korean American relationships in this way:

> A son should be reverential; a younger person respectful; a wife submissive; a subject loyal. And, reciprocally, a father should be strict and loving; an older person wise and gentle; a husband good and understanding; a ruler righteous and benevolent; and friends trusting and trustworthy. In other words, one is never alone when one acts since every action affects someone else. (p. 11)

Generally, second-generation parents tend to be less authoritarian than first-generation parents. Also, they are not likely to assign the first son authority over his younger brothers and sisters (Min, 1988). A strong emphasis is placed on preserving family honor among Koreans. If a child behaves in an embarrassing manner, then the whole family is disgraced. A child in a Korean family is hardly regarded as an independent, whole person. Most decisions directly or indirectly affecting the child are made by the parents or other older members of the family. Children are not encouraged to express their opinions; insistence on doing so in an exchange with a superior results in a scolding. Vocal expression of personal wishes is seldom rewarded. Children are expected to remain quiet, particularly in the presence of adults.

Typical Korean American parents are in their late 30s, usually have two or three children of elementary school age, and most often have a high school or college education. In most households, both parents are employed full-time outside the home, in contrast with the life pattern in Korea. The parents' expectations for their children in school, in both academic and social areas, are very high. Kim (1993) posited that Korean cultural tradition places high value on education as a main channel to higher social position. The Confucian tradition of respecting one's teachers and obeying one's parents have helped children achieve better academic performance.

Religious Practices

Three religious and philosophical traditions in Korean culture—Confucianism, Buddhism, and Taoism—have significantly shaped Korean American attitudes about life and death, self-care, and social interactions. Despite these influences, however, many Korean Americans embrace some form of Christianity. Case studies in Los Angeles, Chicago, and Atlanta indicate that approximately 70% of Korean immigrants regularly attend ethnic churches (Hurh & Kim, 1990). Korean immigrant churches provide fellowship for Korean immigrants, a place to maintain Korean cultural traditions, social services for church members and the Korean community, and social status for members.

An American minister in Seoul, the first physician-missionary sent by the Presbyterian Board of Foreign Missions of the United States, became one of the most trusted of the Korean king's advisers. After his successful treatment of the queen's nephew, who was wounded during a political coup in 1884, he became the royal family's personal physician. Thus, he was able to persuade the king to permit his subjects to immigrate to Hawaii (Choy, 1979). On the day the first group of immigrants left Korea, he went to the port and offered his prayers for the safety of the immigrants to the strange land. He also handed a few of the leaders among them letters of introduction to the superintendent of the Methodist Mission in Hawaii. Therefore, Christians were already among the first Korean immigrants to Hawaii, and a few of them were preachers.

The period between 1903 and 1918 saw a rapid growth in the number of Koreans professing Christianity. Methodist, Episcopal, and Presbyterian churches were established. Several factors seem to have contributed to this growth. First, Korean society in Hawaii lacked strong social groups established on the basis of traditional ties. Second, Christianity may have been used as a means of communicating to the dominant culture that they were attempting to assimilate. Third, the church offered those who were not members of other associations their only opportunity to engage in social intercourse outside the work camps. Fourth, a certain degree of pressure seems to have been applied to get non-Christians to convert, particularly after a significant number of Koreans had already converted. Parents who were not Christians would send their children to church (Choy, 1979).

The period between 1919 and 1925 was marked by disputes over policy on church administration, church financial business, and the operation of the Korean boarding school later known as the Central Institute. In the fall of 1916, a group of 70 to 80 people left their Methodist Church to begin what became known as the Korean Christian Church. They were seeking independence and self-government. Members of the Korean Christian Church were an indispensable part of the Korean national independence movement abroad. They asserted that Korea was ready for independence and self-government. Financial contributions were given for these purposes. The Korean Christian Church eventually became so politically oriented that the spirituality of its members was no longer addressed.

The Korean Christian Church had its own series of internal dissent. One faction wished for the church to once again become a place of worship. Feelings ran so high that force and violence occurred. Almost every Sunday, local police were called in. The controversy was settled by a court, which ordered the two groups to unite in October 1948.

The third period in the history of the church in the Korean American community (1946–1967) was characterized by an effort by the first generation to maintain the status quo and by an attitude of indifference and rebellion on the part of the second and third generations. To the first generation, the church was a place of both social interaction and cultural identification. Their traditional language, values, and customs were reinforced through social contacts provided by the church. The second and third generations did not share the language or culture of the first generation.

The fourth period in the history of the church in the Korean American community began with the new influx of immigrants after 1965. This new wave of immigration promises resources and leadership long needed for a revival of the ethnic church in the Korean American community. This leadership may not, however, be channeled into existing ethnic churches. Because new immigrants arriving in the United States have their own religious preferences, they often look for a church of their own choice or try to establish their own denominational churches (Choy, 1979).

With the exception of holding services in Korean, the churches of Korean Americans and those of the dominant culture do not seem to differ a great deal.

Family Structure and Dynamics

Koreans have generally immigrated in their basic social unit, the nuclear family. Frequently, a family is temporarily separated so that a pioneer member can establish an economic base or because of a bureaucratic delay under U.S. or Korean immigration laws. Favorable conditions for continuing the old family unit or for creating a new family life in the United States were fostered by the Immigration Act of 1965, which permitted reunion of immediate relatives.

The majority of Korean householders are married, with the eldest male, usually the husband, considered head of household. This family structure contrasts with that prevalent among older Korean immigrants, who encountered an immigration law hostile to the creation of families. Even the solution of "picture brides" was not a permanent answer for the extreme shortage of females among older Korean immigrants. Now the opposite phenomenon, a female surplus in the marriage market, has occurred largely as a result of the selective immigration policy of the U.S. government.

Because Korean women outnumber Korean men in the United States, marriageable women face a serious problem in finding husbands. They are further disadvantaged in that Korean men, still concerned with the traditional Korean virtue of female chastity, tend to distrust acculturated Korean women, who, they think, are too aggressive and disobedient—thus the strong tendency among eligible men to take a month-long chartered plane trip to their home country to "pick out a brand-new bride" (Kim, 1981 p. 45). Immigrant Korean women have resorted to the same technique. Both groups have been successful in their marriage ventures because "homeland Koreans are crazy about the Korean Americans" (Kim, 1981, p. 45). When negotiating for their South Korean spouses, Korean Americans tend to inflate their status in the United States. These marriage ventures have facilitated "kinship-centered" immigration because, after marrying in South Korea, Korean Americans have filed for "family reunion" visas on returning to the United States. A high proportion of Korean immigrants send for their entire family once they have acquired citizenship. Spouses and children can enter under "family reunion" visas, but once citizenship is obtained, close relatives can also be brought to the United States.

Koreans have a culture rooted in filial piety wherein care for the elderly from family and kin has been given and accepted as a customary and normative duty. Social supports encompass a range of care and services that include emotional support, advice, guidance, and information (Sung, 1991).

Almost all Korean immigrant families belong to a modified extended-family group. This group includes several nuclear families and is based on the husbands' or wives' common schooling or work experiences in the old or new land, rather than on actual kinship. These groups have also emerged from living in the same neighborhoods or from having identical hobbies. These family associations are different from extended families. They are informal and have few traditions and rituals. At most, they are substitutes for the extended family, designed for the exchange of material and emotional support. During special occasions, such as Christmas, New Year's Eve, and Chinese New Year's Day, they usually meet to enjoy Korean food, dancing, and talk. In many cases, family groups or associations also function as a *gye*, a Korean equivalent of a rotating credit association.

Cultural Values and Attitudes

Korean cultural values and attitudes can perhaps best be described by contrasting them with the dominant culture:

Dominant Culture	*Korean American*
Emphasis on self-autonomy	Emphasis on family
Internal frame of reference (autonomy)	External frame of reference (obedient to elders)
All people are equal	People are ranked in a hierarchy
Informal personal relationships	Formal personal relationships
Student-centered learning (free to question)	Teacher-centered learning (do not question)
Students problem-solve	Students memorize
Equality of sexes	Male dominance

According to Sue and Sue (1990), Asian Americans tend to take a more practical approach to life and problems than do Whites. Well-structured and predictable situations are preferred over ambiguous ones. Asian Americans also appear less autonomous; more dependent, conforming, and obedient to authority; more inhibited; less ready to express impulses; more law-abiding; less assertive; and more reserved. A strong cultural emphasis is placed on suppression of strong feelings, obedience to family authority, and subjugation of individuality to the benefit of the family. Asian Americans are less extroverted than Whites. The cultural influence on formality in interpersonal relations may make Asians uncomfortable interacting with the more spontaneous and informal dominant culture. Asian cultures are family centered and tend to view outsiders with suspicion. Asians have suffered the effects of racism in the United States, and this reinforces mistrust. All of these points concerning Asian Americans in general are applicable to Korean Americans.

Two Korean traditional rituals—*hwangap* (60th birthday) and *jesah* (ancestral worship ceremony)—serve important functions in Korean American communities. Hwangap celebrates passage into old age; jesah honors the dead. Both serve to ensure the continuity of traditions so that older members will be assured of their place in the ancestral order (Chin, 1991).

Whereas the dominant culture of the United States stresses the importance of the individual first, Korean Americans stress family, community, culture, and global influences. Throughout their years in the United States, many Korean Americans have played an active role in the independence movement in Korea.

Implications

Korean cultural values may inhibit Korean Americans from seeking counseling services even when they are feeling psychological distress. Public admission of personal problems is suppressed, and restraint of strong feelings is encouraged. Seeking counseling may be perceived as bringing shame and disgrace on one's family. Physical complaints may be an expression of emotional difficulties.

An awareness of family relationships will help teachers and counselors understand the respect that Korean American parents and students have for teachers and other school officials. This awareness will help counselors become sensitive to many Korean American expectations for guidance and direction. Because Korean Americans are reared believing that their actions will inevitably affect others, they want to ensure that their impact on others will be as they intend it.

Hurh and Kim (1988) reported that work-related variables, such as job satisfaction, occupation, and income, are strongly correlated with positive mental health for males. Positive mental health for Korean females, in contrast, is related to family life satisfaction, ethnic attachment variables (kinship contact, reading a Korean newspaper, Korean church affiliation), and some acculturation variables, such as having a driver's license, being proficient in English, or having United States American friends.

Counselors and educators should be aware that those who seek help may experience guilt and shame because of it. Confidentiality is a factor to be dealt with immediately. The presenting problem may not be the real problem, but a manifestation of something deeper. To build trust and rapport, counselors should deal with the superficial problems first because they are likely to be less threatening to the client. Helping professionals need to employ a logical, structured, directive approach when dealing with Korean Americans.

Questions for Review and Reflection

1. What factors contributed to the rapid adjustment and upward mobility of Korean Americans in the United States? Which of these factors are most consistent with values in the dominant culture of the United States? Which are most inconsistent?

2. How has the size of the Korean American population affected the group's acceptance in the United States?

3. How does the Korean linguistic system influence the communication of Korean Americans in the dominant culture?

4. What information is contained in the order of names of Korean Americans? How is this different from the English system of naming?

5. What knowledge of family relationships among Korean Americans is useful to educators and counselors? How does the concept of family honor affect the rearing of children in the Korean American culture?

6. How has acculturation affected the number of Korean American women who marry Korean American men? What effect does this phenomenon have on the maintenance of the Korean American culture?

7. Korean American culture is said to emphasize an "external frame of reference." How does this value affect Korean Americans and their interactions with the dominant culture?

8. What are the implications for educators and counselors of the teacher-centered learning style of Korean American students?

9. How can an educator or counselor intervene with Korean Americans who are psychologically distressed when the Korean American culture inhibits them from seeking help outside the family?

10. What unique problems might one expect Korean Americans to experience in comparison with other Asian American groups?

References

Chin, S. Y. (1991). Korean birthday rituals. *Journal of Cross Cultural Gerontology, 6*(2), 145-152.

Choy, Bonh-youn. (1979). *Koreans in America.* Chicago: Nelson-Hall.

Hurh, W. M., & Kim, K. C. (1984). *Korean immigrants in America.* Rutherford, NJ: Fairleigh Dickinson University Press.

Hurh, W. M., & Kim, K. C. (1988, June). *Uprooting and adjustment: A sociological study of Korean immigrants' mental health* (Final report to the National Institute of Mental Health, Grant No. 1R01 MH 40312-01). Bethesda, MD: National Institute of Mental Health.

Hurh, W. M., & Kim, K. C. (1990). Religious participation of Korean immigrants in the United States. *Journal of the Scientific Study of Religion, 19,* 19-34.

Kim, E. Y. (1993). Career choice among second-generation Korean Americans: Reflections of a cultural model of success. *Anthropology and Education Quarterly, 24*(3), 224-248.

Kim, I. (1981). *New urban immigrants: The Korean community in New York.* Princeton, NJ: Princeton University Press.

Lee, J. C., & Cynn, V. E. H. (1991). Issues in counseling 1.5-generation Korean Americans. In C. C. Lee & B. B. Richardson (Eds.), *Multicultural issues in counseling: New approaches to diversity* (pp. 127-140). Alexandria, VA: American Association for Counseling and Development.

Min, P. G. (1988). The Korean American family. In C. H. Mindel, R. W. Haberstein, & R. Wright, Jr. (Eds.), *Ethnic families in America* (pp. 199-229). New York: Elsevier.

Patterson, W. (1979). Upward social mobility of the Koreans in Hawaii. *Korean Studies, 3.*

Ramsey, R. S. (1987). Teaching Koreans in America today. In R. A. Morse (Ed.), *Wild asters: Explorations in Korean thought, culture, and society.* Lanham, MD: University Press of America.

Sue, D. W., & Sue, D. (1990). *Counseling the culturally different: Theory and practice.* New York: John Wiley.

Sung, K. T. (1991). Family-centered informal support networks of Korean elderly. *Journal of Cross-Cultural Gerontology, 6*(4), 431-447.

U.S. Bureau of the Census. (1991). *Statistical abstract of the United States.* Washington, DC: Government Printing Office.

8

Vietnamese in the United States

The Indochinese include the Vietnamese, ethnic Chinese, Cambodians (Khmer), Laotians, Hmong, and Mien. They are of diverse ethnic origins and are among the most recent immigrants to the United States. Of the approximately 1 million Indochinese who have come to the United States since 1975, the largest number have come from Vietnam.

An initial, naive thought about the Vietnamese people who immigrated to the United States could lead to the question why these people came. The U.S. Bureau of the Census (1991) reported the Vietnamese American population as approximately 615,000 and projected an increase to 1.6 million by the year 2000. The total Southeast Asian refugee population in the United States was 1,092,000 in 1990. Approximately 90,000 of these refugees belong to a Laotian mountain tribe known as the Hmong. A distinct ethnic group that migrated to the highlands of Laos from southern China during the last century, the Hmong lived in patriarchal clans and survived through slash-and-burn farming. Recruited by the CIA in the 1960s, they became loyal allies of the United States against communism. Large numbers of Hmong have qualified for resettlement in the United States.

The U.S. press in the 1970s would have had readers believe that U.S. troops were none too politely asked to leave Vietnam because the entire North and South Vietnamese population desired Communist domination. Our political leaders astutely pursued withdrawal at the appropriate time, thus avoiding further loss of American life and unfair treatment at the hands of the communism-loving Vietnamese while complying with the wishes of the people we had helped for so long.

Acceptance of the foregoing statements as truth would lead to the assumption that the Vietnamese who chose to follow the U.S. troops to this free nation should have openly and willingly accepted acculturation into the dominant culture of the United States with few problems, negligible suffering, and grateful feelings toward their new country for taking them in. Because most Vietnamese had joined the Communists, those few who still rallied to the United States must have made a deliberate, well-thought-out decision to immigrate. Although some Southeast Asian refugees immigrated to escape untenable situations, others seemed motivated by the possibility of a better lifestyle, including aspirations of wealth, freedom, and the opportunity for a better education.

These ideas, however, are not supported by truth, facts, or research. The Vietnamese who fled their country were taking a path toward which they were driven by a total loss of personal and political freedom, economic deprivation, and a desperate need to survive the chaos in Vietnam.

Vietnam has been mightily affected by global influences throughout its history. Prior to French occupation in the mid-18th century, the tribes of Viets were pursued and slaughtered by other Asians. The Chinese first invaded them and tried to absorb the Lac-Viets, ancestors of today's Vietnamese, thousands of years ago. The Lac-Viets were encouraged by their leaders to fight for freedom from oppression and for maintenance of their separate cultural identity.

Resistance to colonization by France was occasionally vigorous and sometimes sporadic until World War I. The Vietnamese continued to resist and rebel against French rule, but some degree of order and stability was achieved at that time. World War II saw the Japanese arrive as conquerors, and resistance groups again arose. After the war and Japanese withdrawal, the French tried to regain control. The Chinese and the British were also attempting to gain control of Vietnam, and the United States was becoming involved as well.

Modern-day bids for independence in Vietnam died with the Geneva agreement that called for a split in the country. The North was to be ruled by the Communist regime under Ho Chi Minh; the South was to be governed by a system based on Western democracy. It appears that the Vietnamese people have been seeking freedom from global oppression throughout their entire history and over many centuries.

Acculturation

Four categories of refugees came out of Vietnam:

1. The first wave (1975)
2. The second wave (1978–79)
3. The escapees ("boat people")
4. Those who left as a result of the 1979 Memorandum of Understanding Between Vietnam and the United Nations High Commission for Refugees (the Orderly Departure Program) (Haines, 1985)

It is necessary to distinguish among these groups because some researchers have found significant differences in the acculturation process among the Vietnamese refugees on the basis of how and when they came to the United States (S. Nguyen, 1982).

When U.S. troops withdrew from Vietnam in 1975, approximately 135,000 Vietnamese left with them (Hawthorne, 1982). This massive withdrawal was preceded by several years of slow and deliberate abandonment of South Vietnam by the United States. When North Vietnam took over South Vietnam in 1975, the South Vietnamese were astonished by a trail of broken promises and an end to aid and support by the United States. North Vietnam tightened its grip and imposed its totalitarian government on the South. Individual rights and liberties were suppressed, millions of people were jailed or sent to concentration camps without trial, and nearly the entire population was impoverished. The only alternative to imprisonment, death, and destruction of their homes for the South Vietnamese was an abrupt evacuation. They were called refugees, as distinguished from other migrants, because in the vast majority of cases, they did not wish to flee Vietnam (Montero, 1979). Nguyen-Hong-Nhiem and Halpern (1989) described the Vietnamese refugees who fled in 1975 as representing "the urban professional, business, managerial and government elites" (p. 11). Their acculturation has been described as easier and more successful than that of many of the subsequent boat people who were sometimes of provincial working-class or rural peasant backgrounds.

After Vietnam was united under Hanoi's rule in 1976, conditions in South Vietnam became even more intolerable and appalling. More waves of refugees fled South Vietnam, to be met in the United States by significant cultural difficulties: The language barrier itself created overwhelming problems in all attempts to acculturate; the Vietnamese were denied the support of ethnically and culturally similar communities because they were dispersed in small groups across the country; and extended family units had been split and separated in their flight from Vietnam (Montero, 1979). Other factors that have an impact on the issue of acculturation include the escape process, survivor's guilt, and disillusionment with life in the United States.

The Vietnamese boat people escaped a country that had stabilized but with a perceived level of oppression. Nguyen-Hong-Nhiem and Halpern (1989) described the experience of these people:

> For those who survived the trip, safe landing and subsequent arrival at a refugee camp ended the second phase of the personal epic that began with the initial uprooting. Then followed the next stage, the long struggle for a return to "normalcy," with migration to a permanent home, a new norm, a new status, one that can never be equivalent to the old one, but one that does represent the reestablishment and renewal of self in a new sociocultural framework. (p. 10)

Cravens and Bornemann (1990) described a fifth group of Vietnamese in the United States. They reported that, in fiscal year 1989, 8,721 Amerasians and immediate relatives of earlier Vietnamese refugees arrived in the United States. Although these people were technically not refugees, the Amerasian Homecoming Act of 1987 provided the Amerasians with all the federal benefits afforded to refugees, including federal reimbursement to states that were willing to take in refugees. According to Cravens and Bornemann, "although quite diverse, the Amerasians can be described, when compared with their Vietnamese peers, as having fewer years of formal education, fewer skills, and higher levels of general psychological distress" (p. 48).

The Vietnamese acculturation was to be slow and extremely difficult. Many who fled were suspected of having psychological difficulties because of being non-Communists in a Communist-dominated regime in Vietnam (Hawthorne, 1982). Another common dilemma for any refugee also faced the Vietnamese refugee. Refugees often have a kind of love-hate relationship with their new country. They may be grateful to the new country for their freedom and the prosperity they can potentially have there, but they are often unable to accept the new country fully because it cannot provide all the things the refugees lost when they were forced to leave their homeland (Hawthorne, 1982).

Poverty and Economic Concerns

Historically, South Vietnam was comprised of a largely rural population. Continued Communist attempts after World War II to control the rural villages led to a widespread exit from the land to the cities by the South Vietnamese seeking sustenance. By 1974, the homeless rate was 57%, inflation was high, the economy had all but collapsed, and one out of seven South Vietnamese was unemployed (Hawthorne, 1982).

Hanoi created New Economic Zones in the South and gave the army responsibility for boosting the economy in rural areas. People were encouraged to return to the land and the New Economic Zones. Few people, however, were tempted to leave the cities. As difficult as life was in the cities, it was not as harsh as life on the land in the New Economic Zones. The South Vietnamese resisted the government's collective approach to a traditionally family-based working of the land. The economy worsened, and several years of crop failures followed. Food had to be imported and thus created more difficulties, and starvation for many was the result.

Refugees fleeing these conditions found scant relief. In 1977, the median annual income for a Vietnamese individual in the United States was $9,600, compared with a median annual income in the United States as a whole of $13,572 (Montero, 1979). By 1990, the average annual household income was $15,300, with 4.8 persons per household. The annual per capita income was $3,200, and 35% of families had incomes below the poverty level (*Asian Americans: A Status Report,* 1990).

When refugees arrived in the United States, economic self-sufficiency was virtually impossible. Unemployment was at a high 9%. Jobs available to the Vietnamese were low-paying, low-level positions offering little or no opportunity for advancement, when they existed at all. It was almost impossible for the Vietnamese to save their wages to improve their condition in the United States because of their obligations to send money to Vietnam to help support their extended families who remained there. This situation caused emotional crises for the Vietnamese and promoted feelings of loss and deprivation, as well as a loss of prestige (Liu & Muralta, 1977), even though many of the Vietnamese were educated. Some 50% of the Vietnamese in the late 1970s had a secondary education or a university degree; only 35% were either without formal education or had only a primary education (U.S. Committee for Refugees, 1988). By 1990, 62.2% of Vietnamese in the United States over age 25 had a high school education, and 12.9% had 4 years of college (*Asian Americans: A Status Report,* 1990).

Economically, Vietnamese refugees have made a quick adjustment in the United States. The employment picture has steadily improved; in fact, the labor force participation rates of the Vietnamese who have been in the United States for 5 years or longer tend to be higher than those of the general population (Haines, 1985).

History of Oppression

The Vietnamese have been politically oppressed throughout their history. Until 1940, Vietnam was a part of the French colonial empire. During World

War II, the French established a government in Vietnam. Ho Chi Minh became the resistance leader.

After the war, Ho Chi Minh declared independence for Vietnam, and France sought restitution of colonial Vietnam. The United States opposed recolonization at first but later supported France; this move led to the defeat of Vietnam's bid for independence by the mid-1950s.

The Geneva Agreement was to be the signal for peace in Vietnam and the beginning of independence. For the first time, the Vietnamese who were experiencing persecution in the North fled from Ho Chi Minh's regime to the South. At about this time, the United States decided that the pursuit of independence was not correct. No free elections were held, and Diem was put in charge of South Vietnam under U.S. supervision. By 1960, the National Liberation Front had been established in the South to strike at Diem's government as an expression of dissatisfaction with government taxes and attempts to take charge in the villages through the development of Strategic Hamlets.

Diem's assassination signaled the beginning of further U.S. involvement. Repeated attempts were made to seize government power and control of the farming communities. A mass exodus to the cities by people searching for some security and safety followed these attempted coups. The coups ended, and a relatively stable political period resulted. Interestingly, this period during the late 1960s was a relatively peaceful time for South Vietnam, especially in the rural areas, where the people continued their primitive farming relatively removed from the upheaval in the cities. This stable time was short because the National Liberation Front continued to battle in the cities and towns while the United States began withdrawal of troops and aid. U.S. withdrawal afforded the North an opportunity to strengthen its position in the South, and in 1975 the North began to gain control of the South.

The South Vietnamese people were trapped. The protecting U.S. military had deserted them, their rural economy had collapsed, and their leaders had been jailed or sent to camps. The refugees began to pour out of South Vietnam into Malaysia, Cambodia, Thailand, Australia, and the United States, seeking relief from the oppression of the Communist regime. The largest groups in this movement were the approximately 135,000 people who left abruptly with the U.S. military withdrawal and the 85,000 boat people who left in 1978. Freeman (1989) described the misery experienced by the boat people during the course of their flight: Running out of fuel, food, and drinking water; drifting on the open sea; and waiting to be rescued, only to be robbed and raped by pirates, are examples of the hardships that dehumanized them. Haines (1985) reported that even if the boat people "survived the angry waves, mechanical failure, the lack of food and water, multiple robberies, assaults, and rapes, they still had to suffer humiliation, mistreatment, and possibly internment by the countries of first asylum" (p. 201).

Oppression did not end for these people with flight from their country. Arrival in the United States meant continued economic and personal hardship, coupled with a lack of preparation for the cultural differences they encountered. Refugee camps were set up to process the people and resettle them. The Vietnamese were required to remain in the camps until they could meet one of four conditions:

1. They found a sponsor in the United States.
2. They made a decision to return to Vietnam.
3. They could prove that they were able to support themselves financially.
4. They arranged to move to another country, which required verification of that country's willingness to accept them (Hawthorne, 1982).

These were difficult requirements to meet for several reasons. The people of the United States did not view the influx of the Vietnamese as a favorable event. They blamed these people for the loss of loved ones killed in Vietnam and the disruption of their lives as a result of the war. The advent of desperate people willing to work at menial tasks for low wages was interpreted by many Americans as a threat to jobs that should go to unemployed U.S. citizens.

Rodriguez and Urrutia-Rojas (1990) described the host-city rejection suffered by Vietnamese newcomers in the Texas communities of Sea Drift and Seabrook. After settling in Texas between 1976 and 1978, several Vietnamese families left their wage jobs and purchased boats to enter the shrimping business.

> Located 18 miles southeast of Houston, the coastal town of Seabrook become a setting of hostilities against the Vietnamese refugees. Two Vietnamese fishing boats were burned in the town in February 1981. In the same month, the Ku Klux Klan held an anti-Vietnamese rally in the nearby community of Santa Fe. Armed with rifles, Klan members burned a replica of a Vietnamese fishing boat and vowed to return control of Texas coastal fishing to Whites. (p. 274).

A small percentage of refugees did, in fact, return to Vietnam. The third and fourth conditions (listed above) for release from the camps, however, were virtually impossible to meet. Expecting people who have fled their country abruptly and with none of their worldly possessions to show evidence of financial self-sufficiency was ludicrous. And finding a home in another country was equally difficult; these refugees were unwelcome almost everywhere in the world.

Language and the Arts

The Vietnamese language is derived from Chinese. Structurally, the language follows a subject-verb-object pattern similar to English, but the modifier follows the modified term, which is contrary to English structure. The Vietnamese language is non-inflectional. No form changes in words denote gender, case, tense, person, or mood. Words in the Vietnamese language tend to be monosyllabic. Each word has many tones to express differing meanings, however, such as gravity, evenness, interrogation, or sharpness (Do, 1968). The Vietnamese communicate in a quiet, dignified manner even when greeting one another. Smiles may cover anger or rejection, as well as convey positive warmth and happiness (Dung, 1984).

Vietnamese names are written in opposite order from English ones. The family name is listed first to emphasize the person's heritage. The middle name is next, and the given name is listed last. Vietnamese names have no "juniors"; given names are not shared or passed down from one generation to another. Legally, a woman retains her own name after marriage. Formally, however, she uses her husband's name preceded by "Mrs."; her own name may not be used (Montero, 1982). The Vietnamese do not generally use either the given name or the family name on a daily basis. Instead, they use a polite term plus a personal pronoun. The use of actual names is considered impolite.

The Vietnamese refugees found the language barrier to be a big problem for them in their efforts to acculturate into life in the United States. According to Montero (1979), however, no relationship appeared to exist between a proficiency in English and employment figures of the Vietnamese in the United States.

Vietnamese art dates back to prehistoric times (Whitfield, 1976). Stone and metal works are scarce because most such works have not survived the climate, wars, and political strife that are part of Vietnamese history. Traditional Vietnamese painting was limited in scope to religious and mythological subjects, evidenced by the abundance of paintings of the four mythological animals: the dragon, the unicorn, the tortoise, and the phoenix.

Vietnamese architecture is reflective of the theme of harmony and unity with nature. The Vietnamese believe that architecture "should not constitute a struggle against nature, but must instead be in communion with her" (Do, 1968, p. 119). The architecture is often referred to as landscape painting.

The Vietnamese have other art forms as well. Sculpture, however, was never a strong Vietnamese art form. The once-popular art of calligraphy, considered a scholarly art form, is no longer widely practiced. The arts of wood carving, ceramics, embroidery, and lacquerware have been highly developed by the Vietnamese. In general, Vietnamese art reflects the philosophical belief that life on earth is brief. It displays a humility, simplicity, and moderation because grandeur is believed to arise from the spirit, not from physical works of art.

Racism and Prejudice

Race divisions and prejudice are not aspects of life that the Vietnamese initially encountered as refugees in the United States. Historically, the Chinese in Vietnam have been seen as a higher class than the Vietnamese, and they have been attempting to absorb the Vietnamese population for centuries. Do (1968) posited that the Vietnamese race is actually a blending of many racial groups, with a great resemblance among them to the Chinese, Koreans, and Japanese. The Vietnamese constitute approximately 80% of the population of Vietnam. Cultural identity is maintained by physical separation in living areas.

The traditional caste system in Vietnam shows the scholar at the highest level of society. The scholar is followed by the farmer and fisher. The laborer is next, with the merchant or businessperson occupying the least esteemed position in the system (Montero, 1982).

After arrival in the United States, the first-wave Vietnamese encountered different forms of racial bias and prejudice than they would have been subjected to in their home country. These refugees were mainly the young, financially secure, and educationally elite in Vietnam. They were met with resentment of their willingness to accept low-paying, low-level employment while the United States was struggling with economic inflation and high unemployment. The superior education of Vietnamese immigrants was of little use in securing employment, housing, and sustenance for their families. Those in the first waves of refugees were also greeted by hostility from U.S. citizens who only wanted to be finished with the Vietnam War and who did not welcome any reminders of, and association with, the Vietnamese people (Montero, 1979).

Sociopolitical Factors

The arrival of the Vietnamese in the United States was greeted with resistance of all things Vietnamese because of the war. The Vietnamese, however, to whom money is not of primary importance, viewed the lifestyle in the United States as wasteful and luxurious (Hawthorne, 1982). Psychological depression plagued many because of the social and economic pressures of life in the United States. Many Vietnamese lost face, were forced to split from their extended families, and found a culture so different from their own that it was almost impossible for them to reconcile the two.

The Western influence in Vietnam had been considerable during the years before the refugees left their country, but surprisingly, this influence was of little help to the Vietnamese. Even the highly educated were unable to find jobs commensurate with their training; foreign degrees not accepted by U.S. employers, language problems, and the high unemployment level in the United States were all contributing factors. The refugees were concerned about family members left in Vietnam and needed to share with them financially. Awareness of "Western culture" did not mean automatic acceptance of it, nor did it produce a desire on the part of the Vietnamese to let go of their own cultural heritage.

According to McBee (1984), the Vietnamese, Chinese, Japanese, Koreans, and other Southeast Asian Americans are uniting as a political force to overcome social and economic barriers in the United States. The Vietnamese in the United States have formed nuclear community organizations for mutual support and for the preservation of cultural heritage. These mutual aid associations have created a sense of self-confidence and a firm belief in the future. Community life centers are used for public meetings, ceremonies, and cultural performances. Religious ceremonies, holiday celebrations, and social and cultural events help establish a sense of belonging and a sense of identity.

Child-Rearing Practices

In Vietnam, children are considered to be 1 year old at birth. In rural environments, children are generally delivered at home by midwives. Only married women or married female relatives are allowed to attend births or to assist (Montero, 1982).

Sons are more valued than daughters. This belief can be seen as a perpetuation of the centuries-old story of the origin of the Vietnamese people. According to legend, the Vietnamese people are the offspring of the Dragon King and the Fairy Queen, who produced 100 male children. One half of these offspring remained with their mother and went to the mountains to establish a matriarchy. The other half went with their father to the seashore to establish a patriarchy (Do, 1968). It is interesting to note that the Dragon King and the Fairy Queen produced only sons with which to begin the Vietnamese race.

By Western standards, Vietnamese children carry heavy family obligations. The eldest son is responsible for performing ancestor worship at home. Siblings do not kiss or even touch one another and are usually segregated by gender. Girls are under very strict supervision by family members. Educational achievement is stressed, and competition among the children for scholarly progress and success is fierce (N. B. Nguyen, 1982).

The Vietnamese child is trained to think of the family first and to subjugate personal desires and concerns. Parents control their children's behavior by appealing to the children's sense of obligation to others. If this sense of obligation is betrayed, a child may be locked outside the home, isolated from social life, shamed, scolded, or made to feel guilty (Morrow, 1987). According to Chan (1986), the use of pride and shame in Vietnamese families is related to the fact that all individual behavior is considered to reflect either positively or negatively on the entire family. Academic or occupational achievement promotes family pride, whereas disobedience, disrespect, or shirking responsibilities promote family shame.

Caplan, Choy, and Whitmore (1992) found, among Vietnamese students who were high achievers, no perceived discontinuity between family life and what went on in the classroom. By contrast, the Vietnamese children who were most acculturated to the U.S. culture did consistently poorer in school. Difficulties can readily be seen for Vietnamese children in schools in the United States. They face multiple problems of adjustment. The language barrier presents a major problem, but cultural differences appear to present the most difficult obstacles. In addition, it is difficult for Vietnamese parents to lend much support to their children in their academic endeavors because of lack of cultural understanding of Western ways and unfamiliarity with the English language.

Religious Practices

Approximately 90% of Vietnamese people practice some form of Buddhism or ancestor worship (Cohler, 1985). Buddhists try to live by five main precepts: no killing, no stealing, no sexual misconduct, no lying, and no drinking. The religious structure is not a separate entity, but a spirituality that pervades all aspects of society. The Vietnamese believe in Karma and rebirth; that is, they believe that an individual's life cycle is predetermined by good or bad deeds from a previous life. The goal is eventually to achieve spiritual liberation, or release from the perpetual life-and-rebirth cycle. Ancestors are worshipped for four generations after death. Commemoration of a death ceases with the fifth generation because of the belief that, by that time, the deceased either have been reborn on earth or have achieved heavenly bliss.

Buddhism, Confucianism, and Taoism have all influenced Vietnamese culture. All have contributed to the idea of harmony among persons and with nature. Buddhism stresses self-discipline and humility, a following of the "middle path." Respect for elders and a hierarchical rank, loyalty, family orientation, loss of face, shame, and regard for education have come from Confucianism. The avoidance of confrontation, an indirect approach to problem solving, patience, and simplicity are taught by Taoism. As a rule, the three religions are not mutually exclusive, and many beliefs are shared among them (Dung, 1984).

Religion for a Vietnamese is not a specific, closed tradition. It is an acceptance of many religions, based on the fact that all religions are complementary perspectives of human experience. Persons are to live in harmony with nature without striving to dominate it. What can be considered religious rituals or practices in the United States are part of daily life for the Vietnamese. The central room in a Vietnamese house is often a composite of religious area and living and sleeping quarters. Other evidence of this mixing of family life and religion is seen in the preferred custom of having a marriage take place in the home, rather than in a temple or pagoda (Do, 1968). Rutledge (1992) described a group of Vietnamese children in a Port Arthur, Texas, temple singing "Buddha loves me, this I know, for the Sutras tell me so."

Very few first-wave refugees who came to the United States were Buddhists. Although the Vietnamese Catholic population only comprised 10% of the total number of Vietnamese people, Catholics made up 40% of the refugees in 1975 (Montero, 1979). Do (1968) suggested that the few Buddhists willing to relocate in times of political strife may be reflective of the pessimistic and often fatalistic doctrine underlying the Buddhist philosophy.

Because Catholicism is also a part of the Vietnamese culture, immigrants to the United States have been able to continue the practice of this religion. The Vietnamese American population has even boosted the number of ordained priests in Louisiana (McBee, 1984). Vietnamese Catholics and Protestants in large Vietnamese communities are more likely than other religious groups to have chances to worship and participate in religious activities. The availability of ethnic religious services and social activities may have a positive impact on the well-being of the Vietnamese, but it can also have a negative impact on their attempt to acculturate. Vietnamese Catholics and Protestants tend to be less acculturated than other religious groups (Tran, 1992/93).

Family Structure and Dynamics

Traditionally, the family has been the basis of Vietnamese society. The family is the core social unit. The extended family is vitally important to the Vietnamese, as are ancestors. Elders not only are supported by children until their deaths but also are honored and respected for their age and wisdom. Elders, especially males who are heads of households (called *truong toc*), are senior in moral authority and expect deference from others. The extended family resides as a single unit with three or four generations under one roof (Lee & Rong, 1988).

Children remain with the family unit until they are married. Women marry between the ages of 15 and 25; men marry between the ages of 25 and 30. After her marriage, the woman becomes a part of her husband's family and transfers her allegiance and obedience to her spouse and his family. If she is widowed, her eldest son is viewed as the head of the family and is to be obeyed. Until her marriage, a woman is submissive to her father.

Traditionally, parents of both the husband-to-be and the wife-to-be give approval to the marriage. Divorce is legal but not a common practice among the Vietnamese. Most marital difficulties are handled internally by both sides of the family. Until 1959, polygamy was practiced by Vietnamese men. The first wife had primary responsibility for the family, then the second wife, and so forth. All family matters within the household are handled by the wife. The husband attends to all matters related to the outside world.

An extended family of several generations is the norm. The father is the head of the household and supports the family, and the mother manages the household and supervises the education of the children. Vietnamese couples usually have many children so that there will be many to provide for them when they get old. Specific roles are designated for family members, and interaction is structured. Females must be submissive; even widows must show deference to their eldest sons. The mother, as her child's first teacher, trains her child in right and wrong conduct. Children are expected to recognize their mistakes, acknowledge them, and take whatever consequences befall, as Buddha taught (Dung, 1984).

With immigration to the United States, the Vietnamese family has undergone tremendous changes. The woman's role has changed dramatically as the family seeks to cope with social and economic conditions. The extended family unit has often been split, adding to the adjustment problems facing the Vietnamese in the United States. Large families are still desirable, even in the United States, with one third of Vietnamese households containing 6 or more people. Some 10% of Vietnamese families in the United States are composed of 10 or more people. With immigration to the United States, only one marriage per person was accepted by authorities. This brought about the dissolution of subsequent marriages, but often the additional wives were informally accepted as household members of the first marriage. All members of the Vietnamese family are mutually and reciprocally obligated to the family unit.

Cultural Values and Attitudes

Vietnamese cultural values and attitudes are centered around the family unit. A strong emphasis is placed on group loyalty, filial piety, and obedience to elders (S. Nguyen, 1982). Many Vietnamese do relatively well in terms of economic adaptation and educational achievement in the United States because of the cultural values they brought with them, such as a strong belief in education and achievement, a cohesive family, and hard work (Caplan, Whitmore, & Choy, 1989).

The Vietnamese place a value on controlling their emotions in all situations. Impulsive behavior is to be avoided in an effort to promote harmony. Nonconfrontation is valued as a method of promoting consideration of others. The importance of the individual is insignificant. This attitude can be seen in the Vietnamese positive reinforcement of sacrificial behavior and denial of self-gratification.

The Vietnamese are casual in their social arrangements. They approach time in an unhurried, flexible manner. In contrast with this view of the Vietnamese as unhurried and casual, however, the Vietnamese refugees expect structure and predictability in social situations (S. Nguyen, 1982). Another indication of a need for structure is the fact that many refugees consider repetition and practice essential for educational progress. Auerbach (1991) reported that the Vietnamese tend to be more formal and reserved in their style of relating to other people. They "do not consider it polite to look someone straight in the eye or to disagree with them openly. They often smile or say 'yes,' when actually they are upset, so they will not hurt the other person's feelings" (p. 23).

The Vietnamese culture does not emphasize the autonomy of the individual. The family orientation of the Vietnamese promotes individuals with structured mental processes. As mentioned above, the Vietnamese also strive for a lack of outward emotional display of feelings. In an open, impulsive culture such as that of the United States, this conduct often makes the Vietnamese seem rather withdrawn and stoic by comparison. Moral virtue and showing respect for more knowledgeable or elderly people is essential for the Vietnamese. Upholding family pride and honor is extremely important, overriding the importance of the individual.

To demonstrate respect or high regard, a Vietnamese person will bow his or her head. When handing an object to a respected person, both hands are used to hold the object. Greetings are given by clasping one's hands in front of the chest. Vietnamese women never shake hands, even with one another; however, it has become acceptable in the United States for men to shake hands in greeting. To hold one's attention with direct eye contact while conversing is considered disrespectful (Montero, 1982).

The elderly are the only Vietnamese who can touch another's head publicly. This is acceptable only if the older person is touching a child's head. Two Vietnamese of the same gender, however, may hold hands in public or share a bed without the implication of homosexuality. Public kissing is not allowed (Montero, 1982; West, 1984).

The Vietnamese do not call to someone considered an equal with a beckoning, finger-up gesture without creating a provocation. The accepted gesture is to use the entire hand with fingers pointed down. Only animals or inferior people are signaled with a finger-up motion.

Implications

Many Vietnamese had no time to prepare psychologically for immigration to the United States. Others suffered trauma as a result of the Vietnam War, the escape process, and negative conditions in refugee camps. As a result, many psychological disorders have been found among the refugees (Hawthorne, 1982). These disorders are difficult to counsel because of the obligation of the Vietnamese to handle problems within the family framework. To seek outside help is to bring embarrassment and shame to the family (Sue & Sue, 1990).

Bromley (1988) found that refugee youths expressed problems addressing themes of isolation and estrangement, feelings that the values of the homeland are useless, a sense of being devalued in the United States, the loss of power, and the pain of affiliation to a new reference group. Chung and Kagawa-Singer (1993) reported that the Vietnamese at high risk for developing psychiatric disorders are those who

- Suffered greater family loss or separation
- Spent the longest time in refugee camps
- Suffered multiple traumatic experiences
- Are unemployed
- Have the least education or are least English proficient
- Have fewer emotional and material resources

Tung (1985) recommended that counseling with the Vietnamese should be of short duration, limited in scope to the problem, goal directed, actively supportive, and focused on the present and the immediate future. Lee (1988) recommended a chronological approach to counseling that takes into account the client's life in the homeland, the escape process, and life after arrival in the United States.

The Vietnamese disdain for the exuberant lifestyle of members of the dominant culture of the United States must be viewed in an appropriate manner before effective helping can occur. Displays of respect, restraint of public display of feelings and emotions, lack of eye contact, and reluctance to verbalize a problem should not be construed as signs of distrust or reluctance on the part of the Vietnamese. It is possible that a Vietnamese client views the counselor as a teacher, in which case he or she will be waiting for the knowledgeable teacher to convey directions and wisdom.

Because of the nature of the Vietnamese and a reluctance to seek help for problems outside the family unit, the opportunity to counsel them will perhaps be most readily available (or only available) within the school setting. The close-knit organization of the family warrants the use of family therapy whenever possible and appropriate. In cases where the family is experiencing turmoil because of structural realignments, the counselor should make extensive assessments before interventions are begun.

Language barriers create many problems for the Vietnamese. In a school setting, language difficulties accentuate the strangeness that a student may already feel because of the differences in learning style, classroom structure and management, and curriculum format. An educator must be diligent in explaining these differences and constantly aware that styles of schooling in the United States often seem disrespectful to the Vietnamese.

Parents must also be considered when one is counseling students who are experiencing difficulties. Vietnamese parents' concern with their children's success in school is often difficult for them to communicate and can cause them much stress and frustration. An effort to orient parents as well as students to the educational structure and system of the dominant culture of the United States seems necessary for effective education. Understanding the composition and importance of the Vietnamese family is, perhaps, the most important component in the education of the Vietnamese. As the Vietnamese become more involved in life in the United States and familiar with the dominant culture, there may be a rejection of their own cultural heritage or a lack of pride and self-confidence. Educators and counselors must be sensitive to areas such as intergenerational and cultural conflicts that arise between Vietnamese parents and children.

Matsuoka (1993) reported on qualitative differences in adjustment among Vietnamese refugees:

- Men have more mental health problems than women; men were found to be significantly more angry than women.
- Older people have a more difficult time adjusting than their younger counterparts.
- Married people possess more positive acculturation attitudes than single people.

- Highly educated people have a more difficult time adjusting to life in the United States than those with less education.
- Christians experience less displacement and rolelessness than Buddhists and members of other Eastern religious groups. Members of Christian churches possess more Western traits and show fewer signs of helplessness and alienation.
- The Vietnamese who believe that religion is an important and integral part of their lives have a more difficult time adjusting than those for whom religion is less important. Those who believe that their fate is predetermined feel more helpless and are less motivated to evoke change.

An educator or counselor must be aware of, and sensitive to, these factors if teaching and counseling are to be helpful. Exhibiting an appreciation for the differences in the dominant culture and the Vietnamese culture can go far toward developing trust and respect.

Questions for Review and Reflection

1. How might the circumstances surrounding the Vietnam War and the immigration of the Vietnamese to the United States influence their degree of acculturation?

2. What were the major cultural difficulties experienced by the refugees who fled South Vietnam for the United States after 1976? Were these difficulties caused by Vietnamese resistance to acculturation or by the resettlement policies of Vietnamese sponsors in the United States?

3. Why did many citizens of the United States view the immigration of the Vietnamese as an unpopular event? What effect did this have on the Vietnamese?

4. What differences exist between the act of smiling among Vietnamese and among members of the dominant culture? What are the implications of these differences for education or counseling?

5. What cultural beliefs are reflected in Vietnamese art? How might these values influence the work of educators or counselors working with the Vietnamese?

6. How might the Vietnamese practice of determining age (a child is 1 year old at birth) affect age requirements and restrictions in the dominant culture?

7. How do children's obligations to the family differ for the Vietnamese in the United States and members of the dominant culture in the United States?

8. What are the implications of the way teachers are treated in Vietnam for the way the Vietnamese in the United States may interact with educators or counselors?

9. Why are the Vietnamese often unable to help their children with academic endeavors? How can educators or counselors facilitate Vietnamese parental involvement with academic endeavors?

10. What is the influence of Karma in explaining the behaviors of the Vietnamese?

References

Asian Americans: A status report. (1990). Washington, DC: General Accounting Office.

Auerbach, S. (1991). *Vietnamese Americans.* Vero Beach, FL: Rourke.

Bromley, M. A. (1988). Identity as a central adjustment issue for the Southeast Asian unaccompanied refugee minor. *Child and Youth Care Quarterly, 17*(2), 104-113.

Caplan, N., Choy, M. H., & Whitmore, J. K. (1992, February). Indochinese refugee families and academic achievement. *Scientific American,* pp. 36-42.

Caplan, N., Whitmore, J. K., & Choy, M. H. (1989). *The boat people and achievement in America.* Ann Arbor: University of Michigan.

Chan, S. (1986). Parents of exceptional Asian children. In M. K. Kitano & P. C. Chinn (Eds.), *Exceptional Asian youth* (pp. 36-53). Washington, DC: ERIC.

Chung, R. C., & Kagawa-Singer, M. (1993). Predictors of psychological distress among Southeast Asian refugees. *Social Science and Medicine, 36*(5), 631-639.

Cohler, L. (1985, March). New Americans keep old faiths alive. *Scholastic Update,* pp. 17-18.

Cravens, R. B., & Bornemann, T. H. (1990). Refugee camps in countries of first asylum and the North American resettlement process. In W. H. Holtzman & T. H. Bornemann (Eds.), *Mental health of immigrants and refugees* (pp. 38-50). Austin: University of Texas Press.

Do, V. M. (1968). *Viet Nam.* New York: Paragon.

Dung, T. N. (1984). Understanding Asian families: A Vietnamese perspective. *Children Today, 13,* 10-12.

Freeman, J. A. (1989). *Hearts of sorrow: Vietnamese American lives.* Stanford, CA: Stanford University.

Haines, D. W. (1985). *Refugees in the United States.* Westport, CT: Greenwood.

Hawthorne, L. (1982). *Refugee: The Vietnamese experience.* Melbourne, Australia: Oxford University Press.

Lee, E. (1988). Cultural factors in working with Southeast Asian refugee adolescents. *Journal of Adolescence, 11,* 167-179.

Lee, E. S., & Rong, X. (1988). The educational and economic achievement of Asian Americans. *Elementary School Journal, 9,* 545-560.

Liu, W. T., & Muralta, A. K. (1977). The Vietnamese in America: Perilous flights, uncertain future. *Bridge: An Asian American Perspective, 5,* 42-50.

Matsuoka, J. (1993). Demographic characteristics as determinants in qualitative differences in the adjustment of Vietnamese refugees. *Journal of Social Service Research, 17*(3/4), 1-21.

McBee, S. (1984, April). Asian Americans: Are they making the grade? *U.S. News & World Report,* pp. 41-47.

Montero, D. (1979). *Vietnamese Americans: Patterns of resettlement and socioeconomic adaptation in the United States.* Boulder, CO: Westview.

Montero, D. (1982, February). *A mutual challenge.* Paper presented to the U.S. Department of Health, Education and Welfare Region III Task Force.

Morrow, R. D. (1987). Cultural differences: Be aware. *Academic Therapy, 23,* 143-149.

Nguyen, N. B. (1982). *School adjustment of Indochinese students.* Washington, DC: Georgetown University Press.

Nguyen, S. (1982). The psychosocial adjustment and the mental health of Southeast Asia refugees. *Psychiatric Journal of the University of Ottawa, 7,* 26-38.

Nguyen-Hong-Nhiem, L., & Halpern, J. M. (1989). *The Far East comes near.* Amherst: University of Massachusetts Press.

Rodriguez, N. P., & Urrutia-Rojas, X. (1990). Impact of recent refugee migration to Texas: A comparison of Southeast Asian and Central American newcomers. In W. H. Holtzman & T. H. Bornemann (Eds.), *Mental health of immigrants and refugees* (pp. 263-278). Austin: University of Texas.

Rutledge, P. J. (1992). *The Vietnamese experience.* Bloomington: Indiana University Press.

Sue, D. W., & Sue, D. (1990). *Counseling the culturally different: Theory and practice.* New York: John Wiley.

Tran, T. V. (1992/93). Sociodemographic backgrounds and acculturation in a sample of Vietnamese in the United States. *Journal of Applied Social Science, 17*(1), 31-41.

Tung, T. M. (1985). Psychiatric care for Southeast Asians: How different is different? In *Southeast Asian Mental Health.* Washington, DC: U.S. Department of Health and Human Services.

U.S. Bureau of the Census. (1991). *Statistical abstract of the United States.* Washington, DC: Government Printing Office.

U.S. Committee for Refugees. (1988). *Refugee Reporter, 9,* 1.

West, B. E. (1984). New students from Southeast Asia. *Education Digest, 49,* 32-35.

Whitfield, D. J. (1976). *Historical and cultural dictionary of Vietnam.* Metuchen, NJ: Scarecrow.

9

Mexican Americans

Mexican Americans are the second largest ethnic group in the United States, numbering about 13.5 million (U.S. Bureau of the Census, 1991). Mexican Americans constitute about 60% of all Latinos in the United States. Becerra (1988) reported that approximately 86% of Mexican Americans live in the five southwestern states of California, Texas, Arizona, Colorado, and New Mexico. Valencia (1991) projected that, by the year 2060, the total Latino population will number 54.2 million and surpass the African American population (projected to be 53.7 million) as the largest ethnic group in the United States. The Mexican American culture is a mix of Spanish, Indian, and American cultures. The Mexican American identifies with all three but is set apart from all three cultures by language, race, and religion.

Among the choices for identity for individuals in this culture are Mexican American, Chicano, Tejano, Californio, La Raza, Mestizo, Spanish American, Spanish-surnamed, Native American, and Spanish-speaking. *Mexican American* implies that anyone who might identify with the population has origins in what is now Mexico, a fact that may or may not be true. Many Hispanics trace their lineage to the Spanish colonists and eschew the term *Mexican*. *Chicano* was once used as a derisive term and is therefore still offensive to some, but it has become a source of pride for social and political activists in recent decades. Becerra (1988) indicated that the Chicano label is often used to denote a politically alert and active American of Mexican descent. *La Raza* translates literally as "the race" and includes all peoples of the Americas with some Spanish cultural roots (Meier & Rivera, 1981); it is also widely used as a source of cultural pride. *Mestizo* refers to a person of mixed Indian and European ancestry, either racially or culturally. *Spanish American* denies the Native American ancestry and culture, whereas *Native American* denies the Spanish ancestry and cultural contributions. Those who choose to use terms such as *Spanish-speaking* or *Spanish-surnamed* have been considered by activists to be more acculturated into the dominant Anglo culture. Thus, although those in this population share some common experiences and culture, they do not share a common identity.

Matute-Bianchi (1986) identified five major categories of ethnic identity within the Mexican American student population:

1. Recent Mexican immigrant (Mexican born, Spanish speaking, "Mexicano" identity)
2. Mexican oriented (bilingual, strong ties to both Mexico and the United States, disavows identity as "Mexican American")
3. Mexican American (born in the United States, assimilated, prefers English over Spanish)
4. Chicano (identifies as Mexican or Mexicano, alienated from mainstream-oriented activities)
5. Cholo (marginal, disaffected, frequently associated with gangs)

For this chapter, the term *Mexican American* is used to refer to a citizen of the United States either by birth or naturalization who is of Mexican descent, usually of mixed European (largely Spanish) and Native American (Indian) origins (Meier & Rivera, 1981). This term also includes those Mexicans and Native Americans whose homeland is the American Southwest and Texas and whose culture and language are Spanish influenced.

The criteria for identification as Mexican American have changed from census to census (e.g., born in Mexico, parents born in Mexico, Spanish speaking, Spanish surname). Defining Mexican Americans is a complex task involving not only its varied history, language, nativity, and social and economic integration in the United States but also their own perception of ethnicity (Hurtado & Arce, 1987). The main problem in defining the U.S. population of Mexican descent is its heterogeneity combined with its sociopolitical history.

Arias (1986) called the rapid growth of the Hispanic population in the United States one of the "most compelling social developments in the last 25 years" (p. 27). No longer a rural group, they represent a significant number of metropolitan residents.

Historically, Mexican Americans are a conquered people, beginning with Spain's invasion of Mexico in the 1600s and ending with the annexation of

Mexican territories by the United States in 1848 (Kiskadden & Rossell, 1979). It is important to understand that they were living in what today constitutes the Southwestern United States before the Manifest Destiny philosophy made them a minority group with minimal rights. As the Anglo population expanded West, settlers came to live within the Mexican territories and at that time expressed loyalty to the Mexican culture. For some 10 to 15 years, they lived peacefully and in cooperation with their Mexican neighbors. Conflict developed as the Mexicans struggled internally over governmental rule and the United States became anxious to increase its territory. Many Mexicans fought with Americans to achieve an independent state of Texas but soon found themselves foreigners as the Mexican government ceded the southwestern territories to the United States under the Treaty of Guadalupe Hidalgo. Hence, they became Mexican by birth, language, and culture and citizens of the United States by the might of arms (Ortego, 1973).

For the Mexican American, immigration from Mexico is motivated out of a desire for change and opportunity. A heavy value is placed on the need for change and achievement. Prejudice and discrimination against Mexican Americans, however, shut off many usual avenues to achievement. Damaging stereotypes, such as Mexicans being lazy, passive, and failure-oriented, have been reinforced by society and the media. These stereotypes have become internalized by some Mexican Americans who have lost contact with their ancestral culture. In contrast, Mexican Americans who are integrated with their traditional culture have a more positive image of themselves and of their group. Consequently, these persons are in a better position to make headway against prejudice and discrimination and thereby increase their chance for success.

As it is important for Mexican Americans not to disregard their heritage, it is also important for the Anglo culture to regard this culture as valuable. As Anglos expect Mexican Americans to learn the dominant culture, it is also important for Anglos to possess an understanding of the Mexican American culture.

Acculturation

Acculturation is best described as an adjustment process whereby, as a result of sociocultural interactions, a person acquires the customs of an alternative culture. Mexican Americans today have a low degree of acculturation as a result of two factors. First, they are descendants of relatively recent immigrants or are immigrants themselves. Second, most other immigrant groups with large numbers of acculturated members arrived in one or more waves and subsequently successfully acculturated; Mexican immigration has been more like a steady stream, inhibiting the acculturation of residents of longer standing.

Alvarez (1973) described Mexican Americans as

a creation of the imperial conquest of one nation by another through military force. Our people were thrown into a new set of circumstances, and began to evolve new modes of thought and action in order to survive making Mexican American culture different from the culture of Mexicans in Mexico. Because we live in different circumstances we have evolved different cultural modes; just as we are neither identical to "Anglos" in the United States nor to Mexicans in Mexico, we nevertheless incorporate into our ethos much from both societies. This is because we respond to problems of existence that confront us in unique ways, distinct from the way in which Anglos and Mexicans experience them. (p. 938)

Hernandez and Carlquist-Hernandez (1979) used a three-category system to classify Mexican Americans' degree of acculturation.

1. The *traditional* Mexican American identifies strongly with family, community, ethnic group, and members of the extended family.
2. The *duotraditional* Mexican American is semiurban, ethnically heterogeneous, and has moderate ties to his or her family.
3. The *atraditional* Mexican American has been assimilated into the community at large, has few familial ties, is urban, and speaks English as his or her primary language.

Chavez and Roney (1990) used the term *deculturated* to describe marginal Mexican Americans. Deculturated individuals are out of contact with both the culture of their heritage and that of the larger, encasing society. They are people set apart, not just in a spatial sense, but also in a social and psychological sense. They are literally rootless except for the small patch of territory they claim is theirs to defend.

Although Mexican Americans may remain separate, they share some patterns of living of Anglo American society. The demands of life in the United States have required basic modifications of the Mexican cultural tradition. Materially, Mexican Americans are not much different from Anglos. They have acquired English in varying degrees, and their Spanish has become noticeably Anglicized. Although the original organization of the family has persisted, major changes have occurred in patterns of traditional authority, as well as in child-rearing and courtship practices. Still, the Mexican American retains the subtler characteristics of Mexican heritage,

particularly in the conception of time and in other fundamental value orientations, as well as the mode of participation in interpersonal relations.

Many of the most acculturated Mexican Americans have become largely
Anglo American in their way of living, but they retain fluent Spanish and a
knowledge of their traditional culture. They maintain an identification with
their own heritage while participating in Anglo American culture. Mexican
American culture represents the most constructive and effective means its
members have to cope with their changed natural and social environment.
They exchange old ways for new ways only if the new ways appear to be
more meaningful and rewarding than the old, and then only if they are given
full opportunity to acquire and use the new ways.

Poverty and Economic Concerns

Mexican Americans are an economically disadvantaged group. By standards of the dominant culture, they have experienced negligible social
progress even though they have lived in the Southwest United States longer
than most other ethnic groups. As a result of a particular approach to life and
distinct cultural values, which are usually viewed as the opposite of Anglo
American values, Mexican Americans have been prevented from succeeding
in the United States because of discrimination by Anglo society (Duran &
Bernard, 1973). Mexican Americans find themselves markedly behind in the
total amount of education, occupations, income, housing, political representation, and professional identification. At the time of the 1980 census,
19% of Mexican-origin families lived below the poverty line, in comparison
with 9% of Anglo families. Miller, Nicolau, Orr, Valdivieso, and Walker
(1988) reported that, in 1985, Hispanic per capita income had fallen below
that of African Americans, with $6,613 for Hispanics, $6,840 for African
Americans, and $11,671 for Whites and Asian Americans.

Segregation in the Southwest included the establishment of separate
schools for Mexican American children. This practice, continued until the
1970s, left a heritage of barely literate generations, underfunded school
districts, and high dropout rates. In 1985, the average number of school years
completed by Hispanics 25 years old or older was 11.5, whereas the general
population had completed 12.6 years. In 1980, 74% of all 17-year-olds in the
United States had high school diplomas, whereas only 40% of Hispanics had
them (Arias, 1986).

Social scientists who study Mexican Americans invariably end up describing poor Mexican Americans. Those qualities that have been invariably
attributed to Mexican Americans as part of their ethnicity are actually those

of people in poverty but regularly cut across ethnic lives. Despite contributing to the gross national product, paying taxes, and actively supporting U.S. war activities since 1848, Mexican Americans struggle to be acknowledged as worthy, productive individuals with equal rights.

Mexican Americans have always been conscious of the conditions of poverty, disease, hunger, and ignorance in which they live and have always been conscious of the fact that they were forced to live under such conditions in an exploitative society. The problems are "caused by the Anglo society and are not found within the culture itself" (Duran & Bernard, 1973, p. 2).

History of Oppression

Mexican Americans have been reliving the epitome of the immigrant experience in the United States. They come out of distress; they speak an alien tongue; they suffer the uncertainties of the newcomer; they are exploited by their own countrymen who contract their labor and are then exploited again by the employer to whom they are peddled; they are the underclass on whom others look down; they are disproportionally underpaid, uneducated, unacculturated, and unwanted.

In the years following Mexican independence from Spain in 1821, the northern areas of the new nation (America's Southwest) were centers of unrest. In brief wars and a series of conflicts that fell just short of being "official" wars, Mexican Americans were the "enemy." The first war was the War for Texas Independence in 1835; the second was the Mexican War of 1846. The war between Mexico and the United States formally ended with the Treaty of Guadalupe Hidalgo in 1848, but that did not end the actual fighting. Force was used by the Anglos to gain control, and force was used by the Mexicans to retaliate. In New Mexico, an abortive rebellion followed the American occupation.

In the 20th century, during the Mexican Revolution of 1910–1920, hostility between the two countries culminated in the occupation of Veracruz by U.S. forces in 1914 and the famous "Punitive Expedition" into Chihuahua led by Pershing in search of Pancho Villa after the latter's raid on Columbus, New Mexico. Because Mexico was the foe, Mexican Americans suffered indignities.

The Anglo Americans who began to enter New Mexico found that commerce and access to the natural resources of the land were the means to power and wealth. Within a few years after the American conquest, Anglo American and Mexican American merchants were found in virtually all the larger Mexican American villages. The Anglo Americans, through their knowledge of business techniques, were able to eliminate much of their Mexican American competition.

The Santa Fe Ring, a political machine put together by Anglo Americans with Mexican American allies, used violence, manipulation of the land tax, and political chicanery to wrest control of most of the land grants from the villagers by the 1900s. With the erosion of their land holdings, plus the Depression and the drought of the 1930s, the Mexican Americans had to depend on the welfare and employment programs of the New Deal. They lost not only their land and their independence but their pride and self-confidence as well.

In the Southwest during the Depression, local political leaders, welfare organizations, and law enforcement agencies repatriated many Mexican Americans to Mexico, including many who were legal residents and married to U.S. citizens. This exile and a similar roundup in the 1950s sowed permanent seeds of distrust and dislike among Mexican Americans toward American agencies.

Much of the distress in northern New Mexico is a result of the Mexican Americans' loss of ownership or access to the natural resources of the region that have passed into Anglo American or U.S. government hands. Most governmental programs designed to reduce poverty have failed because they have struggled with the symptoms, rather than addressed the fundamental cause of poverty—namely, the alienation of the Mexican American people from the land of northern New Mexico.

In addition to their loss of land, Mexican Americans have been neglected by Anglo American historians whose interest has focused more on the romantic periods of Spanish exploration, conquest, and settlement than on the cultural story of the Mexican American inhabitants of the Southwest. Historians have preferred to dwell on the westward movement of Anglo American frontier people, rather than on the adjustment problems of Mexican Americans. Chroniclers have overlooked Mexican American political and military leaders, explorers, pioneers, ranchers, and businesspeople who played important roles in the history of the Southwest.

Language and the Arts

Many Mexican Americans are bilingual and speak Spanish not only to communicate with foreign-born relatives but habitually and as a matter of tradition. In some areas, some Mexican Americans speak no Spanish, and in other areas some speak no English, but the majority speak both. For years, the state legislature of New Mexico was officially bilingual. The right to speak Spanish was an inalienable right guaranteed to a conquered people. This symbol has gained significance because the right to speak Spanish has been suppressed by public school systems, especially in the Southwest.

In his study of the political integration of Mexican Americans, Garcia (1987) found that almost 70% have no English ability. This statistic seems to support the work of LaBrack and Leonard (1984), who reported that most Mexican American mothers speak Spanish to their children and that Spanish is the dominant language of church activities. This further explains why many Mexican American children have difficulty with English in school and why children must interpret for parents in business outside the home.

The historical suppression of Spanish has tended to degrade the quality of the Spanish that is spoken. Many immigrants to the United States are illiterate agricultural workers who speak a variety of rural Spanish. Years of exposure to the dominant culture has meant that English words have been adapted to Spanish syntax.

Spanish, like any other language, is more than a means of communication; it is the embodiment of a culture. As such, it offers a measure of cohesion, a reason for cooperation, a sense of security, and even a point of pride.

In addition to formal verbal communication, there is verbal play. Mexican Americans "rely heavily on jokes, jocular talk, and in-group humor to relieve tensions and stress caused by cultural conflicts. Jokes are an important means of communication within families and among close friends" (Castro, 1982, p. 277).

The artists of Mexico gained inspiration from the spirit of freedom and the fervent patriotism brought by the revolution. They were inspired as well by a fresh realization of the wealth of Mexico's cultural past. The painters and sculptors avidly studied the great carvings and frescoes created in the ancient civilization of the Maya, the powerful sculptures left by the Aztecs, and the murals found in Mexico's many Spanish Colonial churches and shrines. The primary goal of the painters was to give birth to a new national art as noble as that of the ancient Indians.

In the 1920s, the country's first major exposition of native arts and crafts was organized. The entire range of Mexico's vibrant profusion of folk art, as diverse as pottery and papier-mâché figures and ceramics and lacquerwork, were brought together. The effect inspired a new respect for the country's rich culture. The government was then persuaded to let Diego Rivera and other artists paint murals in government buildings. The painters responded to the challenges of preaching the revolutionary gospel in paint and of restoring the mural to its high place in Mexican art.

The contemporary art movement was an aggressive social protest criticizing the ills of the dominant American culture and the exalted self-worth of that culture (Meier & Rivera, 1981). It also has deep roots in traditional pre-Hispanic and colonial Mexico, with some influence of American art in content and form.

Mural art depicting the Mexican American experience in the United States can be found in many major U.S. cities, particularly in the Southwest. Mural art has two purposes: (a) to teach history and (b) to serve as a voice against oppression. The mural is "an art of advocacy, and in many cases it was intended to change consciousness and promote political action" (Goldman, 1982, p. 111). These murals portray such cultural experiences as violence, "progress" as viewed from the Mexican American perspective, and the negative images of Mexican American culture portrayed in U.S. movies, rodeos, and art. The three most prominent muralists were Diego Rivera, who idolized the Aztec Indians from whom Mexican Americans are descended; José Clemente Orozco, a *hispanista* who embraced the Spanish culture more tenaciously than his own; and David Alfaro Siqueiros, who "used indigenous motifs as allegories or metaphors for contemporary struggles" (Goldman, 1982, p. 116).

Racism and Prejudice

Prejudice, as it presents itself to society, consists of overt acts that deny equal status or opportunity to people because of their racial, religious, or ethnic identity. The term *prejudice* is also used in a specialized sense to describe an individual state of mind or attitude.

Dwerkin (1964), in a study of 280 Mexican Americans in southern California, found significant differences between Mexican Americans born in the United States and those born in Mexico, both in their stereotypes of Anglos and in their own self-images. In general, the U.S.-born Mexican Americans held more negative attitudes toward Anglos and toward themselves than did the Mexican-born. Similarly, Buriel and Vasquez (1982), assessing the stereotypes of persons of Mexican descent held by first-, second-, and third-generation Mexicans, found that, with each successive generation, the stereotype became more negative and more closely approximated the Anglos' stereotypes of persons of Mexican descent.

The range in skin color of Mexican Americans is from white through mestizo and mulatto brown to black. Darker Mexicans typically experience more prejudice and racism in their own country, stemming from their descent. This factor is magnified for Mexican Americans in the United States because of racism and prejudice based on skin color (Ruiz & Padilla, 1977).

In a study by Casas and Atkinson (1981), undergraduate students at the University of California at Santa Barbara were asked to indicate the characteristics that most people would use to describe a Mexican student. The 10 most stereotypical statements generated were poor personal hygiene habits, comes from a violent family, acts defensively when confronted, has a low grade point average, does not come from a middle-class family, does not accept political opinions of others, does not use cocaine, does not plan to attend graduate school, is religious, and does not complete assignments on time.

The Mexican American is representative of a true underclass in the dominant Anglo culture. The dominant culture wants Mexican Americans to speak English but at the same time segregates them into barrios. Anglos expect Mexican Americans to be more like Anglo Americans but will not fully accept them into Anglo society because of distorted stereotypes.

Acculturation among middle-class Mexican Americans was accelerated after World War II. The rapidly expanding Mexican American middle class sensed that acceptance depended on an ability to speak English well, to secure a university or high school degree, to belong to the proper civic clubs, to live in a house in a middle- or upper-class neighborhood, and to maintain Anglo American lifestyles. For many, the attempt to reconcile traditional ties with current pressures led to severe emotional and personal conflicts.

Sociopolitical Factors

Mexican American professionals entered politics to advance their careers. They were defined as approved Mexican American leaders but were denied the power to alter local politics. *La Orden de Hijos de America* (The Order of Sons of America) was founded in 1921 in San Antonio. It was the forerunner of the League of United Latin American Citizens (LULAC), established in Texas in 1928, to demand social and political equality. Today, LULAC has become the Mexican American equivalent of both the Rotary and Kiwanis Clubs. The organization focuses on patriotic, social, and charitable programs to accelerate and smooth Mexican American social mobility into the U.S. mainstream.

Following World War II, the California-born Community Service Organization (CSO) became important and meaningful. The prime objective of the CSO was to get large numbers of Mexican Americans to register and to vote. Two other political groups founded in the 1950s developed similar patterns of political actions. The Mexican American Political Association (MAPA), founded in California in 1958, and the Political Association of Spanish Speaking Organizations (PASSO), organized in Texas, were formed to negotiate with, influence, and/or pressure the political system at the party level.

By far, the most organized Mexican Americans today are in the labor movement. They form a substantial part of the membership of many unions and hold many important policy-level leadership positions.

In the 1960s, many nationwide factors contributed to social unrest. Among these were the influence of the civil rights movement, the political activities of the Kennedy family, the programs of President Johnson's war on poverty, and the appearance of two Mexican American leaders—Cesar Chavez and Reis Lopez Tijerina.

In 1968, high school students began a series of strikes that started in California and then flickered across the entire Southwest. The protest was directed, most of all, against the use of schools to Anglicize Mexican students. Out of the student movements in the late 1960s emerged the "Chicano" movement. As used by students and young people in the barrios, the term *Chicano* refers to an individual committed to the Chicano move- ment. In general, it is associated with the physical and spiritual liberation of the Mexican American people from poverty, welfare, unemployment, a self-image of inferiority, and Anglo American dominance.

The first urban upheavals to involve Mexican Americans were the Los Angeles riots of the early 1970s. Representatives from almost every major Mexican American organization in the United States came to march, protest, fraternize, and discuss the disproportionately high rates at which Mexican Americans were drafted into the army and killed or wounded in Vietnam. Mexican Americans found themselves charged, beaten, and jailed by mem- bers of the Los Angeles Sheriff's Department. The indignation was height- ened by the murder, by deputies, of Ruben Salazar, the most prominent Mexican American journalist in the United States. Out of these events emerged barrio community organizations. Barrio organizations are commit- ted to the improvement of communities through planned programs in hous- ing, economic development, health services, social services, youth programs, worker development, and education.

Child-Rearing Practices

During the early years when children are young, the Mexican American home is usually child centered. Both parents tend to be permissive and indulgent with the younger children. Panitz, McConchie, Sauber, and Fon- seca (1983) observed that "the male child is overindulged and accorded greater status than the female" (p. 37). Children receive training in respon- sibility by being assigned tasks according to their age and ability. Much of a child's self-esteem is related to how he or she perceives self and how others perceive him or her carrying out assigned family responsibilities.

The results of a study by McKenzie, Salis, Nada, Broyles, and Nelson (1992) suggest that Mexican American children tend to spend more time in the presence of adults, to play with fewer action toys, and thus to be less physically active than Anglo children. Differences in patterns of behavior between male and female children are taught implicitly and explicitly from infancy. The male is taught how to think and act like a man; the female is taught how to think and act like a woman. At the onset of adolescence, the difference in patterns of behavior between boys and girls becomes even more markedly apparent. The female is likely to remain much closer to the home and to be protected and guarded in her contact with others beyond the family. Through her relationships with her mother and other female relatives, she is prepared for the role of wife and mother. The adolescent male, in contrast, following the model of his father, is given much more freedom to go and come as he chooses and is encouraged to gain much worldly knowledge and experience outside the home in preparation for the time when he will assume the role of husband and father (Mirandé, 1985).

Religious Practices

Daniels (1990) reported that Mexican Americans are predominantly Roman Catholic. The Catholic Church viewed Mexican American Catholicism as weak and without commitment to faith (Mirandé, 1985). In an attempt to "Americanize" the church, an attempt was made to "Americanize" the Mexican American. For example, Masses were not offered in Spanish, and Catholic schools did not offer bilingual education.

With the shift in social position after World War II, the Mexican American tie to Catholicism was loosened as many began to join Protestant denominations. The Pentecostals especially gained ground among both urban workers and rural villagers.

The church is the center of Mexican Americans' faith. As Mexican Americans are settling into smaller communities, they are beginning to establish their own churches. The Mexican American worship service may be informal, with guitars, accordions, maracas, tambourines, and bongo drums.

Traditional native Mexican American beliefs hold that fate is determined by the gods and that a reciprocal relationship exists between humans and the gods. Some believe that the body contains multiple souls, divine forces, or animistic centers. One force, known as *tonalli*, facilitates interactions between humans, nature, and the supernatural. The tonalli, believed to be located at the top of one's head, can determine a person's temperament, future behavior, and fate (Villarruel & de Montellano, 1992).

Turner (1982) found that, in addition to participation in the Catholic Mass, many Mexican American women keep home altars. These home altars are "distinctive because they represent a personal, private, and most importantly, a creative source of religious experience" (p. 309). Objects typically seen on these altars include statues of the Virgin Mary and the Great Mother of Mexico, the Sacred Heart, and Jesus. According to Turner, the presence of body images "is an indication of the essential desire to bring spiritual and physical, social and profane realms together" (p. 318). Candles symbolize the light of faith, the active acknowledgment of the relationship between the human and the divine. Photographs and statues of political figures also grace these altars. The pictures and statues represent many relationships, and the women who build them are compared to the Virgin Mary, prayerfully interceding for those represented.

Although levels of religious belief, commitment, and actual practice vary greatly among Mexican Americans, it does appear that Catholicism historically has had, and still does have, a powerful influence on the lives of Mexican Americans.

Family Structure and Dynamics

There is no single Mexican American family pattern based on one unique traditional culture. There are literally millions of Mexican American families, all differing significantly from one another along a variety of dimensions. Significant regional, historical, political, socioeconomic, acculturation, and assimilation factors result in a multitude of family patterns of living and coping with each other and with their Anglo environment. These patterns vary in accordance with recency of immigration, place of residence, socioeconomic status, degree of intermarriage, age, urbanization, and employment of women outside the home (Mirandé, 1985).

Among Mexican Americans, the family is the core of thinking and behavior and is the center from which the view of the world extends. Even with respect to identification, the Mexican American self-identity is likely to take second place to the family. Becerra (1988) described family roles of Mexican Americans as more warm and emotional than those of Anglos.

A Mexican American in need of emotional support, guidance, food, or money expects and is expected to turn to family first to meet such needs. A Mexican American may seek help from others only when absolutely no other alternative is available. The strength of the family in providing security to its members is sometimes expressed through a sharing of material things with other relatives even when one might have precious little to meet one's own immediate needs.

Because of the patriarchal nature of the culture, relatives on the father's side of the family may be considered more important than those on the mother's side. Among extended family members there is often much communication, visiting, sharing, and closeness. It is possible that a family may sever all relations with one of its members if that individual, through personal behavior, brings shame or dishonor to the family.

The husband and father is the autocratic head of the household. He tends to remain aloof and independent from the rest of the family. All family members are expected to be respectful of him and to accede to his will or direction. Should he misuse his authority in the family, he will lose respect within the community (Panitz et al., 1983).

In relating to his children, the father frequently serves as disciplinarian. During the children's early years, the father is often permissive, warm, and close. This changes significantly as each child reaches puberty. At this time, the father's behavior toward his children becomes much more reserved, authoritarian, and demanding of respect.

An understanding of the concept of *machismo* is important to an understanding of the use of authority in the family. Mirandé (1988) identified the positive traits of machismo as bravery, courage, self-defense, responsibility, respect, altruism, pride, protection, steadfastness, individualism, androgyny, and honor.

The wife and mother is supposed to be completely devoted to her husband and children. Her role is to serve the needs of her husband, to support his actions and decisions, and to take care of the home and children. Mirandé (1977) described the Chicano woman as the center of the family and the mainstay of the culture. The mother tends to perpetuate the language and values of the culture of origin and is usually the source of warmth and nurturance within the home.

Mexican Americans use an extended family structure that includes godparents (*compradazgo*), who ensure the welfare and religious education of the children. Choosing the proper godparents is essential because "it link[s] the families through the child" (LaBrack & Leonard, 1984, p. 531). Traditional godparents assume serious obligations toward their godchildren and take them into their own households whenever necessary. By extension, godparents become honorary family members. Like the traditional family, the choosing of godparents has been declining, particularly in cities where pressures on Mexican Americans to acculturate are greater and where the dynamics of urban life dilute traditional practices.

Cultural Values and Attitudes

Historical evidence emphasizes the cultural variation among Mexican Americans across time and geographic areas. For the Mexican American, material objects are usually necessities and not ends in themselves. Work is viewed as a necessity for survival, but not as a value in itself. Much higher value is assigned to other life activities in the Mexican culture. Through physical and mental well-being and through an ability to experience, in response to the environment, emotional feelings and to express these to one another and share these, a person experiences the greatest rewards and satisfactions in life. It is much more valuable to experience things directly, through intellectual awareness and through emotional experiences, rather than indirectly, through past accomplishments and accumulation of wealth. The philosopher, poet, musician, and artist are more often revered in this culture than the businessperson or financier.

Mexican Americans are likely to live and experience life more completely in the present. For an individual from the lower socioeconomic portion of society, a limited time orientation may result from immediate survival needs. Another factor contributing to this orientation may stem from the influence of an old Native American Indian cultural belief in the concept of the "limited good." In effect, this is the belief that there is only so much good in the world and that, therefore, only so much good is possible in any one person's life. It matters not how industrious one is, for one will get no more than one's share of good during a lifetime.

In the dominant culture of the United States, being responsible is equated with being punctual. The Mexican American concept of responsibility is based on other values, such as attending to the immediate needs of family or friends, and thus Mexican Americans do not place much value on, and may be casual about, punctuality.

Whereas members of the dominant culture of the United States are taught to value openness, frankness, and directness, the traditional Mexican American approach requires the use of much diplomacy and tact when communicating with another individual. Concern and respect for the feelings of others dictate that a screen be provided behind which an individual may preserve dignity. Much faith is placed in family and friends, such that lasting relationships are developed. Goals do not lie in the accumulation of material goods, but in the good that can be done for all people.

The manner of expression is likely to be elaborate and indirect because the aim is to make the personal relationship at least appear harmonious, to show respect for the other's individuality. To the Mexican American, direct argument or contradiction appears rude and disrespectful. On the surface, one may seem agreeable, manners dictating that one not reveal genuine opinions openly unless one knows the other well and unless there is time to differ tactfully. This concept of courtesy often causes misunderstandings between Anglos and Mexican Americans.

Mexican Americans experience a high degree of sensitivity to the environment. They use the full range of physiological senses to experience the world around them. Thus, they are more likely than Anglos to want to touch, taste, smell, feel, or be close to an object or person on which attention is focused.

Implications

Marin and Marin (1991) described what they saw as basic Mexican American cultural values as collectivism; pleasantness and dignity; agreeableness; simple courtesies; and the avoidance of negativism. They also saw Mexican Americans as more contact oriented, meaning they are comfortable standing close to one another and with body touch. Mexican Americans also view time in a flexible way. Marin (1993) pointed out that "recently arrived Hispanics, contrary to the experiences of other immigrant groups, seem intent on maintaining their language, cultural values, and other group specific characteristics, requiring that attention be given to the group's characteristics whenever community interventions are designed and implemented" (p. 149).

Dana (1993) reported that many Mexican Americans believe illness to be caused by extrahuman forces. Some believe that troubles may cause a person's spirit or soul to leave the body (*susto*). Others believe in hexes (*mal puesto*), the evil eye (*mal ojo*), and the like. Falicov (1996) reported that *Curanderos* (folk healers) are consulted for many maladies and are trusted the most for folk illnesses with psychological components, such as *susto, mal de ojo, empacho* (indigestion), or *envidia* (envy).

Because Mexican Americans show a strong tendency toward being "field sensitive" (Ramirez & Castaneda, 1974), they are likely to prefer working with others to achieve a common goal and are likely to be quite sensitive to the feelings and opinions of others.

More culturally relevant educational programs are needed for Mexican Americans. Educators aware of the Mexican American value system may wish to greet students or clients as soon as they arrive, acknowledging the importance of *personalismo.* The sensitive educator or counselor will use first names with Mexican Americans and will introduce him- or herself by first name. The aware helper will understand that direct eye contact with an older Mexican American may communicate a lack of respect.

Because of potential differences in the perception of time, educators or counselors should make appointments with Mexican Americans immediately, rather than several weeks in advance. A direct approach is likely to be more useful than a nondirect approach to issues or problems.

Helpers must realize that Mexican Americans come from such diverse backgrounds and cultures that they cannot be classified solely on the ability to speak either English or Spanish. The helper must understand that regional differences and differences based on the degree of acculturation into the dominant Anglo culture have major implications for understanding Mexican Americans. The goal of understanding Mexican Americans is to help them find a place in relation to tradition and to feel comfortable in moving between the traditions of the Mexican culture and the traditions of the culture of the United States. Thus, the Mexican American becomes able to function and understand the meaning of being bicultural.

Questions for Review and Reflection

1. The Mexican American population is the fastest growing in the United States. What influence will this growth have on your role as an educator or counselor?

2. Distinguish between Chicano, Hispanic, and Mexican American. What difference, if any, in the degree of acculturation exists between individuals who use different labels to describe the same ethnic group?

3. What is machismo? How does it influence Mexican Americans' interactions within their own culture, with the dominant culture, and with other culturally different groups?

4. What political organization has been most influential for Mexican Americans? Why has it been so influential?

5. What event in the history of Mexican Americans has influenced the dominant culture most in its acceptance of Mexican Americans? Why?

6. How can educators or counselors intervene with Mexican Americans who view family as the primary source of support?

7. What is the impact of Standard English fluency on Mexican Americans? How should educators or counselors approach students or clients who view Spanish as their primary language?

8. What are the unique characteristics of the Mexican American culture? What major problems confront Mexican Americans coming to the United States? How do these factors influence educational and counseling practices?

9. Distinguish between traditional, atraditional, and duotraditional Mexican Americans. What strategies and techniques should educators and counselors use with each group?

10. What influence do the assumptions regarding Mexican American poverty have on educational or counseling programs developed for Mexican Americans?

References

Alvarez, R. (1973). The psycho-historical and socioeconomic development of the Chicano community in the United States. *Social Science Quarterly, 53,* 920-942.

Arias, M. B. (1986). The context of education for Hispanic students: An overview. *American Journal of Education, 95,* 26-57.

Becerra, R. M. (1988). The Mexican American family. In C. H. Mindel, R. W. Haberstein, & R. Wright, Jr. (Eds.), *Ethnic families in America: Patterns and variations* (pp. 141-159). New York: Elsevier.

Buriel, R., & Vasquez, R. (1982). Stereotypes of Mexican descent persons: Attitudes of three generations of Mexican American and Anglo American adolescents. *Journal of Cross-Cultural Psychology, 13,* 59-70.

Casas, J. M., & Atkinson, D. R. (1981). The Mexican American in higher education: An example of subtle stereotyping. *Personnel and Guidance Journal, 59,* 473-476.

Castro, R. (1982). Mexican American women's sexual jokes. *Aztlan, 13,* 275-293.

Chavez, J. M., & Roney, C. E. (1990). Psychocultural factors affecting the mental health status of Mexican American adolescents. In A. R. Stiffman & L. E. Davis (Eds.), *Ethnic issues in adolescent mental health* (pp. 73-91). Newbury Park, CA: Sage.

Dana, R. H. (1993). *Multicultural assessment perspectives for professional psychology.* Boston: Allyn & Bacon.

Daniels, R. (1990). *Coming to America: A history of immigration and ethnicity in American life.* New York: HarperCollins.

Duran, L. I., & Bernard, H. R. (1973). *Introduction to Chicano studies.* New York: Macmillan.

Dwerkin, A. G. (1964). Stereotypes and self-images by native-born and foreign-born Mexican Americans. *Sociology and Social Research, 49,* 214-224.

Falicov, C. J. (1996). Mexican families. In M. McGoldrick, J. Giordano, & J. K. Pearce (Eds.), *Ethnicity and family therapy* (pp. 169-182). New York: Guilford.

Garcia, J. A. (1987). The political integration of Mexican immigrants: Examining some political orientations. *International Migration Review, 21,* 372-389.

Goldman, S. M. (1982). Mexican muralism: Its social-educative roles in Latin America and the United States. *Aztlan, 13,* 111-133.

Hernandez, L., & Carlquist-Hernandez, K. (1979). Humanization of the counseling-teaching process for Latinos: Learning principles. *Journal of Non-White Concerns, 7,* 150-158.

Hurtado, A., & Arce, C. H. (1987). Mexicans, Chicanos, Mexican Americans, or Pochos . . . ¿qué somos? The impact of language and nativity on ethnic labeling. *Aztlan, 17,* 103-130.

Kiskadden, R. W., & Rossell, N. H. (1979). *Mexican American studies: An instructional bulletin.* Los Angeles: Los Angeles Unified School District.

LaBrack, B., & Leonard, K. (1984). Conflict and compatibility in Punjabi Mexican immigrant families in rural California. *Journal of Marriage, 46,* 527-537.

Marin, G. (1993). Defining culturally appropriate community interventions: Hispanics as a case study. *Journal of Community Psychology, 21,* 149-161.

Marin, G., & Marin, B. V. (1991). *Research with Hispanic populations.* Newbury Park, CA: Sage.

Matute-Bianchi, M. E. (1986). Ethnic identities and patterns of school success and failure among Mexican-descent and Japanese American students in a California high school: An ethnographic analysis. *American Journal of Education, 95,* 233-255.

McKenzie, T. L., Salis, J. F., Nada, P. R., Broyles, S. L., & Nelson, S. A. (1992). Anglo and Mexican American preschoolers at home and at recess: Activity patterns and environmental influences. *Journal of Developmental and Behavioral Pediatrics, 13*(3), 173-180.

Meier, M. S., & Rivera, F. (1981). *Dictionary of Mexican American experience.* Westport, CT: Greenwood.

Miller, S., Nicolau, S., Orr, M., Valdivieso, R., & Walker, G. (1988). *Too late to patch: Reconsidering opportunities for Hispanic and other dropouts.* Washington, DC: Hispanic Policy Development Project.

Mirandé, A. (1977). The Chicano family: A reanalysis of conflicting views. *Journal of Marriage and the Family, 39,* 747-756.

Mirandé, A. (1985). *The Chicano experience: An alternative perspective.* Notre Dame, IN: University of Notre Dame Press.

Mirandé, A. (1988). Qué gacho es ser macho: It's a drag to be a macho man. *Aztlan, 17,* 63-89.

Ortego, P. D. (1973). The Chicano renaissance. In L. I. Duran & H. R. Bernard (Eds.), *Introduction to Chicano studies* (pp. 331-349). New York: Macmillan.

Panitz, D. R., McConchie, R. D., Sauber, S. R., & Fonseca, J. A. (1983). The role of machismo and the Hispanic family in the etiology and treatment of alcoholism in Hispanic American males. *American Journal of Family Therapy, 11,* 31-44.

Ramirez, M., & Castaneda, A. (1974). *Cultural democracy: Bicognitive development and education.* San Diego: Academic Press.

Ruiz, R. A., & Padilla, A. M. (1977). Counseling Latinos. *Personnel and Guidance Journal, 55,* 401-408.

Turner, K. F. (1982). Mexican American home altars: Toward their interpretation. *Aztlan, 13,* 309-326.

U.S. Bureau of the Census. (1991). *Statistical abstract of the United States.* Washington, DC: Government Printing Office.

Valencia, R. R. (1991). *Chicano school failure and success.* New York: Falmer.

Villarruel, A. M., & de Montellano, B. O. (1992). Culture and pain: A Mesoamerican perspective. *Advances in Nursing Science, 15*(1), 21-32.

10

Puerto Rican Americans

Puerto Rican Americans are the only migrants who have come to the mainland of the United States as citizens of this country with the rights of naturalized citizens. Even with these rights, the 2.7 million Puerto Ricans who live in the United States are an extremely devalued group (U.S. Bureau of the Census, 1991).

The island of Borinquen, renamed Puerto Rico by the Spanish, is characterized as a mixture of cultural influences, marked by vestiges of the Taino Indians who first inhabited the island, by more than 500 years of Spanish colonialism, and by more than 75 years of domination by the United States. The Spanish influence, with its system of feudal agriculture, the Roman Catholic Church, language, and civil law, remained dominant in Puerto Rican culture until the end of the 19th century.

New economic changes developed for Puerto Ricans late in the 19th century, when the island came into the possession of the United States. The feudal hacienda owners were supplanted by U.S. corporate interests. Until 1932, the U.S. government maintained a relaxed attitude toward the economy of Puerto Rico, with the result that most investment and development in Puerto Rico came from private U.S. capital. Montijo (1985) concluded that "by retaining Puerto Rico as an unincorporated territory and imposing its citizenship on Puerto Ricans, the United States greatly contributed to what could be described as Puerto Rico's national identity crisis" (p. 436).

Under Governor Luis Muñoz Marín, Puerto Rico implemented Operation Bootstrap, a development program designed to raise the standard of living on the island. In 20 years of effort, the Puerto Rican government raised the per capita income more than 300%, and by 1960 some 600 new factories had been established, creating an estimated 45,000 new jobs. Moreover, the government aided in the training of personnel by building factories for rent at attractive rates and through various tax incentives (Rosado, 1986).

Puerto Ricans have benefited individually from the government monies invested in roads, housing, education, health, and welfare. Even so, by 1972, the per capita income was only $1,713, nearly $300 behind the 30-year prediction of Operation Bootstrap. Moreover, an urban, consumer-based middle class had developed with enough political power to oppose increases in the minimum wage standard. As a result, the distribution of income across the island has become increasingly skewed (Lopez & Petras, 1974).

Increased economic and cultural penetration from the United States, displacement of the rural farm community, the creation of an urban under-class as a result of the decline in agriculture, and the lure of U.S. culture all contributed to the heavy Puerto Rican migration to the continental United States. A *Puerto Rican American* can be described as anyone who has at least one parent who was born in Puerto Rico. Individuals residing in the United States can be described as members of four subgroups:

1. Those born in the United States who live in New York City, referred to as "Nuyoricans"
2. Those born in the United States who live in places other than New York City
3. Those born on the island of Puerto Rico who live in New York City
4. Those born in Puerto Rico who live elsewhere in the United States (Lopez & Petras, 1974)

By 1990, more than 2.7 million first-, second-, and third-generation Puerto Ricans lived in the continental United States, representing about 42% of all Puerto Ricans. Although New York City remains the area of heaviest con-centration, Puerto Ricans have moved to other parts of the country (U.S. Bureau of the Census, 1991). Rivera-Batiz and Santiago (1996) reported that more Puerto Ricans moved out of New York City between 1985 and 1990 than moved in during that period. Fitzpatrick (1987) reported that the Puerto Rican population in the United States is becoming more of a second- or third-generation group. In 1970, 58.4% of Puerto Ricans living in New York had been born in Puerto Rico, and by 1980 that number was 42%.

Acculturation

Puerto Ricans are hardworking people who are inculcated with fundamen-tal Catholic ideology. Likewise, a strong sense of self-worth and the concept of personal dignity (*dignidad*), both as an ideal and as a defense, have helped Puerto Rican Americans maintain a sense of community and personal pride despite oppressive socioeconomic conditions. Another factor that has contributed positively to the resiliency of the Puerto Rican community is a need for interaction with others; no great need for privacy exists in the Puerto Rican culture. Another sustaining characteristic is the emphasis on spiritual and human values, rather than on the commercial values of the United States. This last feature has endowed Puerto Rican communities with a flexibility and a source of inner strength in the face of economic hardships.

Adjustments to life in the United States have been eased by the fact that Puerto Ricans are familiar with public education standards, wage systems, large hospitals, mass communication, and the electoral process. This gives them an advantage over other Hispanic migrant groups, which may not have experienced these key structures.

One of the most overt issues of acculturation for Puerto Rican Americans has been language. Employers complain of a labor force with which they cannot communicate. Employment services are reluctant to place workers with little fluency in English. In addition, problems in schools are acute because many Puerto Rican children enter the public school system with little English proficiency.

Puerto Ricans fear the loss of identity as a Puerto Rican with the loss of the Spanish language. However, these people are realistic about the need to master the English language and to adjust to patterns of living in the dominant culture of the United States. Fitzpatrick (1987) suggested that the majority of Puerto Ricans are striving to become bicultural in that they "do not see any form of separatism as either practically possible or socially desirable. But they seek a form of life in which, as New Yorkers, they remain decidedly themselves" (p. 7).

Because the family unit is so important among Puerto Ricans, some adjustments are required by assimilation. For instance, consensual marriage is not recognized in the United States, and in many states, common-law marriage has been outlawed. The mother of children born in a consensual arrangement is ineligible for benefits that might be afforded a widowed, abandoned, or divorced parent. Moreover, the custom of early marriage conflicts with many age-of-consent laws.

Unfortunately, the problems of acculturation are more difficult for younger Puerto Ricans who have grown up in low-income Puerto Rican urban communities in the United States. Children learn the dominant cultural norms in school, and this can result in a devaluing of the Puerto Rican culture in favor of Anglo norms. In addition, the media often portray Puerto Ricans in a negative manner. This lack of a strong sense of cultural identity, compounded by the racial ambiguity faced by new generations of Puerto Rican Americans, results in conflict between the dominant culture of the

United States and Puerto Rican culture. Lacking many of the characteristics of traditional Puerto Rican culture that facilitated the adaptability of first-generation immigrants, later generations of Puerto Rican Americans face real problems of identity as they assimilate.

Being forced to cope with their indigenous culture and the dominant culture of the United States simultaneously frequently generates a high level of stress. Despite the numerous barriers, many Puerto Rican Americans acculturate well, adopting the cultural elements of the dominant society. Other Puerto Ricans cope by attempting to balance elements of both cultures, or they refuse to adopt the dominant culture of the United States.

Poverty and Economic Concerns

Poverty and a lack of opportunity on the island of Puerto Rico are two primary reasons that Puerto Ricans migrate to the U.S. mainland. Chenault (1970) reported that about 70% of all Puerto Ricans who move to New York City settle in Harlem and the navy yard districts. This migration to the slum areas exemplifies the very low economic status of the migrant Puerto Ricans.

The U.S. Bureau of the Census (1990) reported that Puerto Rican Americans living in New York City had a mean per capita household income of $7,989; for Mexican Americans, $8,933; and for Cuban Americans, $14,462. The income levels are slightly higher for all Puerto Ricans living in the United States. Puerto Ricans exhibited substantial income growth in the 1980s; their mean per capita income, adjusted for inflation, increased by close to 30%. This increase was the highest among all major racial and ethnic groups in the United States. Despite this growth, Chavez (1991) depicted Puerto Ricans as occupying the "lowest rung of the social and economic ladder among Hispanics" (p. 140).

Factors related to poverty show Puerto Rican Americans to be behind the general U.S. population. For instance, the dropout rate for Puerto Ricans in 1990 was reported at 32.1% (U.S. Bureau of the Census, 1991). Failure to complete high school, coupled with a decrease in the number of available blue-collar jobs, has resulted in a 12% unemployment rate for Puerto Ricans, about twice that in the United States overall (Rivera-Batiz & Santiago, 1996). Rodriguez (1989) reported that the poverty rate among Puerto Ricans is higher than among Whites, African Americans, or other Hispanic families. Perez (1993) suggested that, if the poverty concerns are to be addressed in a meaningful manner, attention must be given to employment and training programs and policies for young Puerto Rican men; to antipoverty strategies; to social programs; and to welfare reforms that examine poverty and the role of young men in the formation of families.

History of Oppression

Oppressive conditions are not new to Puerto Ricans, who have experienced a history of oppression from external powers for the past 400 years. The original settlers of the island of Puerto Rico were the Taino Indians, who were forced to defend their land against, first, the Carib Indians and, later, the Spanish. In 1508, the arrival of Ponce de León signaled the beginning of official colonization and rule of Puerto Rico by the Spanish empire. The Taino soon realized that they were enslaved by the Spaniards, whose primary needs were to exploit the land and to use a source of cheap labor. The Spanish ruled Puerto Rico until 1897, when the island was granted autonomy. The island was later attacked 26 times by foreign countries and finally ceded to the United States, the 26th attacker. Thus, Puerto Rico continued as a colony of a foreign power. After 2 years of military occupation, the U.S. Congress provided Puerto Rico with a territorial form of government (Cardona, 1974).

In the United States, Puerto Rican Americans form a large part of New York's unskilled labor force and have found employment readily in the lowest-paying jobs. Discrimination at these lower levels of the occupational structure appears to be related to factors of language difference, practices of union discrimination, and monopolies on certain jobs that have been traditionally held and guarded by other ethnic groups. Moreover, certain professional agencies have refused to recognize licenses and training sanctioned in Puerto Rico, making it difficult for skilled Puerto Ricans living in the continental United States to find equivalent work (Lopez & Petras, 1974).

Unemployment among Puerto Rican males continues to be approximately twice that of the general population. Unemployment among Puerto Rican females, though higher than for males, is much nearer the national norm. Median family incomes have historically been lower than those of either Mexican American or Cuban American families.

Language and the Arts

Most Puerto Ricans consider Spanish to be their native tongue, and about three out of every four Puerto Rican Americans report that Spanish is the language spoken in the home. Because Spanish is the native tongue of most Puerto Rican Americans, its usage has increased greatly in communities where migrants reside. These Spanish-speaking areas provide a link to Puerto Rico, as well as help the recent migrant with adjustment to the mainland. The shared language is one major way of preserving the Puerto Rican culture in a new environment (Wagenheim, 1975).

According to Fitzpatrick (1987), awareness of the value of bilingualism among Puerto Rican Americans is increasing. School systems, however, have had difficulty implementing bilingual programs. Questions center around how to teach English as a second language and how to assist children with a mastery of both English and Spanish. As a result of a court case in 1974 brought by the Aspira organization, the Board of Education of the City of New York is required to provide bilingual instruction for Puerto Rican students. Even so, 10 years later "only 30 percent of entitled students receive[d] the full bilingual education that is prescribed by law" (p. 168).

Puerto Ricans have long been famous for their lively and expressive folk art and music, which is evidence of their gusto for life and their high energy. The 19th century is considered to be the Puerto Rican Golden Age of literary, musical, and artistic works. From 1898 to 1920, Puerto Rican authors were primarily concerned with clinging to their past heritage. This literature provides an understanding of the struggles and dreams of those trying to adjust to their country's possession by the United States (Cardona, 1974).

Quero-Chiesa (1974) noted that the Puerto Rican author in the United States has to face a cultural conflict "so serious that it becomes a matter of life and death to him as an artist. Before him rises the wall of the English language, isolating him from the American literary life" (p. 64). Not only is the language a barrier to the writer, but the change in cultural values from honor, romanticism, the sense of family unity, and the hierarchy of intellectual life to pragmatism creates confusion in the minds of the writers that is reflected in their work. Thus, for the Puerto Rican American author, the Hispanic culture is a source from which to draw inspiration. To capture a theme for their writing,

> frequently they latch on to some native motif, such as liberty, folklore, or popular typology. This kind of literature about the idealized motherland with its romantic-nationalistic accent is usually provincial in character and often embodies chauvinism and an exultation of the picturesque. (p. 65)

Along with literary works, music, and accomplishments on the stage, in films, and on television, Puerto Ricans have a folk art, *santeria,* that began in the 16th century. Vice (1974) reported that the "Santeros carved wooden saints for their religious ceremonies and beliefs, and for a very long time, every home had either a set of the Three Kings or some statuette" (p. 144). The *santeros* are generally country folk with little or no training or formal education but with a distinct talent for carving.

Racism and Prejudice

Puerto Ricans did not experience much discrimination based on race until they came to the United States mainland. Prejudice in Puerto Rico was based on class, rather than on race; people were excluded from social participation, not because of color, but because of class. Consequently, an upper-class person's behavior toward the person of color depended not on the person's color, but on his or her class position.

According to Fitzpatrick (1987), nothing is as complicated for Puerto Rican Americans in their effort to adjust to the dominant culture as the problem of color. They represent the first group ever to come to the United states in large numbers with a tradition of widespread intermingling and intermarriage of people of different colors. This blend comes from a mix of Spanish, Taino Indian, and African. The population today ranges from Caucasoid to completely Negroid, with many variations in between. On the U.S. mainland, Puerto Ricans are often expected to fit into racial categories based on color. This categorization has little meaning for Puerto Rican migrants and can be confusing. On the island, Puerto Ricans recognize several racial categories, such as *blanco* (White), *prieto* (dark-skinned), *negro* (Black), and *trigueno* (tan) (Banks, 1987). Puerto Rican Americans who are intermediate in skin color do not fit neatly into a Black/White classification system and are often alienated from both of these two racial groups.

Mainland attitudes have been ambivalent regarding the racial identity of Puerto Ricans. Puerto Ricans who came to the United States before World War II and settled in urban areas were often ostracized by their Italian counterparts, whereas African American ghetto youths were more accepting. During World War II, army camps on the island segregated Puerto Rican troops, and the U.S. Navy refused to enlist Puerto Ricans. Unless very dark and with Negroid features, Puerto Ricans were listed as White in New York City. The proportion of "colored" in Puerto Rican populations dropped with each census (Cordasco, 1973). The 1980 census identified first- and second-generation Puerto Ricans in the United States as "Puerto Rican" (U.S. Bureau of the Census, 1980).

Sociopolitical Factors

In 1947, Puerto Ricans were granted the right to elect their own governor. Shortly thereafter, their first governor, Luis Muñoz Marín, instituted a political status called the Free Associated State of Puerto Rico. This gave more autonomy to the island and established a relationship with the United

States that is similar to commonwealth status (Sociological Resources for the Social Studies, 1974).

Puerto Rico's civil status remains controversial today. Some are proponents of statehood, and other factions argue for complete independence. Those on both sides of this argument believe that their preferred status will strengthen Puerto Rico's cultural identity and political-economic security. Status issues have implications for Puerto Ricans living on the mainland because the communities in Puerto Rico and on the mainland are integrally bound by family ties and a history of migration patterns.

Puerto Ricans are U.S. citizens naturalized by annexation. They have the right to vote in elections, and they are eligible to serve in the military. Until 1964, Puerto Rican Americans in the state of New York were required to take a literacy test before they were permitted to register to vote. Puerto Rican American political strength has been weak in the past because election ballots have traditionally been only in English. In 1969, the Spanish-American Action Committee (SAAC) was formed to further socioeconomic development. This organization "provides services in the areas of housing, employment, education, and community organization. In addition to providing services, SAAC also puts pressure on city officials to get them to respond to the needs of Puerto Ricans" (Cardona, 1974, p. 62). In the political arena, voter registration is high, but "greater political enlightenment of the Puerto Rican community has been hampered by the continuous gerrymandering of several districts with high concentrations of Puerto Ricans" (Cardona, 1974, p. 63). Fitzpatrick (1987) reported that even though Puerto Ricans are participants in a wide range of community organizations and social service programs, they are "still underrepresented in the critical area of the political process, registration and voting. As a result, political representation is low and political influence is weak" (p. 13). The Puerto Rican Forum represents social, political, and business interests of Puerto Ricans at local and national levels. The Puerto Rican Family Institute, established in 1960, works toward the preservation of the health, well-being, and integrity of Puerto Ricans in the United States (Baruth & Manning, 1996). In some parts of the United States, Puerto Rican Americans are still very weak politically, but the Puerto Rican community is growing, learning, and developing the tools to work within the political process.

Child-Rearing Practices

Puerto Ricans demonstrate a strong feeling of love for their children. Obedience and respect for parental authority are stressed in traditional Puerto Rican families, and independence is curtailed. Children are not allowed to question or challenge their parents. High value is placed on being honest and acting with dignity. Relationships with cousins are comparable to that of siblings. First-generation parents do not assign rights to children; they make most decisions for their children (Juarez, 1985). Humility is a highly valued expectation, and children lower their eyes and heads to show respect for their parents. Corporal punishment, if not excessive, is accepted as a disciplinary approach. Simpson and Yinger (1972) pointed out that more "modern" families, usually second and third generations, have different parenting styles, believing that fewer restrictions should be placed on children. The father is still the authority figure, but his authority is more flexible and less imposing.

Boys are given greater independence and, to a great extent, are left to raise themselves. Girls are carefully watched and protected. Simpson and Yinger (1972) suggested that Puerto Rican boys may find friends on the streets who are bad influences, may learn to be disrespectful and disobedient to their parents, and may even get involved with drug addiction and crime.

Compadres are special friends or favorite relatives who act as coparents. Coparents are expected to give and get strong loyalty, affection, respect, and services. It is not unusual for families to add nephews, nieces, godchildren, and children of a husband's extramarital alliances to the extended family.

Religious Practices

Puerto Rico is generally thought of as Catholic territory, but the Catholicism of Puerto Ricans is unique. According to Old World criteria, Puerto Rican Catholicism was of inferior intellectual formation, with undue amounts of superstition in popular devotion (Stevens-Arroyo, 1974). Because of Spanish imperialism, Catholicism was a religion of the town, isolating the people in the hill country from the parish priest. Protestantism was introduced with the U.S. invasion, but the Puerto Rican custom of wearing religious medals was considered to be incompatible with this new religion. The great devotion to the rosary and the cult of the Virgin Mary created a cultural form called *rosaria contao* (Stevens-Arroyo, 1974, p. 120).

Pentecostalism became the largest and fastest growing of Puerto Rican religions because the importance that it places on religious experience reinforced the Puerto Rican desire for intimacy with the supernatural. After migrating to New York, many Puerto Ricans found that Pentecostalism provided a means of escaping the cultural and social aimlessness they experienced in the transition from rural to city life. Nuyoricans continue "to be faithful to religious customs such as baptism and the practice of the *asabache,* which is a black piece of wood, usually in the shape of an arm, meant to protect the child from the evil eye" (Stevens-Arroyo, 1974, p. 128).

As Torres (1995) concluded, however, the Catholic Church has "fallen short of what one would expect. With no Puerto Rican clergy and a severely limited economic foundation in Puerto Rican areas, the Catholic church in New York City has not been particularly aggressive in the promotion of policies and programs to enhance the community's political strength" (p. 71).

Another form of religious practice is *spiritualism,* or the practice of communication with spiritual forces. It is "rooted in the belief that persons in this world can establish contact with the spirit world and can use this power to influence the spirits, either restraining the unfavorable action of evil spirits or effecting the favorable action of good spirits" (Fitzpatrick, 1987, p. 127). Spiritualist activities are conducted by a *medium,* a person who claims power to contact the spirit world. Believers of spiritualism also participate in folk practices that have to do with curing illnesses. In the barrio, there is usually a *botanica* where herbs, potions, prayers, and "voodoo dolls" are sold.

Family Structure and Dynamics

As in most cultures of the world, the individual in Puerto Rico has a deep commitment to membership in the family. The world to a Puerto Rican consists of a pattern of intimate personal relationships, and the basic relationships are those of family. Fitzpatrick (1987) identified a fourfold structural typology among Puerto Rican families:

1. The extended family system, with strong bonds and frequent interaction among a wide range of natural or ritual kin providing a source of strength and support

2. The nuclear family, consisting of the mother, the father, and the children not living close to relatives and having weak bonds to the extended family

3. The father, the mother, their children, and the children of another union or unions of husband or wife

4. The mother-based family, with children of one or more fathers but with no permanent male in the home

Family is often an extended system that encompasses not only those related by blood and marriage but also *compadres* (coparents) and *hijos de crianza* (informally adopted children). *Compadrazgo* is the institution of *compadres comadres* (godparents), a system of ritual kinship with binding mutual obligations for economic assistance and encouragement.

As an alternative to marriage, the *consensual union* is allowed. This is a relatively stable union of a man and a woman who have never gone through a religious or civil marriage ceremony but who live together and rear a family. The number of these unions is steadily decreasing among Puerto Rican Americans. The father is required by law to recognize his children whether he lives with the mother or not. This gives the children rights before the law, including the right to use the father's name, the right to support, and some rights of inheritance (Fitzpatrick, 1987).

Fitzpatrick (1995) found that Puerto Ricans are experiencing internal changes in community in terms of family structure and economic status, which have created two distinct Puerto Rican groups: two-parent families that are well educated and economically well off, and single-parent, meagerly educated families that are living in poverty. Sommers, Fagan, and Baskin (1993) found that, among 1,077 Puerto Rican male adolescents in New York City, values emphasizing family bonds and obligations were powerful in helping the youths avoid delinquency.

A Puerto Rican's confidence, sense of security, and identity are closely tied to relationships in the family. The use of names is an example. The Puerto Rican generally uses the name of his or her father's father and his or her mother's father. In the case of José Garcia Lopez, *Garcia* comes from José's father's family name, and *Lopez* is his mother's father's name. The wife's name in this marriage is Maria Gonzalez de Garcia. She keeps her father's father's name, *Gonzalez,* and adopts her husband's first family name, usually with a *de* (of) (Sociological Resources for the Social Studies, 1974).

The importance of the Puerto Rican American extended family is evidenced in the celebration of holidays such as *Nuech Buena* ("the good night," Christmas Eve), when the family gathers with close friends to celebrate. A feeling of relaxation, of caring, and of temporary retreat from problems is coupled with a diet of yellow rice, pigeon peas, and roast pork (Rodriguez, 1989).

Cultural Values and Attitudes

In many respects, Puerto Ricans share the heritage of the Spanish tradition in their interactions, retention of the language, fundamental Catholic theology, acceptance of class structure, hospitality, gregarious family patterns, machismo, and emphasis on the spiritual and human values of society. Banks (1987) identified the following characteristics of Puerto Rican American values and attitudes: interdependence, group centrality, cooperation, dignity, respect of persons, comfort with human contact, and the need of the presence of human voices to feel at ease.

One of the more obvious value shifts taking place among Puerto Rican Americans is the change in roles of males and females, with females becoming more independent. A shift is also taking place in the role of the child, with children beginning to behave according to dominant cultural standards of self-reliance, aggressiveness, competitiveness, inquisitiveness, and independence. These behaviors are considered disrespectful by Puerto Rican American parents accustomed to more submissive children. Further, migration to the U.S. mainland has weakened the extended kinship bonds and caused the family to find itself alienated in the dominant culture.

Many Puerto Rican values continue, such as *personalism,* a form of individualism that focuses on the inner importance of the person, and the role of the *padrino,* a person of influence who helps the Puerto Rican. This latter role is often operationalized through the personal relationships developed in one's business affairs. Puerto Rican Americans are quite sensitive to personal insult. They also have a sense of destiny and a sense of a hierarchical world. Thus, Puerto Rican Americans are greatly influenced by the family and the community and have been influenced by the dominant culture of the United States. The family and community bonds of Puerto Rican Americans contrast with those of the dominant culture, which are oriented mostly around the individual and his or her accomplishments.

The dominant culture also has a different value of time, in that it encourages planning for the future and requires a compulsive time orientation instead of living for today and having an extended time orientation. Thus, the Puerto Rican orientation toward time causes problems in the dominant culture and often leads to the loss of employment.

Implications

The unique nature of the Puerto Rican migration and of Puerto Rican experiences provides an opportunity to make generalizations about multiethnic curriculum concepts. Banks (1987) identified three key concepts specific to Puerto Rican American experiences and suggested strategies for incorporating them into the curriculum:

1. *Cultural conflict* involves the many problems that Puerto Ricans experience when they encounter new norms, values, and roles on the mainland. Discussions of family case studies can help students understand adjustment problems of Puerto Ricans.

2. The concept of *racial problems* can provide an opportunity to learn about the racial complexity of Puerto Ricans and related identity problems. Teaching activities for this concept can have the value of increasing the sensitivity to

racial problems of other ethnic groups, as well as of understanding Puerto Ricans' concerns.

3. *Colonialism* can be covered by stressing the consequences of control by foreign powers, such as rebellions, political ambiguity, and instability on the island. Another goal for teaching this concept is to generalize the effects of oppression to other ethnic groups.

These concepts can assist students in thinking about their role in making decisions and taking action to help eliminate problems of racism, poverty, and political powerlessness.

Inclan (1985) reminded us that principles of psychoanalytical theory have limited value with poor Hispanic people. There was once an expectation that psychoanalytical practice had promise for all people. When this expectation was not met with poor and ethnic minorities, blame was placed on the client. The rationale was, in Inclan's words, that "they were not verbal, motivated, insightful or able to delay gratification" (p. 332). A more effective theory for Puerto Ricans needs to have a different framework. Inclan recommended therapies that emphasize the here and now and the concrete, rather than take an abstract and future orientation. The therapeutic modalities need to value the lineal family group and an understanding of the role of hierarchies in effecting change. Montijo (1985) emphasized the importance of considering social class values when determining a therapeutic orientation for treating working-class Puerto Ricans. The goal of treatment should be to promote clients' awareness (*conciencia*) of oppression "so that they may fight more effectively for their personal and collective liberation" (p. 436). Delgado (1992) suggested that service providers use Puerto Rican natural support systems as a part of collaborative strategies with the Puerto Rican community. Natural support systems include the extended family, folk healers, religious groups, and merchant and social clubs.

Other studies sought to discover problems unique to Puerto Ricans to develop appropriate treatment modalities. For example, Dongin, Salazar, and Cruz (1987, p. 293) identified specific culturally related difficulties among patients in a Hispanic treatment program:

- Patients had cultural conflicts, as well as a need to explore cultural values, practices, and beliefs to enhance their functioning and well-being.
- Patients had racial and ethnic misconceptions.
- Patients had cultural beliefs that they could not express for fear that others would not understand or would ridicule them.
- Patients had distortions of the macho image and the "submissive" female role.
- Patients related in Spanish only or did not understand English.

A multiethnic curriculum has value for all student populations. Such a curriculum helps all students better understand their own cultures and provides knowledge about other ethnic groups and their contributions. A desired outcome of such a curriculum is to help students function effectively with a range of cultures.

One method that offers promise with Puerto Rican adolescents is the use of *folk hero modeling* (Costantino, Malgady, & Rogler, 1988). This method was developed from the use of *cuentos,* or folktales, as a storytelling technique. In the folk hero modeling technique, stories about heroes and heroines are used to help students gain self-confidence, pride in being Puerto Rican, vocational information, coping strategies, and interest in Puerto Rican culture. Folk hero anecdotes, in both English and Spanish, have been found to produce changes in the group dynamics of participants.

It behooves the educator or counselor to assist in building cultural bridges between the Puerto Rican American culture and the dominant culture. One of the most useful tools in such an endeavor is education. Education for Puerto Rican Americans should be bilingual because the Spanish language is of such great importance to them.

The critical issues of the future for Puerto Rican Americans remain employment, housing, day care, and medical care. Education and local community development initiatives may be effective only if adequate support and resources are available from the dominant culture.

Questions for Review and Reflection

1. What effect, if any, does the fact that Puerto Ricans came to the mainland United States as citizens have on their cultural practices?

2. What role does *dignidad* play in interactions between Puerto Ricans and educators or counselors? How can this concept be used to facilitate relationships between Puerto Ricans and helpers?

3. How can educators or counselors promote bilingualism for Puerto Ricans so that their native culture can be preserved?

4. Why is the issue of skin color an important one among Puerto Ricans? How can knowledge of the skin color issue help educators or counselors who work with Puerto Ricans?

5. Why should or should not Puerto Rico become a state in the United States?

6. What role do *compadres* serve in the Puerto Rican family? How can educators or counselors use the extended family in working with Puerto Rican students or clients?

7. Evidence suggests that traditional roles are shifting among Puerto Ricans. How can knowledge of these shifts help educators or counselors who are working with Puerto Rican students or clients?

8. How does the concept of personalism in the Puerto Rican culture differ from the focus on the individual in the dominant culture of the United States?

9. Why are the therapies recommended by J. Inclan (1985) desirable when working with Puerto Rican clients?

10. What must educators and counselors understand about the "macho males" and the "submissive females" in the Puerto Rican culture?

References

Banks, J. A. (1987). *Teaching strategies for ethnic studies.* Boston: Allyn & Bacon.

Baruth, L. G., & Manning, L. (1996). *Multicultural education.* Boston: Allyn & Bacon.

Cardona, L. A. (1974). *The coming of the Puerto Ricans.* Mesa, AZ: Caretta.

Chavez, L. (1991). *Out of the barrio: Toward a new politics of Hispanic assimilation.* New York: Basic Books.

Chenault, L. R. (1970). *The Puerto Rican migrant in New York City.* New York: Russel & Russel.

Cordasco, F. (1973). *The Puerto Rican experience: A sociological sourcebook.* Totowa, NJ: Littlefield, Adams.

Costantino, G., Malgady, R. G., & Rogler, L. H. (1988). Folk hero modeling therapy for Puerto Rican adolescents. *Journal of Adolescence, 11,* 155-165.

Delgado, M. (1992). *The Puerto Rican community and natural support systems: Implications for the education of children.* Boston: Institute for Responsive Education.

Dongin, D. L., Salazar, A., & Cruz, S. (1987). The Hispanic treatment program: Principles of effective psychotherapy. *Journal of Contemporary Psychotherapy, 17,* 285-295.

Fitzpatrick, J. P. (1987). *Puerto Rican Americans: The meaning of migration to the mainland.* Upper Saddle River, NJ: Prentice Hall.

Fitzpatrick, J. P. (1995). Puerto Rican New Yorkers. *Migration World Magazine, 23,* 16-19.

Inclan, J. (1985). Variations in value orientations in mental health work with Puerto Ricans. *Psychotherapy, 22,* 324-334.

Juarez, R. (1985). Core issues in psychotherapy with the Hispanic child. *Psychotherapy, 22,* 441-449.

Lopez, A., & Petras, H. (1974). *Puerto Rico and the Puerto Ricans.* New York: John Wiley.

Montijo, J. A. (1985). Therapeutic relationships with the poor: A Puerto Rican perspective. *Psychotherapy, 22,* 436-441.

Perez, S. M. (1993). *Moving from the margins: Puerto Rican young men and family poverty.* Washington, DC: National Council of LaRaza.

Quero-Chiesa, L. (1974). The anguish of the expatriate writer. In E. Mapp (Ed.), *Puerto Rican perspectives.* Metuchen, NJ: Scarecrow.

Rivera-Batiz, F. L., & Santiago, C. E. (1996). *Island paradox: Puerto Rico in the 1990s.* New York: Russell Sage.

Rodriguez, C. (1989). *Puerto Ricans born in the USA.* Boston: Unwin Hyman.

Rosado, J. W. (1986). Toward an interfacing of Hispanic cultural variables with school psychology service delivery systems. *Clinical Psychology: Research and Practice, 17,* 191-199.

Simpson, G. E., & Yinger, J. M. (1972). *Racial and cultural minorities.* New York: Harper & Row.

Sociological Resources for the Social Studies. (1974). *Population change: A case study of Puerto Rico.* Boston: Allyn & Bacon.

Sommers, I., Fagan, J., & Baskin, D. (1993). Sociocultural influences on the explanation of delinquency for Puerto Rican youth. *Hispanic Journal of Behavioral Sciences, 15,* 36-62.

Stevens-Arroyo, A. M. (1974). Religion and the Puerto Ricans in New York. In E. Mapp (Ed.), *Puerto Rican perspectives.* Metuchen, NJ: Scarecrow.

Torres, A. (1995). *Between melting pot and mosaic.* Philadelphia: Temple University Press.

U.S. Bureau of the Census. (1980). *Persons of Spanish ancestry* (Supplementary report). Washington, DC: Government Printing Office.

U.S. Bureau of the Census. (1990). *Persons of Spanish ancestry.* Washington, DC: Government Printing Office.

U.S. Bureau of the Census. (1991). *U.S. census of population and housing: Puerto Rico.* Washington, DC: Government Printing Office.

Vice, C. (1974). The Puerto Rican woman in business. In E. Mapp (Ed.), *Puerto Rican perspectives.* Metuchen, NJ: Scarecrow.

Wagenheim, K. (1975). *A survey of Puerto Ricans on the U.S. mainland in the 1970s.* New York: Praeger.

11

_____
_____
___

Jewishness in America

The purpose of this chapter is to describe the customs, beliefs, values, and practices of Jews in the United States. Jewish Americans are difficult to describe because of their diverse origins. Yet, they have retained a high degree of religious and cultural identity. Jewish identity does not rest on the presence of physical traits or religious devoutness, but rather on a sense of belonging that is tied to ancestry. To say that Judaism is a religion ignores too much of Jewish life. The only good way of understanding the Jews is to say that they are a mixture of a religious and a national group, although most think of themselves, their history, and their traditions as mainly religious. According to Dosick (1995), a _Jew_ is a child born of a Jewish mother, or a person who converts to Judaism. If the father is Jewish but the mother is not, then the child in not Jewish. Berger (1986) reported that, in 1983, Reform rabbis agreed to accept as Jews children of intermarriages in which either the father or the mother is Jewish. The term _Jewishness (Yiddishkait)_ is used because of the importance of the religious component in the identity of Jews, making them different from other ethnic groups.

In an article on why Jews should be included in multiculturalism, Langman (1995) pointed out reasons why non-Jews have not included Jews, and why Jews have not included themselves, in multiculturalism. Responses to the first part of the question include "the level of assimilation of American Jews; their classification as White; the idea that Jews are members of a religion, not a culture; their economic success; and the exclusion of anti-Semitism as an issue worth addressing" (pp. 222-223). Issues related to the second part of the question are "the divorce between Jews' public and private identities, the lack of validation of their experience as members of a minority, their fear or anxiety surrounding being publicly Jewish, and the self-hatred that can occur when Jews internalize anti-Semitism" (p. 223).

Judaism is a religion that centers around three ideas: God, Torah, and Israel. Judaism is one of the oldest religions and provides the historical roots for most other religions. It stresses the positive acts of benevolence, kindliness, and encouragement through which the love of one's neighbor is expressed. And Judaism is a system of *mitzvot*. A *mitzvah* (pl., *mitzvot*) is a

> rule of conduct or ritual which is seen as an obligation one owes, not to any human authority, but to God himself, so that in carrying it out one is bringing one's own life, and in some small measure the world, into closer harmony with His will. (Goldberg & Rayner, 1987, p. 293)

Jacobs (1984) reported three distinguishing marks of Jews:

1. Compassion
2. Benevolence
3. Modesty

The content of Jewishness in United States Americans combines retentions with forms and meanings that are infused with United States American values. William Shakespeare expressed the humanity of Jews in a statement made by Shylock:

> Hath not a Jew eyes? hath not a Jew hands, organs, dimensions, senses, affections, passions? fed with the same food, hurt with the same weapons, subject to the same diseases, healed by the same means, warmed and cooled by the same winter and summer, as a Christian is? If you prick us, do we not bleed? if you tickle us, do we not laugh? if you poison us, do we not die? and if you wrong us, shall we not revenge? (*The Merchant of Venice*, Act III, Scene I)

In 1776, only about 2,000 Jews lived in the Colonies. The 19th century witnessed a large wave of Jewish immigration from central and western Europe. By 1820, about 5,000 Jews lived along the East Coast; they established synagogues and auxiliary institutions to maintain their religion. Between 1820 and 1870, their numbers increased to more than 200,000. Between 1870 and 1924, nearly 2.5 million eastern European Jews settled into the larger cities on the East Coast. By the late 1920s, U.S. Jewry was the largest Jewish community in the world (Herberg, 1960). Solomon (1996) reported that, in 1939, about 10 million Jews lived in Europe, 5 million in the Americas, 830,000 in Asia, 6,000 in Africa, and a handful in Oceania, totaling 18 million altogether. Waxman (1992) reported that Jews numbered about 7 million in the United States in 1990. Singer and Seldin (1994) estimated that nearly 45% of the world's Jewish population live in the United States. The majority of Jewish Americans live on the East and West Coasts, with the largest percentages residing in New York, California, Pennsylvania, Illinois, and Florida (U.S. Bureau of the Census, 1992).

Acculturation

Gaining knowledge of Jewish culture is difficult because there is no single Jewish culture. Jewish identity is ethnic, and the degree of acculturation varies for Jewish people. Jewish cultural identity is most often based on a sense of common history. Because not all people of Jewish descent practice Judaism, it is usual to define as Jewish those who define themselves as Jewish.

Solomon (1996) warned against simplistic attempts to reduce Jewish identity to superficial characteristics. "The identity of the individual incorporates many elements, and the Jewish elements are never more than part of a whole" (p. 15). Meyer (1990) reported that three factors have contributed to the formation of contemporary Jewish identity:

1. The *enlightenment,* through which Jews became attuned to modern culture, meant that it became necessary to justify their behavior by reason, the common basis of discourse, rather than by appeal to any authority.
2. *Anti-Semitism,* the rejection by the outside world, led to the reaffirmation of Jewish identity.
3. *Zionism* in the religious sense is a fulfillment of God's promise to Abraham; and in the cultural sense, it is a call to return to the physical land of Israel where a new Jewish culture would be created.

Greeley's (1974) concept of *ethnogenesis,* the theme of ethnic group persistence in later generations as part of the adaptive process, seems appropriate for describing the Jewish cultural experience. Jewish Americans are a composite of three primary groups who came to the United States and forged a distinctive ethnic culture:

1. *Ashkenazi:* from eastern Europe, including Poland and Russia
2. *Sephardic:* from Spain, Portugal, or the Balkans

3. *Edot HaMizrach:* (literally, "the eastern community") from Persia, Yemen, Ethiopia, and other Eastern countries

Differences between the three groups center around customs and cultural influences of the countries of origin. Yiddish, derived from German, is the common language of the Jews. As Herberg (1960) noted, by the 1920s, "American Jewry, despite all internal divisions, already constituted a well-defined ethnic group" (p. 182).

Wouk (1959) reported that Judaism has never tried to extend its influence through conversion. It teaches that "salvation lies in people's conduct before God, not in their taking on the special commands that bind the House of Abraham" (p. 35). Several small groups of African Americans have either adopted or converted to Judaism. Black Judaism had its genesis around the turn of the 20th century in U.S. urban ghettos. Lounds (1981) described a "Hebrew Israelite" as a "Black American of African descent and/or one who is 'of the spirit' " (p. 33). Most Black Jews belong to urban sects that have declared themselves Jewish without going through the traditional conversion process. Brotz (1964) reported that, during the period 1919 to 1931, there are records of at least eight Black Jewish cults that originated in Harlem. Harlem's Black Jews numbered about 1,000 in 1964. The largest congregation is the Commandment Keepers Congregation of the Living God—or as they often refer to themselves from the name of their lodge, the Royal Order of Ethiopian Hebrews, the Sons and Daughters of Culture, Inc.—stated that these groups "have only faint connections to historically recognizable Judaism" (p. 1069). The group contends that African Americans are really Ethiopian Hebrews or Falashas who were stripped of their knowledge of their name and religion during slavery. They believe that both Jacob and Solomon were Black. They believe that they are descendants of King Solomon and the Queen of Sheba, who founded a line of Ethiopian Hebrew kings from Menelik I down to Haile Selassie. Landes (1967) concluded that "this Judaism has never become significant in the Negro life of the United States or elsewhere; and it has been hardly more than a curiosity to American (White) Jews. It has made no impact on social institutions or values, though it can matter in some personal lives" (p. 176).

Culture shock was not great for the Jews because (a) they were literate, (b) the United States represented a permanent home, away from political oppression, and (c) they had no intention of ever returning to their place of origin simply because there was no place to which to return. They were readily adaptable to the new culture, and many were already accustomed to urban living. Zborowski and Herzog (1962) attributed the rapid acculturation and upward mobility of Jews to the favorable fit between their learning- and school-oriented culture and opportunities in the United States at the time of immigration, which made them "first of all Jewish and first of all American" (Zak, 1973, p. 898).

Poverty and Economic Concerns

Krug (1976) reported that many of the 3 million Jews who came to the United States from Russia, Poland, Lithuania, and Hungary had been forced by governmental restrictions in those countries "to make their livelihood as small merchants, peddlers, and artisans" (p. 28). Doctors, teachers, writers, engineers, and other professionals were also represented in the migration of 1880 to 1914 and in the exodus from Germany in later periods. The skills possessed by these immigrants as merchants, traders, artisans, and industrial workers were needed and readily put to use in the United States.

Although financial success is highly valued among Jews, stereotypes have persisted about Jewish attitudes toward money. The reality is that, in Europe, Jews were denied access to many crafts and professions and thus gravitated to pursuits in which money was handled directly. Many people held the stereotype that Jews were conspiring to control the financial empires of the world. Karl Marx's (1844) essay "On the Jewish Question" presented the argument that Judaism is neither a religion nor a peoplehood, but rather the desire for gain. He equated Jews with bourgeois capitalism. The United States American Jew was ultimately characterized as a "clannish, self-seeking lover of money who, shunning hard physical work, made his financial mark through the use of questionable, albeit shrewd, business practices" (Carlson & Colburn, 1972, p. 253).

The extent to which people do not believe that poor Jews or homeless Jews exist is evidence of the stereotype of Jews as economically privileged. Langman (1995) reported that a recent study found that nearly 22% of Jewish households in Brooklyn are below the poverty line. It has been estimated that 3,000 homeless Jews are in New York City. Krug (1976) noted that "responsibility for the plight of the poor, the widows, and the orphans has been a part of the Jewish religion which stresses this worldliness" (p. 46).

History of Oppression

No group has a longer or more varied history of surviving every effect of oppression than the Jewish people. The term *Holocaust* refers to the systematic mass killing of European Jews by the Nazis during World War II. Six million Jews perished during the war (Solomon, 1996). This represented one third of the world's Jewish population and 60% of European Jewry (Schiffman, 1986). Solomon (1996) provided a succinct description of the Holocaust:

> Many people prefer to use the Hebrew term *Shoah* (destruction) to denote the Nazi attempt to exterminate the Jews, since it is less theologically "loaded" than "Holocaust."
>
> Immediately on coming to power in 1933 Hitler began to enact the anti-Jewish legislation he had promised; anybody with one or more Jewish grandparent was defined as racially Jewish. Books by Jewish authors were burned, Jewish businesses boycotted, Jews excluded from the professions; the 1935 Nuremberg Laws consolidated this legislation and extended it to Austria and Czechoslovakia. On Kristallnacht, 9–10 November 1938, synagogues were burnt down, Jewish businesses looted, and thousands of Jews were sent to concentration camps.
>
> Following the invasion of Poland Jews were herded into ghettos where many were murdered and others died from the appalling conditions.
>
> At Wannsee (Berlin) in 1941 the decision was taken to implement the *Endlosung* ("Final Solution"), that is, physically to exterminate all Jews. Extermination camps were established at Auschwitz, Belsen and elsewhere in Central Europe and Jews transported to them in inhuman conditions to be killed, generally by gassing followed by mass cremation; able-bodied Jews were subjected to forced labour under slave conditions before being killed. A systematic policy of humiliation and degradation was practised prior to the actual killing. In all, about six million Jews perished, perhaps two thirds of the Jewish population of Europe and one third of the world Jewish population. (p. 116)

Jews answered the Holocaust by rebuilding their lives and their people. They were determined to be better Jews than they had been before. For many Jews, this meant a country they could call their own, a place where Jews could go and not be turned away. This would be a place where Jews would make the laws and have full rights as citizens. The result of this effort was the establishment of a Jewish state in Palestine in 1948.

Language and the Arts

Hebrew is the language of the Torah, the prayerbook, the Passover Haggadah, and the land of Israel. In addition to Hebrew, three other languages written with the Hebrew alphabet are part of Jewish history and culture: *Aramaic* is an ancient Semitic language and the language of the Talmud. *Yiddish* is a combination of Hebrew, German, and words borrowed from other languages and is still spoken by Jews of eastern European descent

(Ashkenazim). *Ladino* is a combination of Hebrew and Spanish and is still spoken among Jews of Mediterranean background (Sephardim). Both Yiddish and Ladino have a rich literature that includes poetry, lyrics, prayers, and fiction (Diamant & Cooper, 1991).

The Jewish calendar is a prime example of the distinctive culture of Jewish Americans. The Jewish calendar is a solar-lunar calendar. In it, the new day begins at sundown and ends approximately 24 hours later at sundown of the next secular day. Each month consists of 29.5 days; each 12-month lunar year has 354 days arranged on a 19-year cycle. Jewish holidays always occur on the same date on the Jewish calendar; for example, Yom Kippur is always on the 10th day of the month of Tishri; Chanukah begins on the 25th day of the month of Kislev. Jews use B.C.E. (before the common era) and C.E. (common era) instead of the Christian designations B.C. (before Christ) and A.D. (*anno Domini* [in the year of our Lord]).

The tradition of Jewish ritual art and architecture is long and rich. The Jewish religion forbade all corporeal description of divinity. Works of Jewish artists were generally folkloristic and employed simple motifs for decoration. Ritual objects have a religious as well as purely decorative function. They include things as diverse as fine art photographs of Israel, framed examples of Hebrew calligraphy, lithographs, and sculpture. Among artists whose work has been called Jewish art are Marc Chagall, Ben Shahn, Lee Crasner, Louise Nevelson, and Chaim Gross (Diamant & Cooper, 1991; Rubinstein, 1982).

The menorah and the Magen David (Star of David) symbolize the Jewish national awakening, and both are official emblems of the state of Israel. The menorah is the seven- or nine-branched candlestick and was a ceremonial object used in the Holy Temple. The seven-branched menorah has one branch for each of the six days of creation and one for the Sabbath. The nine-branched Chanukah lamp has one branch for each of the eight nights of Chanukah. Menorot carved in wood decorated the entrances of ancient synagogues and constituted a central motif in floor mosaics of Jewish prayer halls. The Magen David, made up of two triangles that interlace to form a six-pointed star, was prominent in 19th-century synagogues. According to legend, the star was on the shields of King David's warriors and soldiers because they wanted their armaments marked with the symbol of God's protection (Dosick, 1995).

Mezuzah is the decorative container and the parchment inscribed with words from the Torah, placed on the doorpost of a Jewish home. It serves as a constant reminder of the obligation to God every time inhabitants enter or leave their home. It also identifies the home as a Jewish household.

Synagogue architecture has two requirements: (a) It should not be so ostentatious as to suggest that the congregation is more interested in externals than with prayer and inwardness; and (b) it must in no way resemble a church (Jacobs, 1984). The latter means that it should not have a steeple or bells. There are no other requirements.

Racism and Prejudice

Jews are people with a multitude of dilemmas. They have been targets for intensely held prejudices. From the Israelite tribes to the prosperous modern-day Israel, bigotry toward Jews has been quite evident. Jews have been blamed for many crises throughout history, including the black plague that swept across Europe in the 14th century. Many eastern European Jews were subjected to pogroms directed at their communities. A *pogrom,* from Yiddish-Russian words for "destruction," is an organized massacre conducted with the aid of government officials.

Despite formal policies concerning religious freedom, periods of anti-Semitism in the United States have been severe. Many Jewish immigrants became prosperous and active in business and politics while facing prejudice and discrimination. Plesur (1982) reported that the industrialist Henry Ford's newspaper, the *Dearborn Independent,* attempted to popularize the idea that Jews intended to monopolize the country's business community and government. Anti-Semitism is rooted in Jewish-Gentile conflicts that have existed for centuries. Discrimination has occurred in all areas of Jewish life, with the form and degree varying with world and national events. Wilson (1978) found that, overall, "religious people tend to be more anti-Semitic than nonreligious people" (p. 316). Despite anti-Semitism, Jewish people became increasingly acculturated in the United States American culture. When Jews were confronted with anti-Semitism in the United States, their response was to emphasize self-employment and self-help, voluntary organizations.

In some parts of the United States, restrictive covenants in real estate contracts were used to keep Jews out of residential areas. Jews were denied access to hotels, restaurants, and country clubs in some areas, and some colleges and universities had quotas for Jews. They were also systematically excluded from many occupations. Despite their apparent similarities, there has been a perceived difference between acts of racism and acts of anti-Semitism. One example of reluctance to include anti-Semitism as an example of racism is found in a major work by Rothenberg (1988). She defined ethnic groups in a way that excludes Jews, whom she identified as "White," thus eliminating them from her discussion of discrimination against ethnic minorities.

Prager and Telushkin (1981) reported that the term *anti-Semitism* was coined in 1879 by Wilhelm Marr, an anti-Semitic spokesman in Germany, to describe the then growing political movement against German Jews. The term is entirely a misnomer, however, since it has nothing to do with Semites. This also explains why we write antisemite as one word. We have adopted the approach of James Parkes, the distinguished Christian historian of anti-semitism, to so write antisemitism, as not to convey the misunderstanding that there is a Semitic entity which antisemitism opposes. (p. 121)

Plesur (1982) stated that, between 1933 and 1941, when the United States entered World War II, more than 100 organizations were active in promoting anti-Semitic propaganda, including charges that the Roosevelt administration was dominated by Jews. Anti-Semitism declined following the war but has seen an increase caused by anxiety over the Israeli-Palestinian conflict, the influence of Christian fundamentalists, and the charge that Jews exploit poor African Americans. Beck (1988) reported that anti-Semitism is fueled in the United States by the

growth of neo-Nazi White supremacists, neo-conservative Christian fundamentalists, and extremists in the Nation of Islam. The increasingly rigid alignment of the political Left with the cause of Palestinians has resulted in the easy elision of "Jew" with "Israel," which has made Jews the world over targets for anti-Israeli sentiments that are often expressed by violent acts of Jew-hating. (p. 96)

Beck (1988) also reported that, in 1987, overt acts of anti-Semitism in the United States rose by 23%. On November 9–10, 1987, the eve of the anniversary of Kristallnacht, Jewish-identified shops and synagogues were vandalized, windows were smashed, and swastikas were painted on walls in dozens of communities. These acts mirrored the events of that night in 1938 when 7,000 Jewish shops were destroyed and synagogues throughout Germany were burned down. During the first 5 months of 1988, the Anti-Defamation League reported 443 anti-Semitic incidents.

A major shift in the views held by United States Americans toward Jews occurred between 1932 and 1982. During this 50-year period, negative traits attributed to Jews as shrewd declined from 79% to 15%; mercenary from 49% to 2%; and aggressive from 12% to 6% (Gordon, 1986).

Suleiman (1988) reported results of a national survey of attitudes of world history teachers and students toward Jews. Students and teachers alike associated Jews with suffering, discrimination, persecution, and the Nazi and World War II experience. Survey respondents viewed Jews as "objects of hatred" who "have been scapegoats for centuries" and who are "struggling for survival" (p. 104). Respondents associated Jews with religion, monotheism, Moses, or the Ten Commandments almost as often as with persecution.

Positive characteristics mentioned included powerful, intellectual, love to learn, industrious, tenacious, builders, energetic, efficient, and brave. Students in the survey articulated one familiar stereotype of Jews, viewing them as rich, exploiting, cheap, money-hungry, stingy, and greedy.

There is a history of hostility between Jews and African Americans. In 1986, in the Howard Beach section of Brooklyn, New York, a group of Whites chased three African American males emerging from a pizza parlor onto an expressway where one of the African American males was killed by an oncoming automobile. The White males were convicted and sentenced for their part in the crime (Binder & Reimers, 1995). This incident most probably reflects the way Plesur (1982) described Jewish-African American relations when he stated that African Americans "are not anti-semitic but anti-white and Jews are the most visible white targets in the ghettos" (p. 149). In the early 1990s, relations between African Americans and Hasids in the Crown Heights area of New York City deteriorated and violence erupted. A major disturbance occurred in the summer of 1991 when an African American child was killed and another injured by a car in a small Jewish motorcade. A rumor spread that the Hasidic-run ambulance driver had tended to the driver of the car and had ignored the children. Some hours later, a Hasidic scholar from Australia was fatally stabbed in apparent retribution for the child's death (Beck, 1991).

African Americans who criticized U.S. support for Israel alienated many Jewish Americans from active participation in African American causes. Prager and Telushkin (1981), distinguishing between anti-Semitism and anti-Zionism, stated that "the consequences of anti-Zionism and antisemitism for the Jewish people are the same" (p. 122). Occurring about the same time were anti-Semitic statements aimed at White merchants and landlords believed to be exploiting African Americans living in ghettos. The reference to New York City as "Hymietown" and to Zionism as the "poison weed" of Judaism by Jesse Jackson in the 1984 presidential campaign and the allegedly anti-Semitic remarks by Louis Farrakhan have exacerbated tensions between African Americans and Jews (Dershowitz, 1991, p. 202).

Perhaps the best description of differences between African Americans and Jews was presented by Pogrebin (1991):

> The differences between blacks and Jews are rarely more obvious than when each group speaks about its own "survival," a word that both use frequently but with quite dissimilar meanings. For blacks, survival means actual physical endurance. . . . For Jews, survival means keeping a minority culture and a religion alive against all odds. . . . In other words, blacks worry about their actual conditions and fear for the present; Jews worry about their history and fear for the future. Black survival is threatened by poverty; Jewish survival is

threatened by affluence. . . . Racism is a bacterium, potentially curable but presently deadly; anti-semitism is a virus, potentially deadly but presently contained. (p. 292)

Sociopolitical Factors

Some Jewish community organizations exist to support individual Jews in their decision to live as Jews. The American Jewish Committee, founded in 1906, has vigorously fought anti-Semitic prejudice and discrimination in the United States. The American Jewish Congress, founded in 1910, has also fought for civil rights for Jewish Americans and has been especially diligent in its pro-Israel efforts. The Anti-Defamation League, set up in 1913, is a major anti-Semitism organization. The United Jewish Appeal, established in 1939, has been a major fund-raising organization for Jewish causes, including war refugees and the state of Israel. The Jewish Defense League was organized in 1968 by Rabbi Kahane in New York City to foster Jewish pride and to defend Jews wherever they were threatened. The North American Jewish Federation is an organization of some 225 local community federations and many social service and educational agencies representing and serving Jewish Americans (Karpf, 1971).

Jewish trade unions sought to improve the lot of early immigrant Jewish workers. In 1888, some Jewish unions formed the United Jewish Trade Union. Cultural activities were expressed through membership societies. Other important Jewish organizations include the Conference of Presidents of Major American Jewish Organizations and the National Jewish Community Relations Advisory Council.

Many Jews have made names for themselves in politics. Abraham Beame, in 1974, became the first Jewish mayor of New York City. He was succeeded by another Jew, Edward Koch. Others who have made impressive contributions in the political arena are Samuel Gompers, Henry Morgenthau; Bella Abzug, Henry Kissinger, Benjamin Cardozo, Arthur Goldberg, and Ruth Bader Ginsburg.

A major focus of political activity for Jews has been on the state of Israel. Zionism is the commitment to the prosperity of Israel. The emergence of Israel as a Jewish state on the former territory of Palestine was a central political issue of the Middle East after World War II. Jews have received vast amounts of financial and military support from Western governments. A major challenge facing Jewry today is discovering how it can contribute to Israeli-Arab reconciliation.

The *Law of Return* is a law that permits any Jew to immigrate to Israel, generally following the Halakhah (traditional Jewish law) in defining who is a Jew. Problems remain, however, for Ethiopian Falashas, the Bene Israel from India, American Black Hebrews, non-Jews who pass as Jews, native Israelis who are "Jews for Jesus," and children of mixed Jewish-Christian couples (Berofsky, 1983).

Borowitz (1979) reported two cases in Israeli courts that failed to separate Jewish nationality and religion. The first dealt with a Jew who converted to Christianity and requested permission to immigrate to Israel under the law that says all Jews have this right. The court turned him down on the grounds that "most Jews consider conversion to another religion as leaving the Jewish community" (p. 76). The second case involved an Israeli Jew who said he was an atheist. He wanted his child registered as a Jew by nationality but without any religious designation. The court turned him down because "if you are part of the Jewish people then you are part of the Jewish religion unless you convert to another one" (p. 76).

Child-Rearing Practices

Bringing up children and teaching them the ways of the Torah are considered to be one of the greatest human privileges for Jewish parents. The essential goal for Jewish parents through the ages has always been to raise a child to be a *mensch,* Yiddish for "a person who cares and shares, loves and studies, and acts righteously in the world" (Diamant & Cooper, 1991, pp. 13-14).

Silberman (1985) stated that "Jewish parents traditionally have seen their children as extensions of themselves rather than separate, still less subordinate creatures . . . children provide their parents with honor and fulfillment as well as with joy" (p. 138). Parenting is often permissive and democratic, with discipline based on reasoning, rather than on corporal punishment. Children are typically free to challenge parental beliefs and are often included in family problem-solving efforts (Rosen & Weltman, 1996). Children are usually taught to delay gratification and to rely on authority, rather than on reciprocity, to justify behavior (Farber, Mindel, & Lazerwitz, 1988). Although children are typically educated in public schools, many receive supplementary instruction in "Hebrew schools" after regular school hours where language and religion are taught.

Religious Practices

It is believed that Judaism originated at Sinai when God entered into a covenant with the people of Israel. Jews are descendants of the tribe of Judah who came out of the Sinai desert into Canaan 3,000 years ago, with a tradition of liberation from Egypt. The Torah, received by Moses and transmitted to Joshua, is the sacred document of that covenant. The Torah, written in Hebrew, presents *mitzvot,* or commandments that govern Jewish life.

Jews can be distinguished in terms of their degree of religious orthodoxy, being liberal (Reform), conservative (Conservative), orthodox (Orthodox), or ultra-Orthodox (e.g., Hasidim). Each of these movements has a central organization with which most individual congregations are affiliated. Each movement trains educators and rabbis and publishes books, magazines, and teaching materials. Although they differ in their approach to theology and practice, they engage in interfaith and intermovement dialogues and actively support the state of Israel. Despite their formal divisions, the hallmark of Judaism is its diversity (Diamant & Cooper, 1991). Some Jews characterize themselves as "secular" in that they are committed to Judaism only in a cultural sense.

Reform Jews, about 30% of the Jewish American population, have instituted many changes in Jewish religious practices, including the use of vernacular languages, musical instruments, and mixed seating for men and women. Reform Judaism rejected the concept of Divine revelation and instead attributed the authorship of Torah to Divinely inspired human beings. Early Reform modernized the worship service by eliminating much of the Hebrew and many of the ritual practices from the services. Borowitz (1979) described Reform Jews as "human beings who would make things right through personal and social ethics" (p. 93). They aimed to create a world of just and merciful, kind and loving, learned and cultured, creative and sensitive people. They vowed to stop talking about the coming of the Messiah and instead work for a Messianic Age. Reform Jews say they accomplish this by working as partners with God to change society, whereas the Hasidic say that Jews must change their own inner lives.

Conservative Jews, about 40% of the Jewish American population, generally practice some balance between religious and modern practices. The Conservative movement was founded by Zacharias Frankel in the mid-19th century. According to the Conservative view, although the law itself changes in response to social, economic, and political realities, individuals are expected to conform to certain classical behaviors, such as keeping kosher, Sabbath and holiday observance, and daily prayer.

Orthodox and ultra-Orthodox Jewish Americans, about 11% of the Jewish American population, attempt to practice traditional Judaism with as few changes as possible. They believe in the direct revelation of Divine law as recorded in the Torah as a guide for everyday life and behavior. About 19% fall into the "secular category" (Diamant & Cooper, 1991; Farber et al., 1988).

The best known of the ultra-Orthodox Jews are the Hasidic Jews, either Satmar or Lubavitch, known for their distinctive dress for men, consisting of long black coats, round black hats, beards, and sidelocks. This group was founded by Rabbi Israel ben Eliezer in eastern Europe in the early 18th century (Dosick, 1995). Binder and Reimers (1995) estimated the Hasidic population to be about 70,000 in 1989. These Jews observe the Sabbath strictly, use the Jewish calendar, segregate the sexes in many social and religious activities, and scorn television. They wear no garments that mix linen and wool. Attending college is frowned upon. Instead, men study the Torah and the Talmud. Women's education consists of instruction on how to run the home in keeping with Orthodox traditions. Married women are required to cover their hair when in public; thus, many wear wigs. Children attend special schools to meet minimum educational standards.

Reconstructionist Judaism was developed in the United States in the early 1920s. Its philosophy rejects the idea of a supernatural God, "understanding God instead as a Power or Process that is the sum of all the forces that give life meaning and worth. Reconstructionism Judaism asserts that Judaism is not merely a religion, but an 'evolving religious civilization,' a peoplehood, a culture, as well as a faith community" (Dosick, 1995, p. 63). These Jews believe that Jews in every generation have an obligation to keep Judaism alive through the process of reconstructing it, reinterpreting ancient rituals and practices and discovering new meanings in them (Diamant & Cooper, 1991).

Judaism has few doctrines, dogmas, or philosophic certainties. The Thirteen Principles of the Jewish Faith, first formulated by Moses Maimonides in his *Commentary on the Mishna* (composed c. 1160), come as close to doctrine as will be found in Judaism. Maimonides took the work of hundreds of sages over the years and recast it into a single book. His purpose was to give the Jews a codified Talmud, a ready reference book of Hebrew law. He "stands without question as the mightiest single legal authority in Jewry from the Talmud to the present" (Wouk, 1959, p. 218). Jacobs (1984) described the 13 principles of faith as "essential to the totality of Judaism" (p. 5):

1. The Creator is Author and Guide of everything that exists.

2. The Creator is One; His unity is unlike that of anything else; He is our God and exists eternally.

3. The Creator has no body or physical characteristics and cannot be compared with anything that exists.

4. The Creator is first and last of all beings.

5. It is right to pray to the Creator, but to no other being.

6. All the words of the prophets were true.

7. The prophecy of Moses is true, and He was the father (that is, the greatest) of all prophets, both before and after Him.
8. The Torah now in our possession is that given to Moses.
9. The Torah will not be changed, nor will the Creator give any other Torah.
10. The Creator knows the deeds and thoughts of people.
11. He rewards those who keep His commandments, and punishes those who disobey.
12. Though the Messiah delay, one must constantly expect His coming.
13. The dead will be resurrected. (Solomon, 1996, p. 135)

Festival celebrations serve as a distinctive feature of Judaism and are as much a matter for the home as for the synagogue. Jewish holidays have two main sources: biblical and historical. The Torah assigns meaning to the biblical holidays. Festival days include the following:

- *Rosh Hashanah* (New Year), the day of judgment, is celebrated in the fall by home visits, greeting cards to family and friends, and festive meals, including the symbolic apples and honey. The central ritual at the synagogue is the blowing of the *shofar,* or ram's horn, 100 times to remind worshipers of the need to atone for their misdeeds.
- *Yom Kippur* (Day of Atonement) occurs 10 days after Rosh Hashanah. The family prays in the synagogue, and after a family meal, the family fasts for 24 hours. Five abstentions are associated with Yom Kippur: (a) eating and drinking, (b) sex, (c) bathing, (d) anointing the body with oil, and (e) wearing leather shoes. Prayers center on repentance before judgment, of release from sin and error.
- *Hanukah* (Feast of Lights) occurs in the winter and lasts for 8 days. A candle is lit each night, and gifts are exchanged among family members. This was once a minor holiday but seems to have taken on greater importance in the United States because it parallels Christmas.
- *Pesach* (Passover) occurs in the spring and lasts for 8 days. The family meal consisting of symbolic foods is eaten, during which time the family recounts the exodus of the Jews from Egypt. The Passover meal, or Seder, features both matzo (unleavened bread) and bitter herbs (Trepp, 1980).

Other festival days, without religious significance, include Yom HaShoah, Holocaust Remembrance Day, and Yom Haatzmaut, Israel's Independence Day.

The Sabbath has special significance in Judaism. The Sabbath is 1 day in every 7 when work stops in honor of the Creator. It is observed from sundown on Friday to the end of twilight on Saturday. It is a gesture of the community, the immemorial collective gesture of stopping work and celebrating. Rest is only half of the ordinance; the day is also holy, set off by changes in dress, manners, diet, and occupations, and by special worship of the Creator. The pious Jew does not travel on the Sabbath, or cook, or use motors or electric appliances, or spend money, or smoke, or write. The main effect of these behaviors is release, peace, gaiety, and lifted spirits.

Dietary rules and practices serve as distinguishing characteristics of worldwide Jewry. *Kashrut,* the system of rules and laws regulating what Jews eat and how Jews prepare food, clearly sets the Jews apart from other United States Americans. Although Muslims and some Christian denominations have dietary rules, none seem as rigid as those of Judaism. Dietary rules in Judaism cut across general manners and ideas. The laws of the Kashrut specify what kinds of foods may be eaten, what foods are prohibited, and how foods are to be acquired and prepared. These centuries-old practices are less about abiding by a list of rigid rules and regulations and more about maximizing one's spiritual, physical, and emotional well-being:

- There is no limit on food that is grown from the ground.
- Animals may be eaten if they are cud-chewing and have a split hoof. This admits beasts that live on grass and leaves, and eliminates beasts of prey, rodents, reptiles, swine, horses, pachyderms, and primates.
- Creatures of the sea are permitted if they have fins and scales; shellfish (shrimps, oysters, and lobsters), sea urchins, snails, mussels, frogs, octopuses, and squids are eliminated.
- No insects are permitted.
- There is a general ban against eating carrion: defined as the flesh of an animal that dies of old age or of disease, or that is torn to death by beasts of prey, or that meets any other violent death.
- Permitted foods must be prepared according to kosher rules. *Kosher* means pure. Animals should be killed by severance of the carotid artery in the neck with a razor-sharp knife. There should be no evidence of disease.
- Rules relating to meat:
  - May not eat flesh cut from a live creature.
  - May not drink blood.
  - May not combine the flesh and milk of an animal.
  - May not use the hard fat formed below the diaphragm.
  - May not eat the sciatic nerve of the hindquarter.

Life-course rituals serve to further identify Jewish ethnicity. The most important life-course rituals of the Jewish tradition are the bris and the Bar and Bas Mitzvah. The *bris* is a religious circumcision used to welcome newborn males to the Jewish community. Boys are circumcised on the 8th day of their life by a person trained in this religious ritual and surgical procedure.

Bar Mitzvah means "son of the commandment" (Wouk, 1959, p. 142). One in not *Bar Mitzvahed;* rather, one *becomes a Bar Mitzvah* or *Bas Mitzvah.* Bar Mitzvah marks a boy's entrance into a responsible religious life. At the age of 13, a boy's mind is capable of grasping concepts and has the discipline to take on religious duties. On the Sabbath nearest his birthday, he receives an *aliya,* a call to the Torah, to speak the blessing over a part of the weekly reading to mark his new status. A child must pass serious examinations in Hebrew, the classics, the laws of the faith, and the history of Jewry.

Girls participate in a *Bas Mitzvah* ceremony, similar to that of the Bar Mitzvah, except that females are exempt from most of the advanced Hebrew studies because they are exempt from most of the Jewish ritual. Girls celebrate their rite earlier than boys, around 12 or 12½ years of age. The Bas Mitzvah is "often a sort of graduation from Sunday-school training, or at least the completion of one stage" (Wouk, 1959, p. 147). The Bas Mitzvah does not occur in traditional synagogues. In most Conservative, Reconstructionist, and Reform synagogues and temples, the Bas and Bar Mitzvah are afforded equal importance.

Practices relating to death and mourning are deeply rooted in religious practice. The Jewish idea of respect for the dead requires the swiftest possible burial in the most austere possible manner. During the first 7 days following death, *Shiva* is a period of mourning when the family remains at home, seated on low stools, receiving a continuous stream of condolence calls. This is followed by the *Shloshim,* a 30-day period when family members resume normal activities, avoiding places of entertainment and continuing to observe certain forms and prayers. At the end of the 30 days, mourning is over, except for one's father or mother, for whom the period of mourning is 1 year.

Kaddish is an ancient Aramaic prose-poem sanctifying God's name and praying for the speedy coming of his kingdom. It is a community prayer that requires a congregation of 10 adult Jews, called a *minyan.* It is spoken during the period of mourning as a pledge of one's undimmed faith in God despite the disaster in the life of the newly bereaved. It may be spoken in unison by all mourners present. On the anniversary of a death, the survivors recite Kaddish year after year.

Family Structure and Dynamics

Fishman (1988) found three clearly discernible trends in contemporary Jewish family life in the United States:

1. The elderly are the fastest growing cohort among the Jewish population. Jewish family life has a strong sense of children's duty to parents. No matter how poor a Jew might be, he or she must support parents.

2. Jewish women are marrying later in life and are bearing children later than earlier generations.

3. Jews are more likely to consider themselves successful human beings when they enjoy marital satisfaction and more likely to suffer lower self-esteem when they experience marital instability or divorce.

Fishman (1988) reported that emphasis on marriage begins at birth, when children "receive a blessing that they mature into marriage and good deeds" (p. 1). She also reported that, in the United States, 95% of Jewish females are married by age 34 and 96% of Jewish males are married by age 39. Married life is characterized by role segregation, with religious tradition specifying by written contract the rights and obligations of each spouse (Guttentag & Secord, 1983). Birth control is generally forbidden. Parental devotion and care, like childbearing, is seen as a religious obligation.

Rosen and Weltman (1996) identified three factors that account for the unusually strong Jewish emphasis on marriage:

1. The child-focused nature of the Jewish family, with children and grandchildren considered the very essence of life's meaning

2. The powerful forces of suffering and discrimination, which imbue the family with the quality of "haven and refuge" when all other social institutions cannot be trusted

3. The strong connection that Jews feel to previous generations and to the obligation to preserve their heritage (p. 613)

Cultural Values and Attitudes

Rosen and Weltman (1996) noted that eastern European Jewish families place primary emphasis on four values:

1. Centrality of the family
2. Suffering as a shared experience
3. Intellectual achievement and financial success
4. Verbal expression of feelings

Silberman (1985) estimated that more than 60% of Jewish adults are college graduates. McGoldrick and Giordano (1996) reported that Jews have long valued cognitive clarity: "Clarifying and sharing ideas and perceptions helps them find meaning in life" (p. 11). Herz and Rosen (1982) pointed out that "success is so vitally important to the Jewish family ethos that you cannot understand the family without understanding the place of success for men and more recently for women" (p. 368).

Goldberg and Rayner (1987) presented an array of Jewish values, among which are the following:

- Four ideal types of persons receive particular praise in Jewish tradition:
  - *Talmid chacham,* the scholar, steeped in Jewish law and lore
  - *Chasid,* one motivated by a constant love of God and desire to do His will
  - *Tzaddik,* the nearest humanly possible approach to perfection, in respect of both inner motivation and overt conduct
  - *Kadosh,* one whose relationship with God is so intimate that the person's whole being is irradiated by exposure to the Divine source of holiness
- Great sensitivity is shown by Jewish tradition when it warns against any action that may damage another person's good name or self-esteem.
- *Tzedakah* (almsgiving) should be done secretly so that the recipient may not be humiliated. A standard feature of Jewish communities is a publicly administered charity chest that preserves the anonymity of donors and recipients alike.
- Judaism is positively concerned with the social dimension of life. Because society is viewed as a family of families, the problem of social ethics is essentially how to transpose the caring characteristics of family life into the larger contests of society.
- Jews are encouraged to identify themselves with the society in which they live and to contribute to its welfare.
- Jewish tradition places major emphasis on the value of work.
- Judaism teaches respect for nature. Particular emphasis is placed on the need to avoid inflicting unnecessary suffering on animals. Respect for nature extends to land as well, where the biblical law required the farmer to let his or her land lie fallow every 7th year.

Other values associated with Jews include giving and receiving; verbal proficiency; valuing children's opinions; using cynicism and criticism to get others to react and respond; and having a well-developed sense of humor. The core of being a Jew is to be different in living habits and to practice a moral way of life based on behavior toward other people (Wouk, 1959).

Implications

Mael (1991) identified career restraints of Observant Jews that are applicable to Jews in employment, school, and other organizational settings.

These include the reminder that Friday night and Saturday activities may be unavailable to participation by Jews. School athletic activities typically scheduled on weekends may be at times when Jewish students may not participate. Jewish holidays frequently occur on school days or workdays and should be taken into account when scheduling meetings or activities. Although food may not be an issue to most, many Jews restrict their diet to kosher foods. Finally, institutions would do a service to its non-Jewish participants if programs were made available to provide knowledge on Jewish holidays, practices, and religious beliefs.

Cohen (1983) summarized general social trends marking American Jewry. Knowledge of these trends may be useful to those working with Jews in a variety of settings:

- Jews are increasingly attracted to those professions accessible through higher education.
- A decline has occurred in institutional affiliation, both with synagogues and with philanthropic and defense organizations.
- A decline has occurred in ritual observance, connected with more and more higher education and entry into the professions.
- Jews have moved away from their early inner-city and Northeastern metropolitan concentrations.
- The Jewish family has followed general trends in United States American society.
- Politically, Jews have been associated with the Democratic Party.
- The more orthopraxic Jews have gained in confidence and prominence.

The Jewish community is facing a crisis. More than half of marriages today are outside the faith. Only one third are raising their children Jewish. There is a projected 50% drop in the Jewish population in the United States. Only 48% of Jews hold formal membership in synagogues or temples (Cohen & Rosen, 1992). Issues that have traditionally bound Jews together—the Holocaust and the establishment of the Jewish state of Israel—are no longer enough to bind young Jews. History has been removed from those who did not live it. Young Jews do not face the same societal barriers their parents did. Today, Jews are included in almost every arena of American life. The challenge is to maintain commitment to Jewish life and traditions while living in the open U.S. society. Many Jewish leaders believe that the solution to this problem is to return to the core of Judaism—the religion that has provided meaning and direction for centuries. Where that spirit of religion is expressed, there is new life. The poet Muriel Rukeyser (1978) expressed these sentiments in a poem entitled "Letter to the Front" where she suggested that being Jewish was a "gift" and the refusal of the gift resulted in "death of the spirit" (p. 239).

Questions for Review and Reflection

1. Define the following terms:

Jewishness	Anti-Semitism
Ashkenazi	Zionism
Sephardic	Rosh Hashanah
Hebrew Israelite	Yom Kippur
Holocaust	Hanukah
B.C.E. and C.E.	Pesach
Magen David	Kashrut
pogrom	Bar and Bas Mitzvah

2. How has the Holocaust influenced contemporary Jewish culture? Why should or should not this event be prominent in a discussion of Jewish Americans?

3. Which Jewish American cultural values are responsible for the relative success of Jewish Americans? How can counselors use this knowledge in working with Jewish students or clients?

4. What stereotypes do you hold about Jewish people? How might the stereotypes facilitate or hinder your work with Jewish students or clients?

5. What has been the major impact of Jewish culture on the dominant culture of the United States?

6. What similarities and differences are likely to be evident among Reform, Conservative, and Orthodox Jews? How can knowledge of these similarities and differences be used in working with Jewish students or clients?

7. What potential advantages or difficulties might exist for individuals who celebrate Jewish holidays? Who practices the dietary restrictions known as Kashrut?

8. What factors have contributed to Jewish Americans' rapid adjustment to the culture of the United States?

9. How can knowledge of the social trends described by S. Cohen (1983) be used in developing educational programs or counseling strategies with Jewish Americans?

10. How are problems faced by Jewish Americans similar to and different from problems faced by other cultural groups in the United States?

References

Beck, E. T. (1988). The politics of Jewish invisibility. *National Women's Studies Association Journal, 1*(1), 93-102.

Beck, M. (1991, September 9). Bonfire in Crown Heights. *Newsweek, 118,* 48.

Berger, J. (1986, February 28). Split widens on a basic issue: What is a Jew? *New York Times,* p. A18.

Berofsky, B. (1983). Jewish self-definition and exile. In E. Levine (Ed.), *Diaspora: Exile and the Jewish condition* (pp. 101-125). New York: Jason Aronson.

Binder, F. M., & Reimers, D. M. (1995). *All the nations under Heaven: An ethnic and racial history of New York City.* New York: Columbia University Press.

Borowitz, E. B. (1979). *Understanding Judaism.* New York: Union of American Hebrew Congregations.

Brotz, H. (1964). *The Black Jews of Harlem: Negro nationalism and the dilemmas of Negro leadership.* New York: Free Press of Glencoe.

Carlson, L. H., & Colburn, G. A. (1972). *In their place: White America defines her minorities, 1850-1950.* New York: John Wiley.

Cohen, R., & Rosen, S. (1992). *Organizational affiliations of American Jews: A research report.* New York: American Jewish Committee.

Cohen, S. (1983). *American modernity and Jewish identity.* New York: Tavistock.

Dershowitz, A. (1991). *Chutzpah.* Boston: Little, Brown.

Diamant, A., & Cooper, H. (1991). *Living a Jewish life: Jewish traditions, customs, and values for today's families.* New York: Harper & Row.

Dosick, W. (1995). *Living Judaism.* New York: HarperCollins.

Farber, B., Mindel, C. H., & Lazerwitz, B. (1988). The Jewish American family. In C. H. Mindel, R. W. Habenstein, & R. Wright, Jr. (Eds.), *Ethnic families in America: Patterns and variations* (pp. 400-437). New York: Elsevier.

Fishman, S. B. (1988). The changing American Jewish family in the '80s. *Contemporary Jewry, 9*(2), 1-33.

Goldberg, D. J., & Rayner, J. D. (1987). *The Jewish people: Their history and their religion.* New York: Viking.

Gordon, L. (1986). College student stereotypes of Blacks and Jews on two campuses: Four studies spanning 50 years. *Sociology and Social Research, 70,* 200-201.

Greeley, A. M. (1974). *Ethnicity in the United States.* New York: John Wiley.

Guttentag, M., & Secord, P. F. (1983). *Too many women: The sex ratio question.* Beverly Hills, CA: Sage.

Herberg, W. (1960). *Protestant—Catholic—Jew: An essay in American religious sociology.* New York: Anchor.

Herz, F., & Rosen, E. (1982). Jewish families. In M. McGoldrick, J. Pearce, & J. Giordano (Eds.), *Ethnicity and family therapy* (pp. 364-392). New York: Guilford.

Jacobs, L. (1984). *The book of Jewish belief.* West Orange, NJ: Behrman House.

Karpf, M. J. (1971). *Jewish community organization in the United States.* New York: Arno.

Krug, M. (1976). *The melting of the ethnics.* Bloomington, IN: Phi Delta Kappa.

Landes, R. (1967). Negro Jews in Harlem. *Jewish Journal of Sociology, 9*(2), 175-190.

Langman, P. F. (1995). Including Jews in multiculturalism. *Journal of Multicultural Counseling and Development, 23,* 222-236.

Lounds, M., Jr. (1981). *Israel's Black Hebrews: Black Americans in search of identity.* Washington, DC: University Press of America.

Mael, F. A. (1991). Career constraints of observant Jews. *Career Development Quarterly, 39,* 341-349.

Marx, K. (1844). *Deutsch-franzosische Jahrbucher.* Paris: Im Bureau Der Jahrbucher.

McGoldrick, M., & Giordano, J. (1996). Overview: Ethnicity and family therapy. In M. McGoldrick, J. Giordano, & J. K. Pearce (Eds.), *Ethnicity and family therapy* (pp. 1 -27). New York: Guilford.

Meyer, M. A. (1990). *Jewish identity in the modern world.* Seattle: University of Washington Press.

Plesur, M. (1982). *Jewish life in 20th-century America.* Chicago: Nelson-Hall.

Pogrebin, L. C. (1991). *Deborah, Golda, and me: Being female and Jewish in America.* New York: Crown.

Prager, D., & Telushkin, J. (1981). *The nine questions people ask about Judaism.* New York: Simon & Schuster.

Rosen, E. J., & Weltman, S. F. (1996). Jewish families: An overview. In M. McGoldrick, J. Giordano, & J. K. Pearce (Eds.), *Ethnicity and family therapy* (pp. 611-630). New York: Guilford.

Rothenberg, P. (1988). *Racism and sexism: An integrated study.* New York: St. Martin's.

Rubinstein, C. S. (1982). *American women artists: From early Indian times to the present.* Boston: G. K. Hall.

Rukeyser, M. (1978). *The collected poems of Muriel Rukeyser.* New York: McGraw-Hill.

Schiffman, L. H. (1986). *Judaism: A primer.* New York: Anti-Defamation League of B'nai B'rith.

Silberman, C. E. (1985). *A certain people: American Jews and their lives today.* New York: Summit.

Singer, D., & Seldin, R. (1994). *American Jewish yearbook, 1994.* New York: American Jewish Committee.

Solomon, N. (1996). *Judaism.* Oxford: Oxford University Press.

Suleiman, M. W. (1988). *The Arabs in the mind of America.* Brattleboro, VT: Amana.

Trepp, L. (1980). *The complete book of Jewish observance.* New York: Behrman House.

U.S. Bureau of the Census. (1992). *Statistical abstract of the United States.* Washington, DC: Government Printing Office.

Waxman, C. I. (1992). Are American Jews experiencing a religious revival? *Qualitative Sociology, 15*(2), 203-211.

Wilson, J. (1978). *Religion in American society: The effective presence.* Upper Saddle River, NJ: Prentice Hall.

Wouk, H. (1959). *This is my God.* Garden City, NY: Doubleday.

Zak, I. (1973). Dimensions of Jewish American identity. *Psychological Reports, 33,* 891-900.

Zborowski, M., & Herzog, E. (1962). *Life is with people: The culture of the Shtetl.* New York: Schocken.

12

_____
=======
___

Muslims in the United States

Early Muslim immigration to the United States began in the late 1800s, primarily from the Middle East. Interest in Muslims in the United States has grown in relation to their increasing presence in urban areas, as well as the development of their distinctive institutions across the country. These include more than 1,500 mosques/Islamic centers, two Islamic colleges, hundreds of parochial schools, hundreds of weekend schools, women's organizations, youth groups, and professional and civic organizations (Haddad, 1991). Gardell (1996) characterized Islam as the "most rapidly expanding religion in the world" (p. 3), and Cooper (1993) called Islam the fastest growing religion in the United States, partly because of conversion by African Americans, estimated to number about 3 million. Although Muslims live throughout the United States, the largest concentrations are in New York, California, and Illinois (Stone, 1991). Less than one fifth of Muslims in North America are of Arab or Iranian origin (Nanji, 1993). Each ethnic group within Islam has its own local culture that determines the way Muslims practice their faith.

One source called the religion of Islam an "American phenomenon" (Haddad & Lummis, 1987, p. 3). Jones (1983) suggested that its philosophical foundations are deeply rooted in the Black-White "crisis situation" (p. 418). The essence of the religious ideology has influence in the social, economic, and political arenas. Although considered a religion, Islam is also a way of life, a set of values and ethics.

Ahmed (1992) estimated the worldwide population of Muslims as about 1 billion people living in about 44 nations. Because the U.S. Bureau of the Census does not record religious affiliation, no official statistics exist on the number of Muslims in the United States. Gardell (1996) reported that Muslims in the United States number between 6 and 8 million. It has been predicted that, by the turn of the century, Islam will replace Judaism as the second largest religion in the United States, behind Christianity. It has also been predicted that one out of four people in the world will be Muslim by 2025 (Suchetka, 1996).

Although the Muslim population originated in the Middle East, the largest Muslim country is Indonesia. About one third of all Muslims in the United States are from India and Pakistan. The term *Muslim* is not synonymous with *Arab.* Thus, *Muslim* and *Arab* are not interchangeable terms. Muslims may be Arabs, Turks, Persians, Indians, Pakistanis, Malaysians, Indonesians, Europeans, Africans, Americans, Chinese, or other nationalities. Twelve million Christians and 10,000 Jews live in Arab countries and consider themselves Arab. An *Arab* is a person whose native tongue is Arabic and who identifies with Arab concerns; a *Muslim* is an adherent of the religion of Islam. For Muslims, their religion, not their country of origin, defines their ethnicity.

The word *religion* in Islam refers to a whole way of life. Watt (1968) stated,

> Islam is not a private matter for individuals, touching only the periphery of their lives, but something which is both private and public, something which permeates the whole fabric of society in a way of which men are conscious. It is—all in one—theological dogma, forms of worship, political theory, and a detailed code of conduct, including even matters which the European would classify as hygiene or etiquette. (p. 3)

The principle that best defines Islam is that of unity even though a wide range of opinions, temperaments, historical experiences, preferences, and convictions are represented and there is no common organizational structure. Nanji (1993) stated that "unity defines the nature of the divine; it is the defining element in the relationship between material life and spiritual life and between human beings as they interact in society and with the natural environment" (p. 232). Muslims use the term *Ummah* for the community that develops out of this unity.

This chapter focuses on all Muslims living in the United States. Special attention is given to the Nation of Islam, or Black Muslims. Readers are reminded that Muslims, like the other ethnic groups described in this book, are heterogeneous. Differences among Muslims may be based on country of origin, branch of Islamic faith, or degree of acculturation, among other things. Topics from the model are more or less appropriate on the basis of these differences.

Acculturation

The tensions that exist around acculturation continue to engage Muslims in the United States. These tensions result from the mingling of ethnic and religious culture, representing a double opposition to the Anglo American culture (Haddad & Smith, 1994). The primary question is whether they will be Muslims who live in an alien culture or United States Americans who happen to be Muslim. Questions of what heritage to pass on to children and how to do so are also primary concerns. Islam teaches its followers to be responsible members of society and requires adherents to the faith to educate themselves and to take responsibility for their behavior and their lives.

Jones (1983) presented evidence of Muslim accommodation (acculturation) to the larger society:

- Relaxation of admission policies to accommodate a more integrationist-oriented religion
- Less emphasis on the separatist aspects of the religion, with greater emphasis on patriotism (including military service)
- Centralization of religious instruction
- Development of a conventional interest in political life
- Accentuation of the spiritual and subordination of the secular
- More interfaith cooperation
- Moderation of expressions of hostility toward Whites

Poverty and Economic Concerns

Because economic matters are regulated by religious teachings, Muslims have directions for relating with each other and with non-Muslims. One Islam direction prohibits interest on money, although some Muslims insist that this rule only applies to excessive interest. Muslims are more likely to adhere to this practice when dealing with fellow Muslims than when dealing with non-Muslims.

The economic politics of the Nation of Islam have fostered business ventures in different sectors: a chain of Salaam restaurants, Shabazz bakeries,

Fashahnn Islamic clothing, clothing stores, food markets, the Nation of Islam Security Agency, Clean 'N Fresh skin and hair care products, Abundant Life Clinics, real estate in some states, fish markets, farmland, and a Chicago mall of supermarkets and restaurants (Gardell, 1996).

The taxation issue of Muslim property has been a major source of difficulty between Muslim communities and local and state governments. These conflicts are not restricted to Muslims but have been a source of conflict for other religious groups as well. The statutory language exempts houses of public worship, provided that the property is used exclusively for religious worship or religious purposes. Church ownership is the sole and sufficient criterion for exemption, and both ownership and specific religious use are required.

History of Oppression

Muslims began arriving in the United States during the last third of the 19th century. On arrival, most Muslims isolated themselves with other followers of the Islamic faith. The development of Muslim communities actually served as boundaries to protect themselves from those who failed to extend a welcome. In doing so, the number of Muslims began to increase, not only from new immigrants but also from conversions to Islam. Islam made inroads to the African American community in the United States by promising liberation of an oppressed people from their oppression.

The overwhelming majority of United States American Muslims keep a low or apolitical profile. This fact is perhaps overshadowed by two unrelated factors: (a) the February 26, 1993, bombing of the World Trade Center and the subsequent arrest of Egyptian Islamist Sheikh Omar Abdel Rahman; and (b) the political activities of Minister Louis Farrakhan of the Nation of Islam.

Naylor (1983) captured many of the common stereotypes of Arabs and Muslims in the following passage:

> Given the long history of political, economic and indeed military conflict, the West has always had its Islamic "bad guy" to color popular culture—be he Salah Ad-Din throwing the Crusaders out of Palestine, the Ottoman Sultan Suleiman, ganging on the gates of Vienna, a Barbary pirate chasing English and French ships out of the Mediterranean, an "oil sheikh" brandishing the so-called "oil weapon," or, as the culmination and personification of the Western world's current prejudices and fears, the image of a Palestinian guerrilla, wrapped in his kaffiyeh, threatening to bring international civil aviation to a standstill. (pp. 392-393)

Language and the Arts

The foremost characteristic of Islamic art is the universal use of Arabic script. The Arabic language is treasured by Muslims because it is so closely related to the Islamic religion. When Prophet Mohammed received the word of God, he recorded it in Arabic. Today, the Arabic of the Qur'an is studied by Muslims worldwide and is understood my most Arabic-speaking people. The art of transcribing the Qur'an into a beautiful script was considered an act of devotion, and its calligraphers have been highly esteemed. The Qur'an is considered the authority on grammatical and idiomatic questions and also on literary style. The use of formal Arabic in everyday conversations is not used. The formal Arabic language cannot be exactly translated into English because it is very structured and the grammatical rules are rigid. Arabic tends to be more abstract and expressive than English. Much emphasis is placed on words and the rhythm and harmony produced by combinations of words. The meaning of words is less significant in Arabic language than in Western languages.

Another feature of Islamic art is the surface embellishment of everyday objects with designs that harmoniously enhance the object. The decorations may include inscriptions, scrolls, geometric motifs, and floral elements. These decorations may be found in bookbindings, textiles, rugs, ceramics, tile, and metalwork.

Ahmed (1992) reported that the tradition that consciously bonds spirituality with art is a continuing one among Muslims. Muslim art often bridges the "trends, styles and ideas between Islamic and Western cultures" (p. 202). Expressing the voices of nationalism and politics while capturing the pull of the Qur'an and the village are themes in Islamic art. Islamic architecture is best seen in the construction of mosques, which range from the historical architecture found in the old Muslim cities to the modern architecture of recently built structures in the United States.

Racism and Prejudice

The rise of Islamic awareness, coupled with the immigration of Muslims as well as the conversion of large numbers of African Americans, has brought about a new sense of what it means to be Muslim in the United States. Muslims are eager to show that the God they worship is the God of Christianity and Judaism. Some evidence suggests a negative image of Islam, especially in the light of recent events in the Middle East. Many people in the United States do not see Islam as a religion, but rather as terrorism in a political arena. Muslims desire that their religion be seen as one of peace and acceptance and that they not be judged by the actions of particular Muslim individuals and groups.

Prejudice against Muslims in the United States is not confined to verbal harassment. Cooper (1993) reported that incidents "range from phone threats to physical attacks on people to bombings and desecrations of mosques" (p. 368). After experiencing discrimination and occasional hate crimes, Muslims are organizing to make their voices heard. In 1990, the American Muslim Council (AMC) was established to represent Muslims in Washington and to provide information to non-Muslims about Islam.

In a report issued by the Los Angeles Commission on Human Relations (Chan, 1991), information was provided on the rise in hate crimes directed toward persons of Arab descent and Muslims before and during the Gulf War. Anti-Muslim evidence in this report included death threats, threats to mosques, negative stereotypes in the media, and minimum coverage of Muslim issues in public school curricula.

Suleiman (1988) reported results of a national survey of attitudes of world history teachers toward Muslims. Although most used neutral language to refer to Muslims and their beliefs, some expressed both positive and negative remarks. Negative remarks included "religious faith that stifles creativity, fanatical, fatalistic, slow in accepting change, holders of anachronistic beliefs, warlike people, and very religious but misguided" (p. 98). On the positive side, Muslims were described as "proud, stubborn, determined, organized, rich heritage, innovative, good people, dedicated, aesthetic, sincere, sincere in belief, appeal to racial equality, tolerant, devout, non-discriminatory, and highly ethical" (p. 99).

Sociopolitical Factors

Islam's appeal to African Americans has hinged on the belief that up to one fifth of all Africans brought to the United States were Muslims before they were forced to convert to Christianity (Cooper, 1993). Islam became an important symbol for African American cultural development during the 1960s. Movements such as the Moorish American Science Temple of Noble Drew Ali and the Nation of Islam provided African Americans the means for affirmation of identity and advancement in the face of White oppression under the religious umbrella of Islamic beliefs and practices (Haddad & Smith, 1994).

The Nation of Islam began in Detroit during the 1930s and by 1959 had grown to 50 temples in 22 states and the District of Columbia (Jaynes & Williams, 1989). What founder Elijah Muhammad provided to African Americans in the 1930s was a social commentary that many perceived as both accurate and powerful in its articulation of the conditions, needs, and aspirations of a large segment of the African American community. He identified Whites as the oppressors and offered specific programs for self-determination, stressing self-knowledge, self-reliance, and self-discipline (Lincoln, 1994).

During the 1960s, the movement achieved national prominence through the personality of Malcolm X, Elijah Muhammad's spokesman, whose forceful articulations of racial pride and Muslim principles made him a cultural hero, especially among African American youths. Malcolm Little changed his name to Malcolm X when Muslims were encouraged to return their surnames to the former slave owners and to retake their original Islamic names as a manifest symbol of their mental emancipation. The X was adopted as a symbol for the original surname, lost during slavery. X also symbolized the mystery of God, the divine power latent in the Black person's nature and manifest through the Nation of Islam. Dropping one's surname and replacing it with an X also meant ex-slave, ex-Christian, and ex-Negro (Haddad & Smith, 1994). After making the Hajj (see "Religious Practices," below), Malcolm X took the name El-Hajj Malik el-Shabazz, the result of converting to orthodox Sunni Islam. In March 1964, he left the Nation of Islam after realizing that Islam is not a religion of hatred, racism, and separation.

A series of changes in the social, intellectual, and spiritual direction and development of the Nation of Islam were effected in the late 1970s under the leadership of Elijah Muhammad's successor, his son, Wallace D. Muhammad. During this period, all precepts of color-consciousness, racism, and the deification of Fard Muhammad (see "Child-Rearing Practices," below) were repudiated, and the organization was renamed the American Muslim Mission. In May 1985, Wallace D. Muhammad announced the dissolution of the American Muslim Mission in order that its members might become a part of the worldwide orthodox Islamic community. The centralized leadership and organization came to an end, although its network of mosques and their attendant religious, educational, and economic programs continued to function. A splinter group based in New York City under the leadership of Louis Farrakhan retained both the name and the founding principles of the Nation of Islam.

Lincoln and Mamiya (1990) estimated that, by 1989, about 1 million Muslims in the United States were African American and that close to 90% of new converts to Islam were African American. Lincoln (1994) described the Black Muslims as "America's foremost black nationalist movement" (p. 2), persistent as a mass movement of protest in the face of "the horror of prison life, the danger of being killed while under arrest, the unevenness and uncertainty of justice in the courts, poverty and hunger, [and] the continuing problem of simply finding a decent place to live" (p. 8). Black Muslim membership is described as young, predominantly male, essentially lower class, almost wholly African American, and predominantly ex-Christian. From the Nation of Islam, other African American groups professing affiliation with Islam emerged. Among them are the Ansaar Allah, the Five Percenters, the Dar ul-Islam, the Islamic Party of North America, the Islamic Brotherhood, and the Hanafi Movement. Mahmoud (1996, p. 114) posited that there are at least three distinct communities of African American Muslims:

1. *Cultural nationalists* stress separation and independence from the dominant community.
2. *Sunni (African American-centered)* adhere to the traditional practice of Islam while stressing self-determination and pride.
3. *Sunni (Arab-centered)* adhere to the traditional practice of Islam, stress the universality of the religion, and are most comfortable in an international, multicultural Islamic community.

The Five Percenters, organized in 1964 under the leadership of Clarence 13X, derived their name from their belief that they are the chosen 5% of humanity who live a righteous Islamic life. They were at the forefront of disseminating the teachings of Elijah Muhammad among the adolescent generation of the 1960s in the New York metropolitan area. Many of the lyrics in contemporary rap music make direct reference or strong allusion to Five Percent ideology (Haddad & Smith, 1994).

Islam is faced with the realization that many relevant decision makers refuse to recognize the movement as a legitimate religion with the same constitutional and legal rights, such as exemption from military service and prisoners' rights, accorded more traditional faiths (Jones, 1983). Lincoln (1994) suggested that it is not necessary for the Muslims to prove they are a valid religious community; rather, the question is whether it can be proved that they are not.

Issues relating to Muslim service in the military have received major media attention. In *Joseph v. United States* (1972), the U.S. Supreme Court declined to affirm or deny whether the Muslims' beliefs against military service were based on religious training and belief. The most famous Muslim objector was Muhammad Ali (born in 1942 as Cassius Clay). He accepted Islam in 1964, and in 1967 he was stripped of his world heavyweight boxing title when he refused to serve in the Vietnam War on moral and religious grounds. In 1970, a court overturned his suspension, and Ali went on to win the heavyweight title two more times before retiring from boxing.

In the area of prisoners' rights, Muslims have been denied the right to purchase or possess the Qur'an by many prison administrators. Many institutions have banned official Muslim newspapers and other religious periodicals. The requirement of Islam that every true Muslim observe the annual fast of Ramadan has been a constant source of conflict between Muslims and prison administrators.

Sunnis and Shiites are Muslims recognized by each other, their differences being political, not religious. The differences between them originated from the central issue of who should rule the Islamic state following the death of Prophet Muhammad. After his death, Abu Bakar, the respected elderly companion of the prophet, was selected by the people as the first Caliph of Islam. After his death, three others, all companions of Prophet Mohammed, succeeded one after another, again selected by the people. The Shiites, about 10% of the world's Muslims, believe that the leaders of the Islamic state, called *Imams,* should not be selected by people's choice, but should be automatically installed from the prophet's descendants. They also believe in a more fundamental interpretation of the Qur'an and often take a position of mixing religion and politics. The Sunnis expound a more moderate interpretation of the Qur'an and are strong believers in peace.

Ahmed (1991) discussed the organizational structures of Muslims in the United States and the constituencies they serve. The Islamic Society of North America, founded in 1981, is an umbrella organization of five constituent organizations (Muslim Student Association, Muslim Community Association, American Muslim Social Scientists, American Muslim Scientists and Engineers, and Islamic Medical Association) and four autonomous service institutions (Islamic Teaching Center, North American Islamic Trust, Canadian Islamic Trust, and Foundation of International Development) designed to represent the Islamic mainstream. The American Muslim Mission (AMM; historically, the Nation of Islam, predecessor of the AMM), with headquarters in Plainfield, Indiana, incorporated the tradition of both the Moorish Science Temple and the International Negro Improvement Movement of Marcus Garvey. Darul Islam has been the main and largest indigenous Sunni organization in the United States. Ansarullah originated in the 1960s and attempted to accommodate Black nationalism, radicalism, and Islam into a single focus. In November 1976, the Nation of Islam became the World Community of al-Islam in the West (WCIW), only to be renamed the American Muslim Mission in April 1978 (Gardell, 1996). In January 1976, the "temples" were renamed "mosques," and in March 1977, "masjids." At the same time, many mosques substituted their number with a meaningful name.

The largest Islamic center in the Los Angeles area is the Islamic Center of Southern California, with approximately 1,000 active members and serving some 10,000 Muslim families. The most distinctive aspect of this mosque is its broadly based commitment to outreach activities, geared both to serving

Muslims who are spiritually floundering and to correcting negative stereo-types about Islam with the non-Muslim public. The center sponsors a half-hour television program on Saturday, hosts multireligious panels about public and international affairs, and provides speakers to discuss Islam at churches, schools, and community associations (Haddad & Smith, 1994). Cooper (1993) reported that 15 predominantly African American mosques are located in the South under the leadership of Jamil Al-Amin, formerly H. Rap Brown.

The Nation of Islam is a combination of the notion of militant Islam and the legacy of classic Black nationalism. The leader in 1997 was Minister Louis Farrakhan Muhammad, the strongman behind the 1995 Million Man March. He has accepted financial aid from Libya, expressed sympathy for Manuel Noriega, and pledged support for Saddam Hussein in the Gulf War. He has stated that "violence was the last resort of the oppressed and stressed that unless justice is created, America will be doomed" (Gardell, 1996, p. 5).

Child-Rearing Practices

The religious laws of Islam determine family roles. The traditional family is based on a patriarchal model in which the husband is the senior male and indisputable head of the household. The Qur'an provides directions for children with statements such as "To cherish one's parents is second only to the worship of God," "Your Sustainer has decreed that you worship none but Him, and that you be kind to your parents," and "Paradise is under the feet of mothers" (Elkholy, 1988, p. 451). The Qur'an establishes that Muslim children must be protected and cherished and that children must be obedient and committed to the will of parents. Sons are expected to obey their fathers even after marriage. As somewhat of a balance for the stern and dictatorial attitude of the father is the leniency of the mother (Ghazwi & Nock, 1989).

Pryce-Jones (1989) described the place of children in providing honor for Muslim men and women. For men, honor is related to fulfilling the masculine role and fathering children, especially sons. For women, honor involves modesty, faithfulness, and the bearing of many children, especially sons.

Education assumes a prominent place in child-rearing for Muslims. The first University of Islam was started in Detroit in 1932 as an elementary and secondary school. It was called a "university" to indicate that its curriculum was universal. It was established by Fard Muhammad, who began to teach poor African Americans that they were members of the tribe of Shabazz who had been separated from their original culture and homeland (Lincoln, 1994). One of Fard Muhammad's first converts to Islam was Elijah Poole, who later changed his name to Elijah Muhammad, in whose home the first school was located. The goal of the school was to enable Muslim children to receive instruction in an environment consistent with Islamic philosophy. Rashid and Muhammad (1992) identified the role of the Islamic school as "to produce self-reliant, competent, and above all, God-fearing Muslims who are not afraid to place Al-Islam in the marketplace of ideas competing for the soul of America" (p. 185).

Religious Practices

Islam had its beginning in the Middle East with an Arab named Muhammad ibn 'Abd Allah, who was born in the city of Mecca. Mecca was an important trading center, as well as a center of pagan worship. Drinking, gambling, and corruption were widespread. In time, Muhammad became troubled with the conditions in the city and wanted to change them. He began to spend time alone praying and fasting.

According to Islamic tradition, an angel appeared to Muhammad and told him that God wanted him to be His messenger. Over a period of 22 years, the angel reappeared to Muhammad and spoke God's words to him. Muhammad memorized the words, and they later became the Qur'an. The Qur'an is a work roughly the same length as the New Testament. The *Hadith,* not considered infallible, is the report of the sayings, deeds, and approvals of Prophet Muhammad as recounted by his companions. The most famous collections of Hadith are those of Bukhari (A.D. 870) and of Muslim (A.D. 875). The prophet's sayings and deeds are called *Sunnah.* The *Seerah* is the writings of the followers of Muhammad about the life of the prophet. These documents provide guidance for many of the practical issues encountered by Muslims.

Muhammad urged the citizens of Mecca to give up their idols and submit to God. He stressed that submission—the word *Islam* in Arabic—should be made to no other god but *Allah*—the word for God in Arabic. Muhammad said that Allah was the same god as the God of the Jews and the Christians.

The year 622 is an important date in Islam. It marks the beginning of the Muslim calendar. It is the year when Muhammad fled Mecca for Yathrib, a city 250 miles to the north. There, the people accepted Muhammad as God's messenger and as the ruler of their city. Yathrib was given the new name of al-Medina al-Munawara, "the enlightened city," and became known as Medina. There, Muhammad continued to teach and to gain many converts. Within 10 years, he had defeated the leaders of Mecca and returned to that city in triumph. Muhammad died in 632.

Muslims believe that divine revelations began with Adam, the first human, and that Muhammad was the last in a chain of prophets. According to the

Qur'an, God gave revelation to Muhammad just as He did to Adam, Abraham, David, and Jesus. Although Prophet Muhammad is regarded as the last and the seal of the prophets, Muslims recognize and accept all the previous prophets of God because they are acknowledged in the Qur'an.

Muslims have respect for all the prophets, as well as for the Bible, Judaism, and Christianity. They refer to Jews and Christians as "People of the Book" and hold Abraham in special esteem. They believe that Arabs are descendants of Abraham through his son Ishmael and that Jews are descendants of Abraham through his son Isaac. Abraham is considered to have been a Muslim and a major Muslim prophet.

The Qur'an consists of 114 chapters, called *suras,* which are divided into verses, called *ayas.* Three major topics comprise the theme of the Qur'an: law, previous prophets, and the final judgment. Ruling over all of the Qur'an, and the reference point for all the developments of the themes, is the figure of the all-mighty, all-powerful, and all-merciful God, *Allah* in Arabic. To Muslims, God has no equal and there is no god but God.

In addition to containing the basic beliefs of Islam, the Qur'an provides Muslims with specific guidelines for daily living. It forbids the eating of pork, the drinking of liquor, and gambling and provides guidelines for marriage and divorce. It also spells out the Five Pillars of Faith, the essential religious practices that Muslims must fulfill:

1. The first pillar is that of the confession of faith, or *shahēda.* This pillar requires Muslims to believe and say that there is no god but God and that Muhammad is the messenger of God.

2. The second pillar involves prayer. Muslims perform the *salēt* at five prescribed times each day—namely, *fajr,* or dawn; *zuhr,* or midday; *'asr,* or afternoon; *maghrib,* or sunset; and *'ishē,* or evening (Watt, 1968). The group prayers help create a sense of familiarity, friendliness, selflessness, and equality among Muslims. The recitation of the Qur'an during prayer represents a continuous chain of teaching, listening, and memorizing Qur'anic sayings and is a reminder that the Muslim's daily life and faith are continuously intertwined (El Azayem & Hedayat-Diba, 1994).

3. The third pillar focuses on care for the poor and needy. Muslims must give money, or *zakēt,* to charity annually. The equivalent of 2% of one's assets is recommended, and those who can give more are asked to do so. Some of this money in spent on education.

4. The fourth pillar requires fasting. Once a year, during Ramadan, the ninth month in the Islamic calendar and the month in which the first verses of the Qur'an were revealed to Muhammad, Muslims must demonstrate obedience to God by refraining from all eating, drinking, smoking, and sexual intercourse from half an hour before sunrise until half an hour after

sunset. Pregnant women, children under 7 years of age, travelers, and those who are ill are excused from the obligation.

5. The fifth pillar is the *Hajj,* or pilgrimage to Mecca. All Muslims who are able and can afford it are expected to make the pilgrimage at least once in their lifetimes. Annually, about 2 million people from all over the world pilgrimage to Mecca to unite in testimony of their faith (El Azayem & Hedayat-Diba, 1994). The pilgrimage, lasting up to 7 days, takes place during the Feast of Sacrifice, which commemorates Abraham's offering of his son to God. The pilgrims pray facing the religious shrine, the *Ka'ba,* that sits at the center of the courtyard of Mecca's Sacred Mosque.

The holy day of the Muslims is Friday. Muslims have two celebrations (*Eid*)—namely, Eid of Sacrifice and Eid of Fast-Breaking. The Eid of Sacrifice is in remembrance of the sacrifice-to-be by Prophet Abraham of his son. The Eid of Fast-Breaking comes at the end of the month of fasting, Ramadan. The *mawlid* festival, celebrating the birth of Muhammad and the informal *du'a* prayers, are two additional ritual-type activities considered by Muslims to be significant in terms of the expression of their faith. Among Shiites, the festival of *Ashura,* ceremonies connected with the 10th day of the first month of the year, *Muharram,* re-creates historical events from the early history of the Shiite movement (Rippin, 1990).

The head of the mosque is the *Imam,* the person who leads Friday prayers. Haddad and Lummis (1987) reported that the Imam may be called on to do counseling. One Imam stated,

> Most of the counseling problems I deal with fall into two categories, one being economic, another being marital. Many of the Muslims new to this country do not like to reveal their private life to a stranger. But if the matter is tense, and they have to do something about it, they will come to a place they trust, the mosque. If it is something confidential, it is easier to talk to the Imam than to some social worker. (p. 60)

The heart of Islamic practice is the public worship, or *salēt.* It consists of a series of bowings and standings, accompanied by exclamations of praise, and concludes with the worshippers touching the ground with their foreheads in recognition of the supreme might and majesty of God. The *salēt* is always preceded by ablutions (ceremonial washing). Unless one has performed the rite of ablution, one may not touch the Qur'an or perform prayer. During the *salēt,* passages from the Qur'an are recited. Groups arrange themselves in parallel rows behind an Imam and stand, bow, and prostrate themselves in time with the leader. At the end of the *salēt,* Muslims pronounce "peace" to worshippers to their right and to their left. In a traditional service, the call to prayer and the *salēt* are both in Arabic. In most Mosques, passages from the Qur'an and Hadith are also read in Arabic.

Family Structure and Dynamics

Islam considers marriage to be one of the most virtuous and approved institutions. It is considered compulsory. Families tend to be large, nuclear, and extended because Islamic practice requires that families respect their aged members and take care of them. Traditional family members tend to live in proximity with one another. Women have not usually worked outside the home, thus making it easy for families to care for elderly relatives. The Qur'an stresses that parents must be well cared for in their older years, but it does not specify how or where that care should be provided.

The family is a key social unit in the Islamic religion, where each member is valued and each plays a special role (Ahmed, 1992). Compassion, goodness, and piety are important values. The Qur'an stresses piety, love, and mercy in marriage. Sexual fidelity is demanded, and adultery is severely punished. The crisis for Islam today is how to preserve timeless moral precepts in a rapidly changing world.

Love, obedience, mutual help, and respect are the cornerstones of the traditional Muslim family, which for most is an extended family that includes grandparents, aunts, uncles, and cousins, as well as parents and brothers and sisters. Modesty was regarded as a great virtue by Prophet Mohammad. Individuals find their identity through membership in the family. Religion and traditional customs have influenced the roles of men and women in marriage and family.

In the past, women were considered subordinate to men. They were expected to obey and please their husbands and to stay at home and raise their children. *Purdah,* the seclusion or separation of women from men, was practiced by many women. The Qur'an prescribes certain measures to elevate the status of women and to protect them. One such practice is the wearing of a head covering, called the *hajib,* while in public. Although many Muslim women are moving out of these traditional roles, many find it difficult to break the old patterns and traditions. Opinions are divided over such issues as veiling, social and professional relations outside the family, and leadership in the mosque community.

Gulick (1955) found that the strongest sense of values in Middle Eastern communities is attached to kinship, residence, nationality, religion, and language. He reported an example of the way the "average" Arab would verbalize fundamental family values:

The strongest tie which binds one person to another is the tie of blood, reckoned on the male line. The only people in this hard world in whom I can trust are my relatives. Therefore, the best people in the world are my relatives—my brother, my father, my father's brothers and their sons, and beyond them, everyone in my father's lineage. When one marries, one chooses the best person one can find, and the best person is to be found among one's kinsmen—the closer the better. (p. 127)

Mahmoud (1996, p. 120) identified family issues that may be helpful to counselors and therapists:

- Contraception is allowed, and abortion is not allowed after the fetus is fully formed.
- The best of believers are those who are good to their wives.
- Among all lawful things, divorce is most hated by Allah.
- A representative from the husband's family and the wife's family are often appointed to settle marital disputes that the couple cannot solve themselves.
- Fathers retain custody of their children after divorce unless otherwise arranged by the couple.
- Muslims are not allowed to change the birth name of adopted children because the children should always know their lineage.
- Anything that intoxicates is forbidden (*haram*): alcohol, other mood altering drugs, and so on.
- It is considered modest for a man or a woman who is not married to look down and away when speaking directly.

Cultural Values and Attitudes

One universal element of Islam is the awareness of human life as determined and limited by factors beyond human control and greater than humans. The individual in Islam is an independent member of the group who makes decisions to satisfy his or her needs and interests without hurting the group. Nydell (1987) identified core values of Islam:

- A person's dignity, honor, and reputation are of major importance.
- Loyalty to one's family takes precedence over personal needs.
- One is to behave at all times in a way that reflects well on others.
- One is to believe in God and acknowledge his power.
- Humans are unable to exert control over all events in their lives and must acknowledge that they depend on God.
- Piety is an admirable human characteristic.

Watt (1968) presented the religious values of Islam as follows:

- Man's finiteness and dependence, or the insistence on a certain inevitability in events and on man's inability to control them, is recognized.
- There is no deity but God, and God is merciful and compassionate.
- There is a day of judgment at the end of the world, and on that day, God will judge men and assign them to Paradise or Hell.
- Men have knowledge of the sphere of transcendence. This knowledge is known as revelation, and the persons through whom it is transmitted are called messengers or prophets.
- Ethical norms have been revealed in the Qur'an and Traditions.
- Muhammad is the embodiment of the Islamic vision in a human life. There is a formula which is central to Islam: no Prophet, no Qur'an; no Qur'an, no Islam.
- The system of marriage and family has contributed to the stability of Islam.
- Islam obtains a balance between moralism and laxity by its doctrine that all Muslims will eventually go to Paradise, but those who have sinned will first suffer some punishment. The one sin which brings a man to Hell is *shirk,* treating as divine certain beings other than God.
- The integration of communal life and the sense of brotherhood are divinely founded.

Implications

Banawi and Stockton (1993) discussed several features of Islamic faith and Muslim practice that may likely affect counseling:

- Limiting touching to members of the same sex
- Reluctance to reveal secrets or important information outside their extended family
- A special respect for authority figures, an attitude that may limit frank and open discussion of opinions and feelings
- Avoidance of confrontation
- A likelihood of struggling with two kinds of identity problems, one intrapersonal and the other interpersonal, which are mutually interactive

Counselors are encouraged to assess the specific backgrounds of Muslims regarding the degree of religiosity, their length of time in the United States, and their ethnic background.

Islam's principles of forbearance, perseverance, and forgiveness are believed to enhance willpower and self-confidence and to support feelings of hope and optimism, all of which either protect against or alleviate symptoms of depression. Suicide is rare in Islamic society because the faith incriminates this attitude (El Azayem & Hedayat-Diba, 1994).

Georgia (1994) presented a set of questions that may prove helpful to a counselor working with a Muslim client. These questions provide a structure whereby the counselor can translate the components of counseling into the language and belief structures of the Muslim client, thus enhancing the outcomes:

- As a precondition, have I adequately explored and evaluated my own religious values and beliefs so that I can identify possible biases, presuppositions, limitations, doubts, and still-open questions?

- How can I familiarize myself with Islam, and particularly the branch of Islam with which my client is affiliated, so that I appreciate the intellectual and historical context of Islamic teaching? What literature should I review to gain a comprehensive, open-minded, nonjudgmental understanding of the religion, particularly its influence on human functioning?

- How can I experience Islam in practice so that I can develop a personal sense of the familial, social, and cultural dimensions and expressions of the religion? What Islamic community and religious activities are accessible to me?

- How can I communicate openly and honestly with my Muslim client about religious values and beliefs?

- How can I make my Muslim client feel comfortable and confident enough to describe to me his or her religious values and beliefs, religious experiences, and how these have influenced his or her current life?

- How can I help my Muslim client feel that his or her religious values and beliefs are an accepted part of the therapeutic process and that they will play an important role in the cooperatively determined goals of counseling?

- How can I help my Muslim client see his or her religious values and beliefs as part of the solution to his or her problem, and not just as part of the problem, without my trying to challenge or change those values or beliefs?

- How can I convey my therapeutic expectations and treatment approaches to my Muslim client both in my accustomed counseling language and in the language of his or her value and belief structure? (pp. 147-148)

Abdudabbeh (1991) suggested that cognitive therapy be used with Arab American clients because they are likely to resist expression of feelings to strangers. He also indicated that many Arab Americans consider it impolite to use the personal pronoun *I* and suggested that counselors strive to maintain respect of clients by using statements such as "It is my professional opinion . . ." rather than "I think . . ." when sharing psychological insights.

Questions for Review and Reflection

1. In what ways are Islamic beliefs similar to and different from Christian beliefs?
2. Why do Muslims have great respect for the prophets, the Bible, Judaism, and Christianity?
3. Discuss the Muslim concept of "family" and the roles of men and women in a traditional family unit. Describe Muslim women in the context of women in the United States.
4. What about Islam was attractive to African Americans? To individuals in prison?
5. What role does the Qur'an play in the life of a Muslim?
6. What is the significance of the Hajj?
7. What factors help Muslims maintain their ethnic identity in the United States? What are the consequences of maintaining this ethnic identity?
8. What Islamic practice do you find most appealing to you? Most potentially useful to the dominant culture? Why?
9. How can United States American institutions accommodate Islamic religious days and events?
10. Which characteristic of Muslim culture will most likely positively influence counseling? Which characteristic will most likely negatively influence counseling? Why?

References

Abdudabbeh, N. (1991, April). Cultural differences should be considered in treating Arab Americans. *Psychiatric Times: Medicine and Behavior, 8*(4), 15-17.

Ahmed, A. S. (1992). *Postmodernism and Islam.* New York: Routledge.

Ahmed, G. M. (1991). Muslim organizations in the United States. In Y. Y. Haddad (Ed.), *The Muslims of America* (pp. 11-24). New York: Oxford University Press.

Banawi, R., & Stockton, R. (1993). Islamic values relevant to group work, with practical applications for the group leader. *Journal for Specialists in Group Work, 18*(3), 151-160.

Chan, C. (1991). *Violence and intimidation: Rising bigotry toward Arabs and Muslims.* Los Angeles: County Commission on Human Relations.

Cooper, M. H. (1993). Muslims in America. *CQ Researcher, 3*(16), 368-383.

El Azayem, G. A., & Hedayat-Diba, Z. (1994). The psychological aspects of Islam: Basic principles of Islam and their psychological corollary. *International Journal for the Psychology of Religion, 4*(1), 41-50.

Elkholy, A. A. (1988). The Arab family. In C. H. Mindel, R. W. Haberstein, & W. Roosevelt, Jr. (Eds.), *Ethnic families in America: Patterns and variations* (pp. 438-455). New York: Elsevier.

Gardell, M. (1996). *In the name of Elijah Muhammad.* Durham, NC: Duke University Press.

Georgia, R. T. (1994). Preparing to counsel clients of different religious backgrounds: A phenomenological approach. *Counseling and Values, 38,* 143-151.

Ghazwi, F., & Nock, S. L. (1989, July). Religion as a mediating force in the effects of modernization on parent-child relations in Jordan. *Middle Eastern Studies, 25*(3), 363-369.

Gulick, J. (1955). *Social structure and culture change in a Lebanese village.* New York: Fund Publications in Anthropology.

Haddad, Y. Y. (1991). Introduction: The Muslims of America. In Y. Y. Haddad (Ed.), *The Muslims of America* (pp. 3-8). New York: Oxford University Press.

Haddad, Y. Y., & Lummis, A. T. (1987). *Islamic values in the United States.* New York: Oxford University Press.

Haddad, Y. Y., & Smith, J. I. (1994). *Muslim communities in North America.* Albany: State University of New York Press.

Jaynes, G. D., & Williams, R. M. (1989). *A common destiny: Blacks and American society.* Washington, DC: National Academy Press.

Jones, O., Jr. (1983). The Black Muslim movement and the American constitutional system. *Journal of Black Studies, 13,* 417-437.

Joseph v. United States. 405 U.S. 1006. (1972).

Lincoln, C. E. (1994). *The Black Muslims in America.* Grand Rapids, MI: W. B. Eerdmans.

Lincoln, C. E., & Mamiya, L. H. (1990). *The Black church in the African American experience.* Durham, NC: Duke University.

Mahmoud, V. (1996). African American Muslim families. In M. McGoldrick, J. Giordano, & J. K. Pearce (Eds.), *Ethnicity and family therapy* (pp. 112-128). New York: Guilford.

Nanji, A. A. (1993). The Muslim family in North America. In H. P. McAdoo (Ed.), *Family ethnicity: Strength in diversity* (pp. 229-242). Newbury Park, CA: Sage.

Naylor, T. (1983). Canadian mass media and the Middle East. In E. Ghareeb (Ed.), *Split vision: The portrayal of Arabs in the American media* (pp. 391-401). Washington, DC: American-Arab Affairs Council.

Nydell, M. (1987). *Understanding Arabs: A guide for Westerners.* Yarmouth, ME: Intercultural Press.

Pryce-Jones, D. (1989). *The closed circle: An interpretation of the Arabs.* New York: Harper & Row.

Rashid, H. M., & Muhammad, Z. (1992). The Sister Clara Muhammad Schools: Pioneers in the development of Islamic education in America. *Journal of Negro Education, 61*(2), 178-185.

Rippin, A. (1990). *Muslims: Their religious beliefs and practices.* New York: Routledge.

Stone, C. L. (1991). Estimate of Muslims living in America. In Y. Y. Haddad (Ed.), *The Muslims of America* (pp. 25-36). New York: Oxford University Press.

Suchetka, D. (1996, January 20). A month of meditation. *Charlotte Observer,* pp. G1, G3.

Suleiman, M. W. (1988). *The Arabs in the mind of America.* Brattleboro, VT: Amana.

Watt, W. M. (1968). *What is Islam?* New York: Praeger.

Epilogue

Increased knowledge of multicultural issues contributes to better relationships between educators and counselors and their students and clients. This epilogue provides a summary of themes and issues that emerge from the model of multicultural understanding presented in this volume and the model's application to specific population groups. The model is designed to serve as a framework for gaining information on diverse ethnic groups so that those working with students or clients from these groups might have increased personal awareness and information about individuals and the groups in general. The model has potential usefulness in teaching, individual counseling, family counseling, group counseling, and other interventions with diverse populations.

Principles of Multicultural Practice

Several principles serve as the guiding philosophy for the model of multicultural understanding. These are discussed in turn below:

1. *Culturally diverse individuals and groups should be the primary source of information about their situation, condition, or direction.* Any efforts directed at identifying, developing, or evaluating information related to the culturally diverse should involve individuals from the specific population, preferably in leadership roles. When teaching or counseling individuals from diverse ethnic groups, helping professionals should include strategies appropriate to those groups. These strategies should take into account both the historical and the contemporary status of the groups.

2. *Multiculturalism encourages the treatment of culturally diverse group members with dignity, respect, and responsibility.* People from diverse ethnic groups should be treated with the same dignity and respect that any person receives in the particular setting. Educators and counselors need to bear in mind that ethnically diverse status does not diminish or eliminate the responsibility of the individual client for meeting her or his own needs. The needs may be met within a different structural framework than might be used by a member of the dominant culture or by a member of another ethnic group, but the responsibility remains with the individual.

3. *Ethnically diverse populations are heterogeneous.* Any knowledge gained about members of a particular group must be balanced with the view that each person is also a unique individual, different from any other individual. Individual dimensions of behavior exist within culturally diverse groups. What might be viewed as a particular style or pattern for the ethnically diverse group may not represent a specific style or pattern for any given individual within the group. Counselors and educators are encouraged to keep in mind that students or clients from ethnically diverse populations bring with them many beliefs, values, and attitudes that result from membership in their ethnic group. The way these beliefs, values, and attitudes are expressed is influenced by an individually unique adaptation based on personal style.

4. *Educational institutions should have well-defined policy statements and curricula regarding the significance, purpose, and thrust of their multicultural efforts.* The multicultural focus should be a part of the core of what is done in any setting, rather than peripheral in nature. In too many cases, attention to multicultural issues is an afterthought, rather than a part of the foundation of program efforts, as it should be. Multiculturalism is not simply the addition of content about ethnically diverse peoples; it involves rethinking the policy related to all parts of the curriculum.

Individuals interested in moving toward a multicultural program should begin by (a) recognizing that education or counseling or both are not value-free; (b) identifying current biases and deficiencies in the existing program by conducting a critique of the environment; (c) acquiring a thorough knowledge of the philosophy and theory concerning multiculturalism and its application to the specific setting; (d) acquiring, evaluating, adapting, and developing materials appropriate to the multicultural effort being undertaken; and (e) determining an effective means of involving members of the ethnically diverse population(s) in the effort to make the program responsive to all persons served. These preparatory efforts should lead to a solid foundation upon which to build a multicultural program that is reasonably sensitive to the needs of the various populations served. Instructional and counseling methods should be selected for what is to be accomplished and because they reflect the cultural background of the participants.

5. *Multicultural efforts must focus on normal behaviors and wellness, rather than on abnormal behaviors and illness.* Too many efforts at meeting the needs of ethnically diverse individuals fail because they begin from the point of abnormality, rather than from the point of normality. Factors such as low self-esteem and self-hatred are frequently assumed to be characteristic of ethnically diverse group members without any investigation of the basis on which such claims are made. We must also use care in how we translate research results and generalize to populations different from those used in the research investigation.

6. *Multiculturalism requires that educators and counselors be aware of the systemic dimensions of racism and alienation and thereby attempt to understand the experiences, lifestyles, and values of students and clients.* As convenient as it might be to pretend that racism does not permeate most of the culture of the United States, we must be aware of it, how it affects members of the dominant culture, and how it affects members of ethnically diverse cultural groups. If schools and other institutions are to be successful with all students or clients, the prevailing values in the system must be acknowledged. Because awareness is the initial step in dealing with any problem, representatives of the institution and members of culturally diverse populations must understand how racism affects both groups.

7. *Educators and counselors must be trained who are capable of demonstrating effectiveness with individuals from culturally diverse ethnic groups.* Training programs must be expanded beyond single course offerings into areas that deal directly with the needs of culturally diverse populations. Training must move beyond rhetoric about cultural pluralism to what is real in the lives of the culturally diverse. Programs should focus on training counselors and educators for roles as change agents who will challenge the system, rather than modify the behavior of culturally diverse students or clients to fit the system.

General Guidelines to Enhance Multicultural Understanding

Guidelines, adapted from Locke (1989), are presented here to extend what teachers and counselors use from either the model of multicultural understanding or the information on a specific culturally diverse group.

1. *Learn as much as possible about your own culture.* One can appreciate another culture much more if one first appreciates one's own.

2. *Work at being open and honest in your relationships with culturally diverse populations.* Leave yourself open to different attitudes and values, and encourage those different from yourself to be open and honest with you about issues related to their cultures. Attend to the verbal and nonverbal communication patterns between yourself and your culturally different students or clients.

3. *Seek to develop genuine respect and appreciation of culturally diverse attitudes and behaviors.* Demonstrate that you both recognize and value the cultures of those different from yourself. Respect can be demonstrated by starting with the life experiences of the student or client, and not the experiences of the teacher or counselor.

4. *Take advantage of all available opportunities to participate in activities in the communities of culturally diverse groups.*

5. *Keep in mind that individuals from culturally diverse groups are both members of their group and unique individuals as well.* Strive to keep a healthy balance between your view of students or clients as cultural beings and as unique beings.

6. *Learn to examine cultural biases, prejudices, and stereotypes.* Eliminate all of your behaviors that suggest prejudice or racism, and do not tolerate such behaviors in your colleagues or in other members of your own cultural group. Teach your students or clients how to recognize bias and how to challenge stereotypes.

7. *Encourage administrators or supervisors or both in your school or agency to institutionalize practices that acknowledge the diversity among your students or clients.*

8. *Hold high expectations of your culturally different students or clients, and encourage others who work with diverse populations to do likewise.*

9. *Ask questions about the cultures of ethnically diverse groups.* Learn as much as possible about different cultures, and share what you learn with others.

10. *Develop culturally specific strategies, techniques, and programs to foster the psychological development of culturally diverse individuals and groups.*

A Vision

In 1972, the Commission on Multicultural Education of the American Association of Colleges of Teacher Education (AACTE) issued a statement titled "No One Model American." The document stated that multiculturalism "recognizes cultural diversity as a fact of life in American society, and it affirms that this cultural diversity is a valuable resource that should be preserved and extended" (AACTE, 1973, p. 264).

By 1997, the Association for Multicultural Counseling and Development, the Association for Counselor Education and Supervision, and the American School Counseling Association had adopted multicultural counseling competencies (Arredondo et al., 1996). These competencies were designed to guide interpersonal counseling interactions with attention to culture, ethnicity, and race.

These statements communicate a vision of a better society, one that is possible if current efforts to create a truly multicultural outlook are implemented and sustained. They recognize the multicultural and pluralistic nature of U.S. society and call for the development of comprehensive approaches to meeting the needs of all students or clients. To make a difference, we must continue theory development relevant to the culturally different, conduct quantitative and qualitative research on diverse populations, and ensure that curricular offerings are inclusive of all groups within this society.

The need for new and different models for working with culturally different populations in the United States is imperative. The United States is a richer nation as a result of the many cultures that have contributed, and continue to contribute, to making the country what it is. We must be aware of the many values that each culturally diverse group adds to the quality, vitality, and strength of the nation. We also must be aware of the differences that exist among the culturally diverse populations.

The differences that exist between members of the dominant culture and members of ethnically diverse cultures are real. Many differences are grounded in the cultures from which individuals form their worldviews. Others are the result of unique differences between individuals regardless of cultural background. Counselors and educators must be aware of these differences and the ways these differences complicate interactions between themselves and their students and clients. The ideas discussed here may be useful toward that end.

References

American Association of Colleges of Teacher Education (AACTE). (1973, Winter). No one model American. *Journal of Teacher Education, 24,* 264-265.

Arredondo, P., Toporek, R., Brown, S. P., Jones, J., Locke, D. C., Sanchez, J., & Stadler, H. (1996). Operationalization of the multicultural counseling competencies. *Journal of Multicultural Counseling and Development, 24*(1), 42-78.

Locke, D. C. (1989). Fostering the self-esteem of African American children. *Elementary School Guidance and Counseling, 23,* 254-259.

Name Index

Subject Index

About the Author

Don C. Locke is Professor and Director of the North Carolina State University (NCSU) Doctoral Program in Adult and Community College Education at the Asheville Graduate Center. Immediately prior to his current position, he was Head of the Department of Counselor Education at NCSU in Raleigh. He began his career as a high school social studies teacher in Fort Wayne, Indiana, where he also worked as a high school counselor for 2 years. He earned his doctorate at Ball State University in 1974. He has been active in state, regional, and national counseling organizations and has served as President of the North Carolina Counseling Association, as Chair of the Southern Region Branch of the American Counseling Association (ACA), as Secretary of the Association for Counselor Education and Supervision (ACES), and as Chair of the American Counseling Association Foundation. He has also been a member of the ACES Editorial Board, President of the Southern Association for Counselor Education and Supervision (SACES), and a member of the ACA Governing Council. The recipient of numerous awards including the Ella Stephens Barrett Leadership Award from the North Carolina Counseling Association, the Professional Development Award from ACA, and the Provost's African-American Professional Development Award from North Carolina State University, this author or coauthor of more than 50 publications is currently focusing on multicultural issues. He was named to the Chi Sigma Iota Academy of Leaders for Excellence in 1997.

Breinigsville, PA USA
09 May 2010
237617BV00001B/8/P